"I found this book interesting and stimulating. It is well written and I loved reading it ... the book is an important contribution to the existing literature."
David Clapham, University of Glasgow

"With the madness of 'build, baby, build' tragically ascendant, even hegemonic, Rob Imrie's powerful, wide-ranging and fascinating book systematically and cogently injects urgently needed sanity and judiciousness into the policy discourse."
David Imbroscio, University of Louisville

"A book that should be acted on rather than being simply read. We're drowning in an endless sea of concrete and, as Imrie potently argues, we must build less and better."
Federico Cugurullo, Trinity College Dublin

"A critical call for an ethics of care in a world obsessed with reconstruction in cities from an eminent global urban scholar."
Loretta Lees, University of Leicester

D1612487

CONCRETE CITIES

Why We Need to Build Differently

Rob Imrie

BRISTOL
UNIVERSITY
PRESS

First published in Great Britain in 2021 by

Bristol University Press
University of Bristol
1–9 Old Park Hill
Bristol
BS2 8BB
UK
t: +44 (0)117 954 5940
e: bup-info@bristol.ac.uk

Details of international sales and distribution partners are available at bristoluniversitypress.co.uk

© Bristol University Press 2021

British Library Cataloguing in Publication Data
A catalogue record for this book is available from the British Library

ISBN 978-1-5292-2051-3 hardcover
ISBN 978-1-5292-2052-0 paperback
ISBN 978-1-5292-2053-7 ePub
ISBN 978-1-5292-2054-4 ePdf

Cover design: Namkwan Cho
Front cover image: Rob Imrie
Printed and bound in Great Britain by CMP, Poole
Bristol University Press uses environmentally responsible print partners

Contents

List of Figures

About the Author

Rob Imrie was previously Professor of Sociology at Goldsmiths University of London and retains a visiting professorship. He spends much of his time working as a bicycle mechanic and riding his cycle around the Surrey Hills and beyond. He has written widely on issues relating to architecture and urban design, urban policy and politics, and disability and the built environment.

Preface

At the heart of this book is an existential issue of why we build, and why we build in the ways that we do. The premise is that we build far too much and too badly, and in ways whereby many of the needs of people remain unmet, while despoiling and degrading ecology and the environment, or the very biospheres that we depend on for our existence. There is an unprecedented expansion in the rate and scale of urbanisation, and building activity is occurring everywhere on the planet, from the construction of major hydroelectricity installations, to transcontinental road and rail infrastructure. The rationality of building revolves around a system of supply shaped by speculation, or a political economy of construction that knows no bounds or limits to building. Here, a building is conceived more as an object than a liveable, vital, part of the biosphere, and as a commodity or means to realise monetised value through its production and exchange.

This translates into a bewildering range of building projects and products shaped by one of the most powerful, corporate, global industries. The construction sector has its imprint in every aspect of our lives. It has the world's largest ecological footprint by using materials like concrete with high levels of embodied energy and constructing office environments that use energy-intensive air-conditioning systems, and it is implicated in the large-scale, and escalating, conversions of green space to buildings and constructed infrastructure. Its ecological impact extends from the sourcing of forestry products from Amazonia used in flooring and related building products, to the construction of dams that are implicated in the drowning and destruction of settlements, and the displacement of different species. There is no part of environments that is not affected by the actions of actors in the construction sector, yet they operate with few restraints or checks.

Building is likely to be even more important in a post-COVID-19 world, or part of a post-pandemic economics that, in the words of British Prime Minister Boris Johnson (2020), is to 'build, build, build'. This is a depressing scenario, whereby what is offered is more roads, motor vehicles, speculative development, vanity projects and construction-related pollution and environmental despoliation. The world is awash with buildings and concrete infrastructure, many of which are the outcome of illicit and corrupt practice, and often constructed for a minority, private interest. Much building activity is not well attuned to any sense of the commons, despite intruding onto, and being a significant part of, environments used by all. How might it be possible to think otherwise, beyond building, or to recraft our building cultures in ways whereby ideas of care and respect, for nature, objects and fellow human beings, conjoin to create a different series of 'construction mentalities'?

In developing these ideas and bringing the book to fruition, I am thankful to Emily Watt of Bristol University Press (BUP) for giving me the opportunity to write the book, and providing invaluable advice and guidance throughout the process. My thanks to Caroline Astley, Freya Trand and other staff at BUP, who also provided excellent support. My thanks to Gail Welsh and the production team at Newgen Publishing for their guidance and advice in the final production of the book, and particularly to the copy editor who did an excellent job in reviewing the manuscript. Three individuals gave permission to reproduce photographs, and I thank: Erik Mulder, architect at RAU Architects, Amsterdam, for permission to reproduce his image of the Tridos Bank building in Utrecht, the Netherlands; Paul Hede, Senior Principal at Bickerton Masters, for permission to use three of his images of the Northern Autistic School in Melbourne, Australia; and Phillippa Flannery for her permission to reproduce her photograph of the Te Kura Whare building, Taneatua, New Zealand.

I am grateful to participants in my research projects, who taught me much about the interrelationships between design, buildings and space. In this regard, my thanks to Paul Hede of Bickerton Masters, Mike Westley of Westley Design Ltd., and to participants in my research in Esher, including Alex King, Ian McGuire, Chris Whelan and Joan Leiffer. My thanks also to Ann, Reiko and Elaine, who, as individuals with insights into how to navigate the perils of places constructed with little attentiveness to bodily impairment, provided me with understanding of the disabling, and disablist, nature of the built environment. I am also thankful to the staff at the Getty Research Institute in Los Angeles for giving me access to the archives of the American architect Frank Lloyd Wright, and for guidance on how to use their facilities. Part of this research was funded by the European Research Council (grant number 323777).

I have had the support of research colleagues and I am grateful to Dr Mike Dolton for sharing ideas with me and for joint work that we carried out into the regeneration of a Tesco's site in East London and Nine Elms in Battersea, south-west London. I benefitted too from working with Dr Luna Glucksberg, and we cooperated on a pilot project investigating the emergence of a super-rich neighbourhood in the small town of Esher, part of the 'stockbroker' belt on the western fringes of London. My thanks to Dr Emma Street for her close and critical reading of a version of Chapter 7, and to an anonymous reader and Dr Sarah Fielder for reading a draft of the manuscript and pointing out its weaknesses. I am particularly indebted to Dr Fielder for her copy editing, which helped me to improve the flow and feeling of the text, and for her work in editing the references. My thanks also extend to Dr Marian Hawkesworth and Will Hawkesworth, who read a draft of the manuscript and made telling comments that made me rethink some of the book's arguments.

Finally, my thanks to Goldsmiths University of London, and particularly the Department of Sociology that restored my faith and belief in the power of academia to do good work by providing a supportive environment to develop the ideas for the book.

Rob Imrie
Goldsmiths University of London
August 2021

Introduction: The Omnipresent Nature of Building

In July 2015, I was based in Japan and had been spending most of my time working in Tokyo. While Tokyo is a spectacular city, it is the epitome of a concrete jungle and so an invitation by a colleague to visit the southern Japanese island of Kyushu seemed like the opportune time to experience some of Japan's green spaces. The train ride from Tokyo to the main city in Kyushu, Fukuoka, is 1,100 km and takes six hours to complete. The route traverses the populated south coast of Japan that, as was evident from my journey to Fukuoka, is dominated by a strip of major urban settlements. The views from the train's window were fleeting glimpses of urban Japan interspersed with 'blackouts' as the train rapidly entered and exited numerous tunnels. The experience was like looking through a kaleidoscope with a bewildering array of 'quick-fire' glimpses of buildings and urban infrastructure. There were rare sights of green spaces, though these were never without buildings in view. By the time I arrived in Fukuoka, I could have been forgiven for thinking that countryside does not exist in Japan.

My Japanese experience is illustrative of most of the contemporary world, in which the built environment is integral to our everyday lives and fundamental in influencing how we interact with one another and patterns of living and habitation. There are few places left untouched by the excavation of the earth's resources for construction and this, along with the combination of materials to create new structures, ranging widely from houses to roads, and dams to water pipelines, is the defining feature of people's domination of the planet. Wherever one goes, the sounds, sights and smells of construction are evident, and our environments are increasingly shaped by what often feels like a never-ending process of building. From the endless construction of domestic dwellings to the excavation of new roads and railways into frontier areas such as Western China and Amazonia, building work is omnipresent to the extent that it can be thought of as a formative process shaping contemporary economy and society.

Such is the rate of new (re)construction that we are living in a period of unparalleled building, characterised by trillions of dollars pouring into property development. Whatever measures one uses, the construction of buildings and infrastructure has never been greater or more ambitious in its scale and form. The expansion of the global population, combined with economic growth, has precipitated a worldwide building boom, characterised by the rapid suburbanisation of cities, the proliferation of infrastructure, and a massive increase in the consumption of raw materials used to create the basic components of construction. Illustrative of this is the production of cement, which totalled 1,100 million metric tons globally in 1990, increasing fourfold to 4,370 million metric tons by 2020 (Garside, 2020). Urbanisation has also proliferated, with, for example, 27,020 hectares of built-up area added to New York City between 2000 and 2011, and 19,762 hectares added to Mumbai in India between 2001 and 2014 (United Nations Habitat, 2016).

These patterns are evident in most parts of the world, and they are indicative of the urbanisation of society, in which the extent of built-up, and built-on, places is proliferating. Land-cover surveys of Europe for the period 2000 to 2018 show that land take, or building on greenfield sites, exceeded 921 km^2 per year, an area larger than Berlin, and that over the same period, urban areas increased by 9 per cent (European Environment Agency, 2019). In places such as China, the changes have also been dramatic, with the size of built-up areas increasing from 2.3 million hectares in 2000 to 8.8 million hectares in 2013, or an annual change of 8.5 per cent (see United Nations Habitat, 2016). The use of concrete as the building block of construction has proliferated, ranging from its use in the large-scale construction of commercial buildings to the production of domestic dwellings, including the conversion of permeable front gardens to hard, concrete, surfaces. As Watts (2019: 1) observes, this material is the basis of 'a developmental model that replaces living landscapes with built environments'.

The transformation of nature and its reworking through the creation of synthetic environments shows no signs of abating, and we are living in a time of ecological destruction in which building and construction are at the forefront in contributing to the despoliation of ecology, environment and our non-human worlds.[1] From the sounds and smells of demolition and building work to the release of carbon dioxide in the production of cement, the environment is pervaded by the activities of actors involved in a constant stream of construction. Much of what is built is ugly and disfigures the environment, and it is part of a political economy that encourages a never-ending supply of concrete objects, or a rationality of 'building without limits'. The proliferation of constructed artefacts is part of an ideology of building that regards construction as a natural act, beyond question or reproach, with little sensitivity to what is needed. Instead, building and construction, in themselves, are regarded as 'good'.

This book takes exception to the almost-ubiquitous, 'self-evident', understanding that building is 'a good thing', and calls for an end to the mentalities of construction and building that are failing many people and places in different ways. These failures include: archaic building industries that design and construct too many poor buildings inadequate in responding to people's physiological and emotional needs; the extraction of minerals and resources, such as sand and gravel, for use in construction at rates greater than their natural replenishment; systems of governance that encourage too much building and are ill equipped to regulate building and construction activities; the dominance of speculative building and a vast oversupply of property built for investment, not occupation and use; the shortening of building life cycles and the supplanting of refurbishment and reuse by demolition and rebuilding; and, the ongoing colonisation of space by building, and the despoliation and degradation of ecology and environment.

The overarching premise of the book is that we not only need to build better, but also need to build less, and to transform the corporate political and governance structures that encourage a constant expansion in building and construction activities. The book advances the argument that urban policies, and related government programmes, are integral elements of 'construction states', in which governments, in partnerships with powerful private interests, propagate a political economy of building that is wasteful of resources and neglectful of people, places, ecologies and communities. Through a series of interlocking chapters, the book makes a case for a renewed, ecologically sensitive, building culture, including the democratisation of building practice and the devolution of construction to local people and places, while 'building for life', or design sensitised to people's needs and to nature and the environment.

The book will develop a number of key, integrative, themes:

- Building and construction are part of a value-creation process that is never-ending and based on a problematical rationality or logic that does not encourage critical reflection, or much thought for the human and ecological consequences of (building) actions and outcomes.
- This rationality is predisposed towards the production of more and more or, in the context of building, the construction of a built environment that embodies waste and wastefulness, while being inattentive to what is needed for the reproduction of people and nature.
- Building and construction is a disruptive process that involves disturbance to socio-ecological systems, and it is implicated in the social dislocation

and displacement of people and nature. It has the capacity to perpetrate actions that are destructive of the natural world and meaningful human experience.

- Such destruction is part of the banal, often invisible, ways in which violence is perpetrated by building and construction, ranging from the design of buildings that do not permit ease of access for disabled people, to air and water pollution caused by mining and demolition activities.
- Building is often insensitive to the human senses and sensory matter, and it rarely relates to the body, or the multiplicity of ways in which people seek to interact with(in) the designed environment. There is a disconnect between building cultures and people's bodily interchanges and interactions with the built environment.
- Construction is an uneven process and implicated in the (re)production of socio-spatial inequalities. Infrastructure is not evenly distributed or equally accessible and shared, and its construction reflects and reproduces social divisions and inequalities.

While construction, in whatever form, will disturb and transform the socio-ecological relations of a place, this does not mean that there ought to be no building activity. It does mean that there needs to be much more attentiveness to the rationale for a specific building, in terms of who or what it is for, and greater seriousness shown by politicians about what is acceptable or not as a built environment, relating to its social and ecological effects. This includes challenging, and changing, some of the *predominant ways* in which buildings are conceived, designed and constructed, particularly the construction of buildings as speculative monetised objects. In the book, I argue that the dominance of speculative building detracts from the *raison d'être* of what building, and the built environment, ought to be, that is, the creation of nurturing and life-affirming spaces integral to the health and well-being of people and non-human species.

Instead, our building cultures are predisposed towards the construction of 'stuff' shaped by an economic rationality in which what is built is conditioned, largely, by what buildings can command as a market value, rather than their usefulness, and suitability, in meeting the needs of people and responding to the fragilities of the natural world. This is compounded by a building process that, in most countries, is not particularly open or transparent, and primarily occurs through large corporate construction companies, backed up by private equity funding and state support. These institutions are remote from public scrutiny and while most building projects follow formal, legal, planning processes, these are barely democratic, and tend to present development projects as a fait accompli. For most people, the built environment is an imposition, or something that transpires out of an opaque process, particularly with regard to large-scale mega-projects and housing programmes.

These programmes can be inappropriate and wasteful, and the globe is littered with half-finished and abandoned projects that are testimony to the irrationality of a building culture that often pursues construction that fails to recognise, or respond to, the needs of people. An illustration is housing abandonment in Mexico, which reflects a series of poorly thought-through, and executed, projects that due to the financial terms of access to them, their poor build and design quality, and their failure to provide safe and secure environments, were either left unoccupied or people did not stay in them. This summarises why over 4 million residential properties in Mexico are empty, while numerous housing estates are half-built and semi-abandoned. This situation originates with an ambitious building programme from 2001, devised and developed by the Mexican government, and supported by the World Bank, Wall Street financiers and a host of private equity and real estate interests.

The aim was the construction of decent, affordable, housing for Mexico's working-class population, in which ease of access to mortgages was the means to incentivise the building industry to build, what Marosi (2017: 1) describes as 'a dream scenario for hundreds of developers, large and small'. Marosi (2017) notes that between 2001 and 2012, an estimated 20 million people relocated out of shanty towns and rural areas to live in newly constructed settlements. By the early 2010s, with economic collapse, the building industry in recession and people tied into complex loans, defaults on mortgage payments were common, and many housing estates were left incomplete and bereft of basic infrastructure. Martínez (2018) observes that over 5 million homes were empty in 2018, testimony to what is wrong with the prevalent construction culture, in which a building is treated more as a commodity or financial asset than a useful, and useable, part of an environment. In this instance, while large construction companies and investors made money out of government contracts, there was a failure to deliver or provide the requisite means for people to live.

The illustration also highlights the propensity to build anew rather than to adapt or renew existing stock, and the logic of the building culture is to continuously develop new products and objects for consumption, and to extend the market into every aspect of building and construction. This logic encourages speculation and continuous construction, creating what Frank Lloyd Wright (FLW) (1994 [1947]: 313) described as an 'amazing avalanche of material'. This material is manifest in the ever-expanding rates of urbanisation and the depletion of the non-renewable resource base to provide for urban expansion. This is the antithesis of an adaptive culture, or one with the onus on mending and repairing, and working with what exists. An adaptive approach prevents, potentially, the use of precious, disappearing spaces, and by its reworking and reuse of existing infrastructure and materials, can contribute to the preservation of the world's diminishing resource base.

There is a paradox of sorts at play in relation to building, in that while construction often attracts political opposition and contestation, particularly in relation to large-scale projects, there is also a quiescence or lassitude among many communities, in which building activity is seen as acceptable or, as Edwards (2003: 185) suggests, part of a 'naturalised background, as ordinary and unremarkable to us as trees, daylight, and dirt'. A potential effect is to render construction as an apolitical activity that is conceived, by some, as revolving around the reproduction of inert and inanimate physical objects that have no agency and no politics. Such conceptions of construction are to the fore in many academic and popular accounts of building that present it, primarily, as a technical or process-based activity in which the activities of the actors involved in the sector are rarely problematised, or, otherwise, are conceived as benevolent and in the interests of society as a whole (see Simpson, 2020).

The book takes issue with these naturalised conceptions of construction and seeks to develop Fry's (2011: 6) understanding of construction as an inherently partisan and political process that 'gives material form and directionality to the ideological embodiment of a particular politics'. Here, the design and building of places is the insinuation of values about what the character and content of an environment should be. From the targeted demolition of buildings in war zones to ethnically cleanse neighbourhoods, to the construction of upscale condominiums in areas previously occupied by low-income groups, the political, and politicised, nature of building and construction is omnipresent, and every act of building is a purposive action that has distributive consequences for people and nature. The acceptance of this observation entails the recognition of building as a moral act, where the responsibility, of all involved, is to question, and deliberate, not only what ought to be built, but also what is acceptable as a constructed object.

This understanding shapes the structure and content of the book, in which I draw on illustrations from different parts of the world, and from a wide range of building types and construction projects. The countries include, among others, Japan, Australia, Turkey, Egypt, Spain, Brazil, China, the US and the UK, in which I explore everything from mega-projects to residential property development and small-scale, domestic refurbishments. While each country and construction project has specific socio-political, economic and technical nuances, or specificities that shape building types and effects, there are many commonalities that reflect, in part, a globalising building culture. This culture revolves around building as part of an exchange-value economy dominated by a host of global financiers, private equity firms and construction companies.

Throughout the book, I refer to 'building culture' in ways whereby there is the danger of an essentialising and totalising effect or conception of the subject matter. This is not the intent, as I recognise the significance of local, contextual variations relating to the specifics of a place's political and economic systems. However, these important variations are interconnected to, and interact with, broader, global processes, and there is commonality that cross-cuts placed-based building contexts. This relates, primarily, to the ascendency of the market in shaping construction, and, specifically, to the rise of neoliberal governance, or the opening up of spaces to investors to engage in the thoroughgoing commodification of land and its resources. From the rapid deforestation of Amazonia to feed the furniture and flooring sectors, to the rapid gentrification of the inner areas of places such as Seoul, Melbourne and Luanda, the tentacles of a globalising political economy of building are a defining feature of contemporary construction.

In developing these, and related, ideas, I have used a wide range of secondary and primary research materials to evaluate and illustrate the key arguments, including information derived from published reports, academic papers, newspapers and social media websites. The evidence assembled from secondary sources is variable in its quality and coverage of a topic, and one of the tasks that I undertook was to interrogate the veracity of these sources. In a so-called 'post-truth world', where fake news and fakery of data appear to be rife, it was important to sift and sort through the published data that I have used, and whenever I refer to a particular source and the data it refers to, whatever claim it is making, I will have triangulated it or tried to corroborate it by sourcing other papers or publications relating to the same subject matter and information set.

This is not an easy task, as it raises the question of what is a fact that is not also simultaneously a value, and there is recognition that data, in whatever form, are a partial representation and never definitive of their subject. There is the issue too of the interpretation and analysis of information outside of one's purview, or, as Irwin (2013: 297) notes, 'by those who come to it from a distance, uninvolved in the process of data creation'. Mindful of this, my approach is one of avoiding taking data out of their research context, but rather to subject the context, and the data relating to it, to evaluation. This is part of a necessary process of seeking to develop an argument, or disposition, towards the subject, in which there is always a selection of material, and a certain, select deployment of data, that may be regarded as a partial approach. My response is that while the arguments in the book are shaped, inevitably, by my values, they revolve around an abundance of incontrovertible information that adds up to the general thesis that we build too much, and too badly.

The primary research that I refer to in the book, and that forms the bedrock of Chapters 4, 5, 6 and 8, was developed and implemented between 2000 and 2017. These were a mixture of projects ranging across a variety of themes, including: a study of disability and mobility and movement in the UK; architects' conceptions of the human body; inclusive design and housing; regulation and the design process; universal design and the crafting of inclusive spaces; wealthy elites and urban displacement in suburban London; and the construction of buy-to-leave properties in the redevelopment of Nine Elms in South-west Central London. In addition to these projects, I refer to data gathered from archival research on the work of the American architect FLW. Here, I made two visits to the Getty Research Institute in Los Angeles, where an archive of FLW's work is based. In drawing on the data, I divide the rest of the book into a further nine chapters.

In Chapter 2, I outline and evaluate the building culture that shapes the design and construction of the built environment. Primed by a political economy of building, the prevailing approach to construction is a continuous output, shaped by a corporate, global construction nexus, or deeply embedded interests propagating building as a primary source of investment and wealth. I develop the argument that while constructing habitats is intrinsic to human life, the rationality of construction is to propagate building far in excess of what people need, and much is wasteful and harmful. The chapter demonstrates that there is an imperative to build, or a building culture that rarely stops to question why we build or what building is for. Rather, an ideology of building permeates society that encourages a never-ending supply of bricks and mortar, developed and delivered by a building industry that has long lost any sense of craft or constructing in ways that 'brings something that cares into being' (Fry, 2011: 140).

In Chapter 3, I consider the importance of building and construction in relation to the growth and development of nation states, in particular, in facilitating the social and economic goals of governments. The argument is that construction is integral to the socio-development goals of state actors, ranging from early, pre-modern forms of defensive construction to assure the protection of populations, to contemporary mega-projects that seek to open up new territories for political control and economic exploitation. The proliferation of building, including its form and performance, is closely intertwined with its institutionalisation, and governance, through the interrelationships between powerful corporate organisations, which include organised crime and state policies and programmes. I discuss the significance of state involvement in propagating building and construction, and the rise and the role of what I refer to as 'construction states' in shaping the proclivity to build and construct.

Chapter 4 explores the most significant dynamic of building and construction, that is, the speculation in land and real estate. I relate it to the emergence of so-called super-rich enclaves in cities, and the construction of buildings only affordable to wealthy investors. In major cities like London and New York, the construction of, primarily, residential buildings is part of a broader process of creating investment portfolios. Such properties are less to be lived in than regarded as economic assets that enable global investors to accumulate wealth. This phenomenon is part of a casino capitalism in which the built environment is regarded as comprising tradable objects to be exchanged as part of a system of technocratic asset management. In the chapter, I discuss the significance of 'building as assets' and the impacts on the socio-spatial development of cities, including pricing people out of local housing markets and rendering neighbourhoods as 'dead zones'. Buildings are built but rarely inhabited, or are part of a daytime economy that, at best, includes partial human presence and, at worst, perpetuates 'ghost places'.

The construction industry continues to benefit from major state support for property-led development that has fuelled the growth of market-oriented building, often in areas of low-cost housing and small businesses. As outlined in Chapter 4, major cities are awash with speculative building projects that encourage gentrification, including upward pressures on rents that exacerbate problems of affordability. Such city building, evident almost everywhere, is analogous to a process of unsettlement and social destabilisation, or what Till (2012: 8) describes as place-based colonisation involving 'settlement clearances [and] geographies of displacement'. Buildings and spaces increasingly serve and service private places in which much of the built environment is foreclosed to the public and only accessible under specific conditions of entry. In Chapter 5, I consider how state-sponsored 'building for profit' in cities is enacting swathes of clearances of people from places, and contributing to new forms of social inequality.

As much as we build, we demolish and destroy, and building cultures are defined, in part, by the tendency towards obsolescence of products and objects, and the restless urge to renew and reconstruct. The sounds and sights of demolition are ever present, ranging from the visibility of wrecking machinery to the production of rubble dust and dirt in the atmosphere. The effects are irrational, often disruptive and include: the loss of scarce materials; the increase in waste and landfill; particulate and noise pollution due to demolition processes; disturbance to, and destruction of, local ecologies; and the loss of scarce, usually low-income, housing, contributing to shortfalls in housing stock. In Chapter 6, I conceive of construction as dominated by a demolition paradigm in which there is rarely consideration by actors in the sector of the life cycle of buildings and the appropriate means to salvage, reuse and/or adapt them. There is a rush to demolish instead of 'creating a value in the end of life of a structure' (LaMore et al, 2018: 1).

A fallacy of our building culture is that there is a shortage of housing that is the root cause of a crisis that includes unaffordability and homelessness. A proffered solution is to build more housing, a supply-side argument that, as Pettifor (2018: 1) notes, is a conventional wisdom 'bought into' by everyone, 'from the government, to housing charities, to housebuilders'. This 'wisdom' goes more or less unchallenged, and propagates swathes of volume house building that do little to tackle the problems of housing shortfalls. In Chapter 7, I challenge the 'building as solution' argument, and argue for a 'less is more' approach that tackles the complexities relating to people's inability to get access to good-quality housing. Part of an approach ought to be to build less and to work better with what exists, including bringing back into use the 210,000 long-term empty homes in England (Westwater, 2019). It also means changing how people get access to housing, including reforming housing finance, rent controls and a paraphernalia of other systems that, if left untouched, will mean that building more housing is ineffective.

While building cultures are predisposed towards creating systems that enable basic human needs to be met, such as enabling water to enter and exit a building, they are less attuned to constructing spaces that respond to people's diverse psychological and physiological needs. This is the theme of Chapter 8, where I develop the proposition that the processes by which building actors design and construct a place, and the methods they deploy to understand how objects and people interact, are estranged from, and insensitive to, the human context, or fail to consider the relationships between spaces and the functioning of the human body. Construction practices are disembodied insofar as practitioners rarely relate their work to human scale, or the manifold complexities of the body. As a consequence, what we build is implicated in the (re)production of debilitating spaces, or environs that degrade, and undermine, the body's capacities to work well within the built environment.

The idea of ecological or green building has become big business, and corporate building and construction companies have not been slow to attach themselves to the rising popularity of building for sustainable development. This chimes with the rise of alternative building cultures, such as self-build, that express, in part, people's disaffection with volume house building, and the emergence of smart technologies that offer potential to minimise the environmental impact of buildings. In Chapter 9, I argue that there is no such thing as sustainable or green building because no building can be green or ecological. Building is a disruptive and violent process, ranging from the destructive extraction of non-reproducible materials from the earth, to the colonisation of land from nature and the disturbance of socio-ecological systems. Instead, a radical greening needs to inform how, when and why we build, which incorporates limits to building and building that respects ecological integrity and well-being.

The final chapter, Chapter 10, begins by noting that there are much better ways to build than at present. Different worlds can be crafted that enable people to live in more humane ways that are respectful of ecology and the environment. Building and construction practices need to reject the 'more of everything' approach, and shift towards a quality-based paradigm in which crafting becomes the basis for the design and production of the built environment. The chapter considers how far an ethics and politics of care and caring can be instilled into the construction of places, and discusses what a caring building ethic refers to and may entail in practice (see Bates et al, 2017). Here, an important focus relates to learning about how care and building may be conjoined, including discussion of the pedagogic and practical challenges in creating caring building values and practices.

While building is always, unavoidably, part of people's presence on the earth, there is no inevitability to the continuation of the deleterious socio-ecological effects of building and construction. These effects are symptomatic of a failing political culture based on an economic rationality that, if left unchecked, will continue to perpetuate building without limits and the (re)production of wasteland environments that fail to respond to the needs of people and nature. There has to be a greater politicisation of people's interrelationships with nature and the development of political projects that, in Fry's (2011: 211) terms, create the capacities of 'living otherwise'. This will require a systemic transformation in how people live and how society is organised that rejects conventional politics and economics, including consumerism and greenwashing and its platitudes.

2

The Significance of Building
and Construction

Introduction

Since the beginning of human occupation on the earth, roughly 200,000 years ago, building and construction have been part of people's activities to create habitable and liveable environments. Building is necessary in enabling human beings to function, ranging from the provision of shelter, or nurturing spaces that provide the means for people to reproduce themselves, to the construction of public buildings that support everyday life. Construction has gone well beyond the (re)production of the built environment purely as a means of subsistence, or to assure basic reproduction, to become the defining, ecological and environmental imprint of people upon the earth. In contrast to other species, which (re)produce constructed artefacts as a survival strategy, humans have evolved construction to create a culture and political economy of building, in which what is constructed far exceeds, and is often irrelevant for, subsistence and species survival.

The world we live in has changed from one where until the 18th century, building was relatively sparse, to one where it is now difficult to find a place that has not been built upon. Everywhere has the imprint of human intervention in nature and bears the marks of a world (re)made by people combining materials to create constructed artefacts. What many regard as wilderness areas, such as Amazonia and the polar regions, have long been places of industrial and infrastructural construction, and reflect what Fry (2009: 1) describes as 'our anthropocentric mode of worldly habitation'. This habitation includes the construction of 100,000 km of roads in Amazonia, with a further 12,000 km planned, and the extensive building of research installations in Antarctica (see Butler, 2012; Brooks et al, 2019). Construction also extends beyond the earth, and the largest, and most expensive, project to date is the International Space Station, started in 1998 and likely to be an ongoing site of building work until the mid-2020s.

The space station is emblematic of a global culture in which building is integral to one of its key characteristics, that is, the expansion of people's territorial footprint. Urbanisation is the obvious manifestation. For example, as Vidal (2018: 1) describes, in the 1960s, the Nigerian capital of Lagos was a small city 'surrounded by a few semi-rural African villages'. However, by 2018, its population had grown 100-fold from 200,000 to 2 million people, sprawling across 1,000 km^2. Lagos' experiences are repeated across the globe and are typified by the rise of mega-projects that, in their scale and deployment of material and human resources, are unparalleled in human history. From the construction of Al Maktoum international airport in Dubai, extending over 21 square miles, to the South-North Water Transfer project in China, a system of three long distance canals exporting water to China's arid areas, and each exceeding 600 miles in length, the 21st century appears to be the 'century of construction', in which unprecedented levels of building are taking place.

In this chapter, I develop the argument that while building and construction is intrinsic to species survival, much of the constructed environment is not necessary and is often inattentive to, and neglectful of, the needs of people and nature. Construction is propagated by a politics shaped by an economic culture that Douglas (2007: 547) refers to as 'growthism', or the notion that people's best interests are served by an ever-expanding economy. The growthist ideology reflects the dominant rationality of society, which is to propagate 'more of everything', including the construction of buildings and infrastructure. Here, construction is not only a means to an end by providing the physical supports to facilitate economic development, but also an end in itself by (re)producing monetised objects, or infrastructure that reflects, and reproduces, the values inherent in a growthist culture.

In pursuing this argument, I divide the chapter into three. I begin by considering the emergence of building as part of survival, or the means to secure the biological necessities of life. Early, pre-modern building was a response to bodily needs to assure water supplies and food sources, and the provision of shelter from physical threats to personal safety.[1] The small size of populations, coupled with the relatively unsophisticated nature of technology, led to minimal human impacts on ecology and environments. By 100 BC, however, there was acceleration in the quantity and range of human-made materials being produced, such as concrete and lead pipes. These were part of building and infrastructure projects, and were the basis of an emerging techno-fossil society, in which humans were increasingly using, and dependent upon, the production of materials that were more or less indestructible and being absorbed into, and becoming part of, the composition of the natural world.

After the 18th century, industrialisation and urbanisation led to what Zalasiewicz et al (2014: 35) describe as 'an orders-of-magnitude increase in the production of human artifacts', shaped by an ideology that conceived of nature as random and valueless. The logic of growthism was in ascendency, including attendant rationalities and value systems that served to legitimise unfettered building and construction. In a second section, I discuss the emergence of building within the broadcloth of modernity, or the system of ideas that serves to legitimise growthism and people's domination of nature, as well as the pursuit of profit without recourse to costing, or valuing, the impact of human actions on the environment. I refer to the 'great acceleration' or how, since the early 1950s, human activity, including unprecedented increases in the rate and scale of building and construction, has become the prime factor in the deleterious transformation of habitats and environments (see Steffen et al, 2015).

The final part of the chapter notes that the logic of a growthist ideology, as reflected in, and reproduced by, building and construction practices, is waste. Construction is wasteful and it is implicated in the production of waste materials, as well as in laying to waste particular places and environments. The notion of waste is a useful descriptor of the values and practices of the construction industry. It provides a basis to make visible many building practices that remain hidden or rarely thought of as anything other than a normal, everyday part of society. Popular narratives about construction tend to portray it as positive, or benign, in which waste is an externality, or by-product, of the rational process of building. I suggest that waste is anything but this, being symptomatic of a failing (building) culture and economy that is harmful to the well-being of people and nature.

Formative building and the imprint of construction

From the earliest presence of people on the earth, there is evidence of construction, where human beings sought to colonise space, and build upon it, as a prerequisite for their survival. To construct was as instinctive as breathing, whether that took the form of crude shelter carved out of rock, or the use of bones, animal hides or stones to craft basic structures. Prehistoric structures were usually temporary or part of a nomadic culture. Harvie (2019) suggests that there is evidence of these structures being built and occupied in the Siberian Steppe over 44,000 years ago. They were constructed from animal skins placed over sticks, and were easy to disassemble and reassemble. Variations included the tipi, a temporary structure used, primarily, by the

Indigenous peoples of the Great Plains and Canadian Prairies (see Laubin and Laubin, 2012). The tipi was made with buffalo skin placed over a frame of wooden poles, and was built close to the ground to blend in with the natural landscape.

Formative building was simple and reflected the biological necessity for shelter and protection from weather and other dangers. Such shelters left few traces and they were crafted and constructed by inhabitants developing a strong knowledge of local materials and the skills to excavate and craft them into buildings. Building was vernacular and composed of materials indigenous to a place, reflecting the local traditions and customs (Tilley, 1996). As societies began to farm, fixed building structures emerged as part of the human environment, albeit of a semi-permanent nature. The Neolithic or New Stone Age, associated with the coming of sedentary lifestyles, is characterised by a complexity of building types, constructed from either stone or timber and typically rectangular in shape. This period, spanning 9000 BC to 2000 BC, saw the construction not only of dwellings, but also of religious and ceremonial buildings, including tombs and burial spaces (see Figure 2.1).

Neolithic settlements varied in size, with some being substantial and among the forerunners of urbanisation. The first documented urban site was the

Figure 2.1: Göbekli Tepe

Note: Göbekli Tepe is located near the settlement of Urfa in south-eastern Turkey. Curry (2008: 1) describes it as the 'world's first temple constructed over 11,000 years ago'.

Source: https://en.wikipedia.org/wiki/Göbekli_Tepe#/media/File:Göbekli_Tepe,_Urfa.jpg

Mesopotamian city of Eridu, constructed 7,000 years ago from mud bricks or bundled marsh reeds. Mallowan (1970) notes that Eridu was a large city of 25 acres with a population of 4,000 people. The emergence of such settlements was characterised by increasing levels of technology, including the means to quarry stone and to combine different materials to create new building products. For instance, the city of Uruk, founded 5,000 years ago in Mesopotamia, was crafted, primarily, from adobe brick and limestone, and many buildings were plastered with lime mortar. Clay brick walls, 9 km in length, enclosed the city, and its hinterland included roads and hydraulic systems, or a sophisticated infrastructure that provided the basis for life in the city (Leick, 2002).

Urban settlements, such as Uruk, presaged the rise of construction as a dominant force in shaping society and nature. The last 2,000 years have been characterised by the development of a bewildering array of building materials, technologies and applications. These reflect the primacy of human-centric values that, over time, have shaped what Lewis and Maslin (2015: 171) refer to as the 'variety and longevity of human-induced changes' to the planet. These changes have been characterised by an increase in the intensity and scale of people's interpenetration of nature, including significant transformations of the land. While early urbanisation, such as Uruk, was disruptive of local ecologies and left visible traces of settlement, it was only after 200 BC, with the emergence of empires and territorial expansion, that building and construction began to leave indelible, irreversible imprints on the earth's surface.

This was the beginning of the period that, for some scholars, marks the emergence of the Anthropocene, in which human impacts upon the earth began, in Graham's (2016: 1) terms, to 'forge the very ground beneath our feet – to manufacture our own geological history'. Prior to this, people had inhabited the earth for over 200,000 years with little evidence of their occupation by way of physical traces of human settlement or constructed artefacts. The emergence of empires, including the rise of Alexander the Great and the Hellenistic period from 356 BC to 146 BC, and, subsequently, the Roman Empire from approximately 150 BC to AD 476, began to change this by the construction of new, durable networks of cities and infrastructure. Alexander the Great, for instance, founded a series of cities across his empire that involved major excavations of earth and the reshaping of ecologies and landscapes that remain to this day (see Figure 2.2).

This pales into insignificance when compared with the Roman Empire, which Mumford (1961: 239) described as 'a vast city building enterprise'. At its height, the Roman Empire was 5 million km^2 and comprised thousands of settlements, roads, aqueducts and ancillary infrastructure. These were served by a network of mines and quarries that ran into tens of thousands

Figure 2.2: Ruins of Alexandria in Arachosia in 1881

Note: Alexandria in Arachosia is one of over 70 cities founded or renamed by Alexander the Great, and it occupies a site of the present-day city of Kandahar in Afghanistan. It was founded in AD 329.

Source: https://en.wikipedia.org/wiki/Alexandria_Arachosia#/media/File:Ruins_of_old_Kandahar_Citadel_in_1881.jpg

across the empire, and were the basis for a fast-expanding construction sector. Roman building activity substantially altered local and regional landscapes, and, as Malhi (2017: 92) suggests, it left 'a distinct stratigraphic record of altered anthropogenic soils'. This is evident in the geology of the earth, where excavations continue to reveal layers of buildings and artefacts constructed during the Roman period, as well as evidence of large-scale resource extraction and waste production. The material remnants are what Haff (2013) refers to as techno-fossils, or preservable materials and records of human activity on, and upon, the earth.

The Roman period saw the emergence of a host of new techno-fossils, including the development of concrete that, more than any other material, symbolised the techno-colonisation of the earth by construction.[2] The earliest varieties of concrete used in Roman society involved the burning of limestone to create a quicklime paste that when combined with volcanic ash and seawater, reacted to create a durable mortar that, unlike modern variations, endures for thousands of years (see Brune et al, 2010). Aggregate,

Figure 2.3: The Pantheon, Rome

Note: The Pantheon temple was constructed in AD 126 and its standout feature is the concrete dome roof, crafted without the use of steel rods or any material that is now commonly used to support concrete to prevent its break-up.

Source: https://upload.wikimedia.org/wikipedia/commons/2/2e/Pantheon_Rome-The_Dome.jpg

such as stone or volcanic rock, was added to the mortar to increase its strength. For Roman builders, the virtue of concrete, in contrast to the use of cut stone, was its plasticity, which, combined with its strength, expanded the range of what could be built and enabled experimentation in design. These ranged from the development of curvilinear interior spaces to the formation of domed structures and arches, as exemplified by the Pantheon and Coliseum in Rome (see Figure 2.3).

The epithet of 'concrete revolution' applies to innovations in Roman architecture and construction, when concrete came to define, and give identity to, the development of buildings and infrastructure throughout the empire (Mark and Hutchinson, 1986). Its imprint was akin to a new type of rock or a substance that once used in construction, was difficult to remove or to destroy and reintegrate its material parts back into nature. Its durability is evident in the preservation of Roman artefacts, such as the city of Caesarea Maritima constructed on the Sharon Plain located in present-day Israel (see Figure 2.4). The city and harbour were constructed between 22 BC and 10 BC, with the breakwaters of the harbour set in underwater concrete. The harbour is one of 58 constructed in the Roman Empire using

Figure 2.4: Remnants of Caesarea Maritima

Source: https://upload.wikimedia.org/wikipedia/commons/b/bb/Caesarea_maritima_%28DerHexer%29_2011-08-02_098.jpg

concrete, and today, 'vast numbers of concrete blocks ... dot the seafloor' (Hohfelder et al, 2007: 410).

By the onset of the Roman Empire's decline from the mid-4th century AD, anthropogenic changes to the environment relating to building and construction were widespread, and, as Ehrlich and Ehrlich (1980: 1) suggest, this was due to the Romans' 'strictly utilitarian view of their environment: The land was there to be exploited.' This was manifest in deforestation and air pollution: the former caused, primarily, by the production of wood for the construction of dwellings; the latter caused by the smelting of metals, discharging toxins into the atmosphere (Havlíček and Morcinek, 2016). One of the primary metals that the Romans mined was lead, used to make pipes for large-scale plumbing systems, to bind together limestone and marble blocks, and as gutters for villas. Research shows concentrations of trace metals in Mont Blanc's ice fields that indicate high levels of atmospheric lead pollution in Europe during the Roman era, with significant spikes in the 2nd century BC and the 2nd century AD (see Lipuma, 2019).

Notwithstanding the eco-environmental effects of Roman building and construction, human colonisation on the earth grew at a slow pace until the late 17th century, and constructed artefacts were sporadic and low density. The impact of building was not extensive, though there were local concentrations and effects. One of these was in China between 960 and 1279. Several cities of more than 1 million in population emerged, and extensive road and canal networks were constructed, and monumental, stone buildings were built (see Wu and Gaubatz, 2013). Likewise, in Renaissance Europe between approximately 1300 and 1600, networks of urban centres were established, encouraged by a political ideology premised on the distancing of people from nature, or what Opie (1987: 15) regarded as the devaluing of nature as no more than 'an extension of autonomous human activity'. This was to become the dominant trope shaping the coming of the modern, urban world, a theme I now turn to.

Modernity and the scaling of building and construction

A familiar storyline in the social sciences is the emergence of modernity in shaping society, and the rise of technology as part of the human quest to control nature and the environment. Mass construction is linked to the rise of a modern, technocratic society, and the omnipresence of building is due, in part, to the development of the technical know-how to both excavate the resources required to construct and assemble them as constructed artefacts. While building pre-dates the rise of modernity, it is the emergence of an industrial society from the mid-18th century that develops human values often dismissive of nature, and regarding its conquest as a prerequisite for people's well-being. To construct was conceived as the building of a better world in which nature was regarded as an object of exploitation, to supply the material means to build and to be built upon with the infrastructure to support, and enable, people to pursue the point and purpose of life.

This was defined as the pursuit of people's happiness, in which building was regarded as a manifestation of human ingenuity, or the appliance of science and technology to engineer a world that promised people fulfilment through material acquisition and gratification (Smith, 1776). The *raison d'être* of society was understood as seeking to satisfy individuals' wants and desires, or the belief in the inviolate rights of people to dominate and control nature for their own ends. These ends were the realisation of life by providing the infrastructure to (re)produce places not only able to sustain human habitation, but also to be the basis for supporting the paramount objective of society. This was construed as creating the conditions for individuals to maximise their own gains, or, as Adam Smith (1776: 184) noted in *The Wealth of Nations*, 'to render the annual revenue of the society as great as he can'.

Smith's (1776) views chime with the emergence of growthism as a belief in the virtues, even inevitability, of endless material growth, in which it was argued that human ingenuity and inventiveness would always ensure a plentiful supply of the earth's resources to satisfy consumption. By the early 18th century, a growthist ideology dominated the political and economic strategies of states, in which human actions revolved around the production of goods and services to consume. Economic growth, including continuous increases in productivity and output, was conceived as a natural, rational outcome that justified not only the exploitation of nature, but also the unlimited production of objects for consumption. This was an understanding of a world without limits or ends, in which the pursuit of 'more of everything' was deemed to be compatible with the purpose of human organisation.

This purpose was characterised by rapid territorial expansion and the onset of what has since become the continuous geographical spread and development of built environments. The opening up of new territories, such as the Americas, was symptomatic of the impulses of modernity, in which construction of infrastructure, including the mining and extraction of non-renewable materials, was construed, and justified, as the epitome of modernisation, or the power of infrastructure to facilitate a progressive and desirable future. Building was not only symbolic of the onward march of a progressive culture, but also part of a process of political control and economic development, in which to construct was to create the means of conquest by building (see Figure 2.5). Colonial histories bear witness to the potency of building as a political and development strategy, ranging from roads and railways to enable the ease of settlement of new territories, to the building of defensive architecture, such as walls and buffer zones, to segregate populations and control their movements.

With the coming of industrialisation and urbanisation after the 18th century, the power and potency of modernity in shaping the built environment, and the role of construction in the making of the modern world, became centre stage. This was a world that was slowly, if inextricably, drawn into an exchange economy and characterised by building and construction projects that began to spawn major industrial and urban environments. Not only was building part of the means to support a significant expansion of population and economy, but, in and of itself, it quickly developed into a major commodity form and a vital part of the emergent urban and industrial economies of the 19th century. These economies were the embodiment of modernity's quest for scientific and technical progress, or part of an ongoing project of modernisation in which building was conceived as a civilising act by providing people with the means to live a good life.

These values reflected a human centricity that shaped advances in knowledge about materials and construction techniques, and their application to an array of constructed artefacts. In the 18th century, the emergence of iron as a building material enabled a new generation of bridges to be

Figure 2.5: The Transcontinental Railway, USA, 10 May 1869

Note: The image shows the completion ceremony of the Transcontinental Railway. Karuka (2019) describes the railway as an instrument of American colonialism and empire building by dispossessing Native Americans of their land.

Source: https://upload.wikimedia.org/wikipedia/commons/5/5d/East_and_West_Shaking_hands_at_the_laying_of_last_rail_Union_Pacific_Railroad_-_Restoration.jpg

constructed, and the invention of cast iron piping became a feature in some cities to carry water and filter sewage (Antaki, 2005). Here, the promise of modernity to facilitate human progress was reflected, in part, by the construction of plumbing fixtures that replaced unhygienic portable washbasins and chamber pots. Iron technology also enabled an expansion in the types of building that were constructed, and the invention of iron frames was the basis of numerous, often spectacular, buildings, including the Crystal Palace, erected in Hyde Park in London for the Grand International Exhibition of 1851 (see Figure 2.6).

The development of building materials and technologies continued unabated, and by the late 19th century, a new material, steel, was revolutionising the construction of high-rise buildings. This was typified by the Home Insurance Building, constructed in Chicago in 1885 and the first tall structure to be supported by a fireproof structural steel and metal frame (see Figure 2.7). The use of concrete, reinforced with steel bars, also transformed building technique, and by the early 20th century, reinforced concrete was the staple material of buildings and infrastructure, including

Figure 2.6: The Crystal Palace, London

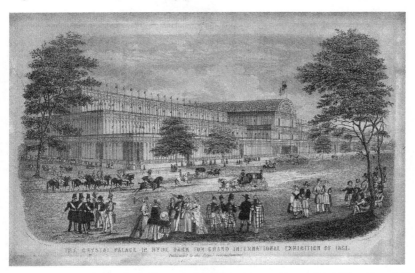

Source: https://upload.wikimedia.org/wikipedia/commons/thumb/a/a8/The_Crystal_Palace_
in_Hyde_Park_for_Grand_International_Exhibition_of_1851.jpg/1280px-The_Crystal_
Palace_in_Hyde_Park_for_Grand_International_Exhibition_of_1851.jpg

the Ingalls Building, constructed in Cincinnati in 1903 (see Witcher, 2018). Other advances included slip forming, in which concrete was poured into a continuous vertical element of planar or tubular form, enabling tall buildings to be constructed, as well as self-supporting, long-span structures with no need for trusses, frames or support posts.

By the late 19th century, the construction industry had developed scale economies and standardised methods of production, and building activity expanded at phenomenal rates, primarily in the context of rapid urbanisation. In the US, the proportion of people living in urban settlements was less than 20 per cent in 1860 but rose to 50 per cent by 1950, and by 2019, it was over 85 per cent (Ritchie and Roser, 2019). This pattern was repeated across Western nations and has taken hold globally, particularly in Africa, and Eastern and South East Asia. In 1978, 170 million people in China resided in urban areas, and by 2018, the number was 850 million, or 60 per cent of the total population (United Nations, 2019). Shanghai's population grew from 11 million people in 1987 to 26 million by the end of 2018, with China's urban population projected to be over 70 per cent by 2050 (United Nations, 2019). Similar urban population growth rates are evident in Africa, with cities such as Nairobi in Kenya growing by over 500 per cent from 862,000 to 4.7 million people between 1980 and 2020 (Macrotrends LLC, 2020).

Figure 2.7: The Home Insurance Building, Chicago

Source: https://en.wikipedia.org/wiki/Home_Insurance_Building#/media/File:Home_
Insurance_Building.JPG

Rapid urbanisation is part of a 'great acceleration', not only in the exponential rates of growth of building and construction, but also in energy use, non-organic fertiliser consumption, deforestation, greenhouse gas emissions and water use (see Steffen et al, 2015). Another measure is the production of sand and aggregates, which, along with cement, are the main ingredients of concrete. The global output of both aggregates and sand is 50 billion metric tons each per year (Cousins, 2019). They are the most mined and consumed resources on the planet, and the Organisation for Economic Co-operation and Development (OECD, 2019) forecast that their output will double by 2060. Their applications are many and varied, ranging from road building to the construction of rail tracks and water infrastructure. In China, for example, sand has been incorporated into 85,000 dams built there since 1957, including the construction of 294,104 km of embankments and dykes, as well as 43,300 water gates (Ministry of Water Resources, 2011).

While this increasing scale of building and construction has attracted much comment and critique, so too has its form and content, or the design and performance of the built environment. The ethos of modernist city building was to create spaces that were functional and utilitarian, being premised on facilitating economic growth and efficiencies of movement and circulation. The scale economies of construction were predicated, primarily, on speculation by supplying property and infrastructure that provided rapid returns on investment. This model of building encouraged value engineering, in which the objective was to strip away elements of the construction process to assure cost-effective solutions. This evolving culture was part of the standardisation of building and the reduction of construction to an instrumental process in the pursuit of technical outcomes, or what FLW (Lloyd Wright, 1992 [1894]: 21) described as the production of 'boxwise' buildings crafted in 'utter humiliation of every natural thing in sight'.

FLW highlighted the debasing of design by its subjugation to the economics of building, and for some, such as Lewis Mumford (1961), modern building cultures represented the antithesis of 'the good city'. Mumford (1961: 523) was pointing to the ugliness of the modern, sprawling city and its retrogression from previous urban forms, or what he described as 'the massing of industries ... and its effluvia absorbed by the surrounding landscape'. He related his ideas to the specificity of American urbanism and, in particular, to suburban sprawl, which he described as the building of 'a multitude of uniform, unidentifiable houses, lined up inflexibly, at uniform distances, on uniform roads, in a treeless communal waste' (Mumford, 1961: 553). For Mumford (1961: 553), far from suburbia providing people with an ideal life, or the promised escape from the problems of the inner city, including noise, air pollution, crime and high-cost living, it provided no more than 'a low grade uniform environment' (see also Chapter 4).

Mumford's (1961) observations chimed with others who described the construction of the modern city as in thrall to the automobile and insensitive to human scales of interaction (Jacobs, 1961). Mumford (1956: 388) argued that road construction, particularly in suburban locations, was anti-nature by undermining 'the surviving agricultural and wilderness areas' while sterilising 'ever larger quantities of land'. Echoing Mumford, Jacobs' (1961: 6) critique of the American city noted the design of dead and not living streets, or, as she described, 'promenades that go from no place to nowhere and have no promenaders [and] expressways that eviscerate great cities'. For Jacobs,

Figure 2.8: The M8 motorway, Charing Cross in Glasgow

Note: The M8 motorway cuts through the heart of Glasgow, and its construction destroyed many historic buildings and communities. Thousands of dwellings were demolished and people were decanted to peripheral housing estates, often against their wishes.

Source: https://en.wikipedia.org/wiki/M8_motorway_(Scotland)#/media/File:Glasgow_Charing_Cross_Interchange.JPG

building in cities sought to facilitate the interchange of things and objects as part of a value-creation process, and encouraged the construction of infrastructure, such as urban motorways, that ripped the sociability out of places by destroying local landmarks and character and displacing people (see Figure 2.8).

Modern urbanism, as described by Jacobs, was the antithesis of what many regarded as appropriate for creating 'the good city', that is, the organic settlement that FLW (Lloyd Wright, 1932: 62) outlined as 'buildings qualified by light, bred by native character to environment, married to the ground'. Rather, the modernist culture and political economy of building encouraged the rapid production of buildings and infrastructure in which the imperative to build was the extraction, by construction companies, of maximum value and profit. This meant the development, and use, of 'cost-effective', mass-produced materials that, once assembled, created places that often resembled one another, and were shaped by planning typologies that provided limited variation in building forms and spatial patterns. By the end of the 1950s, many towns and cities across the globe were beginning to resemble one another, being constructed with limited reference to, or acknowledgement of, their surroundings.

This decontextualisation of modern building is an important theme in the critique of modernism and the built environment (Mumford, 1961). It reflects the emergent culture of construction in which many construction projects appeared to be responsible for the (re)production of places that no longer offered 'common living', and where 'most modern buildings exist in a "nowhere" ... all qualities are lost' (Norberg Schulz, 2019: 40). For Lynch (1960: 116), the modernising impulses of construction were destroying vernacular traditions of building, and, as he observed, the intensity and scale of building provides 'no time for the slow adjustment of form to small, individualised forces'. Lynch (1960) could well have been thinking about volume house builders, who rarely design a dwelling with respect to the fine grain of a place or with knowledge of, and regard towards, local tradition and custom. Rather, the construction of volume-build housing is a perfunctory approach to the built environment, akin to what McCormick (1997: 42) describes as products 'spurting quickly and efficiently without any serious consideration of their ethical worth'.

This indicates a construction culture constantly pushing its products and developing building portfolios whatever the costs to people and the environment. The rush to build since the 1950s has been characterised by swathes of demolitions, loss of green open space, the destruction of ecosystems, the displacement of people from neighbourhoods and substantial sums of public finance invested in speculative, privatised, property-led projects. This is reshaping places around high-value buildings and infrastructure propagated by a panoply of property agents seeking to sell the built environment as 'an investment opportunity'. It is also reshaping existing buildings, with one manifestation being the growth in basement building, or super-rich people creating subterranean residential spaces. In London, 7,350 basements have been constructed underneath existing residential properties since 2008. Some 1,500 of these are two or more storeys deep, and over 500 have swimming pools (Baldwin et al, 2019).

This is the tip of the construction iceberg in which the form and functioning of the built environment is far removed from the origins or genesis of building as integral to, and motivated by, survival.[3] Contemporary construction is intertwined with conspicuous consumption, and lifestyle media have elevated the acquisition of property, and its internal and external decor, as important aspects of the personas of people. From the DIY culture to the emergence of manicurists to cater for gardens, the built environment is an expansive 'cash flow', or an assemblage of commodified parts that are sold to people as intrinsic to good living. This is reflected in the boom in housing extensions in the UK, with a fad for the conversion of lofts to bedroom spaces and for 'open-plan' living, leading to the demolition of internal walls. In each instance, the selling of 'lifestyle' is crucial to people's demands for more space, of which one of the net effects is to increase the quantity of concrete and techno-fossils.

This seems to matter little to actors within the construction industry, whose culture operates within short time cycles, which rarely encourages critical questions, or scrutiny, about who or what may be affected by their actions. There is little 'future-proofing' of their activities or acknowledgement of the longer-term impacts and legacies of what they build. The focus is the pursuit of building as an end in itself, rather than as a means to an end, or an object that is never complete or divisible from its context or environment. Nothing ends with the completion of buildings and they are never neutral or benign, as Fry (2009) notes, to build is to create but also destroy. For Fry (2011: 120), this recognition ought to require actors in the construction industry to confront the question, 'Does what we create justify what we destroy?', prior to a building project being given consent to proceed, with the need to take responsibility for the ways in which construction interacts with, and transforms, people and nature.

Construction and the (re)production of waste

Construction is implicated in the production of waste, in which objects that do not have economic value are considered to be disposable. This is an apt way of thinking about the building and construction sectors, in which the (re)production of waste is one of the main outcomes of their operations. From the oversupply of buildings that are not needed or ever used to the fly-tipping of construction waste and emissions of carbon dioxide from cement manufacture, the notion of waste is a useful descriptor of the building industry. The industry is more wasteful than any other, and in the UK, it contributes over 60 per cent of total material waste, including wasting of concrete, wood, asbestos and plastics, and 50 per cent of carbon dioxide emissions; over 50 per cent of British landfill sites are also filled with often untreated construction waste and fly-tipping has become endemic (see Department for Environment, Food and Rural Affairs, 2020).[4] Globally, the volume of construction waste is enormous and projected to double to 2.2 billion tons by 2025 (Slowey, 2018).

The production of construction waste is symptomatic of a culture of wastefulness, or a throwaway society wedded to personal convenience and seemingly unaware of, and not concerned about, the consequences of unfettered consumption. Unlike discussions about, and awareness of, the impacts of air pollution on health and well-being, there is little public debate about the deleterious human and ecological effects of construction waste, reflecting Lynch's (1990: 22) observation that 'wasting is a pervasive (if valiantly ignored) process in human society'.[5] While actors in the construction industry are increasingly aware of, and seeking to respond to, the high volumes of waste produced by the sector, for some observers, there is still much to do (Sharman, 2018). This is particularly so in relation to changing the industry's record relating to the wasted lives of those killed or maimed by working in construction in different parts of the world, as well as the laying to waste of countless micro-ecologies and environments affected by building operations (see Steed, 2019).

The nature of waste relating to building is captured, in part, by Lynch's (1990: 12) definition, in which waste 'is a lessening of something ... it is loss and abandonment, decline, separation and death [and] the spent and valueless material left after some act of production and consumption'. This sums up some of the negative characteristics of construction, including not only the waste of materials, but also the wasting of physical space, or what Lynch (1990) refers to as 'the waste of place'. Such wasting involves the displacement and destruction of the earth, including rock strata and minerals that, as Fry (2005: 126) observes, took millions of years to form but are 'combusted in but a few seconds' to supply the building industry. The production of aggregates, including crushed rock, sand and gravel, is the staple of construction, yet these materials are fast disappearing and leaving behind wasted spaces, particularly in coastal and riverine environments (Dan Gavriletea, 2017).

An example is the Mekong Delta, Vietnam, where sand mining has led to the infiltration of saltwater into domestic water supplies and local ecologies have been destroyed. Dredging of sand has led to riverbanks collapsing into the water, 'taking with them farm fields, fishponds, shops, and homes' (Beiser, 2018: 1). In documenting the illegal pillaging of sand for construction in Vietnam, Beiser (2018: 1) notes that 'thousands of acres of rice farms have been lost' and numerous people have been evacuated from places at risk of landslides. The waste of place by sand dredging is also evident in many Chinese rivers and lakes, including Lake Poyang in China, where hundreds of dredgers daily extract sand to fuel China's urbanisation boom (see Figure 2.9). The lake has been described by Beiser (2018: 1) as 'the biggest sand mine on the planet', and the impacts range from a decline in water quality to the destruction of fishing habitats and local livelihoods.[6]

The exploitation of sand and other resources reflects a construction sector in which the despoliation of places is conceived by actors in the industry as an unfortunate yet necessary by-product in seeking to satisfy the more or less insatiable demand for buildings. This attitude is also reflected in the industry's approach to externalising, by dumping, materials that are deemed to be valueless. One of the major forms of wasting perpetrated by construction is dumping rubble and demolished materials in landfill sites. The consequences

Figure 2.9: A sand-mining operation in the Red River, Jinping County, China

Source: https://en.wikipedia.org/wiki/Sand_mining

range from dumping material, such as concrete, which take thousands of years to be reabsorbed into the environment, to catastrophic incidents involving loss of life. Elinoff et al (2017) recount a landslide of construction waste in the Chinese city of Shenzhen in December 2015 that covered 25 acres, killing 73 people and destroying 33 buildings. The waste was built up over a number of years, being described by Elinoff et al (2017: 580) as 'the detritus from the city's building frenzy of the last 30 years'.

The wasting of lives appears to be a feature of construction, in which structural and other failings of buildings and infrastructure regularly occur. They reflect a mixture of incompetence and lassitude, even corruption, by politicians and the attitudes of actors in the construction industry that do not prioritise the health and well-being of users of the built environment. One example is the collapse of a walkway in the Hyatt Regency Hotel in Kansas City in the US in 1981, a year after the building opened. A total of 114 people died and 200 were injured, with the immediate cause being the structural failure of a double-rod system that anchored the walkways (Morin and Fischer, 2006). The design did not meet minimum safety standards, but it circumvented the building control process and was incorporated into the final structure. The inquiry into the walkway's failure concluded that the project's engineers failed to check changes to their original design by fabricators, who, inadvertently, introduced weaknesses into the final product, with the consequences that followed (Morin and Fischer, 2006).

There are other examples of such failures, in which certain people's lives are more at risk than others from building failure, as they are less likely to be provided with a quality of habitation and environment that mitigates harm and risk from poor construction. The Grenfell Tower fire in London in June 2017, in which 72 people lost their lives and a further 70 were injured, illustrates this point. Preliminary evidence from a public inquiry into the causes of the fire suggests that materials used in the construction of Grenfell Tower were substandard (Moore-Bick, 2019). This was particularly so with cheap cladding that, once alight, enabled the fire to spread quickly throughout the building. The cladding did not comply with building regulations, and 'it acted as a source of fuel for the growing fire' (Moore-Bick, 2019: 557). Other design issues compounded the problem, including fire doors that did not close, the absence of water sprinkler systems and windows that broke under heat stress, enabling smoke to enter flats in the building.

Grenfell Tower comprised social housing occupied by poor people, many unemployed and from minority ethnic backgrounds, who had little political power or social status to shape their living environments. It is doubtful that the fire would have happened in the richer, privileged parts of Kensington and Chelsea where Grenfell Tower is located because a class politics was at play that did not value public infrastructure, as reflected in the neglect of social housing by years of underinvestment. For years, residents in Grenfell Tower had complained about fire risk and the poor quality of the building, yet the local authority and the landlord responsible for the residences either ignored them or invested piecemeal in low-cost solutions (Booth and Wahlquist, 2017). The result was the completion of the cladding of the building in June 2016, comprising an aluminium composite material with a polyethylene core, a highly flammable combination. The cladding was only £2 cheaper per square metre than fire-resistant alternatives and had been banned in several countries (Davies et al, 2017).

Grenfell Tower is one example of many in which building and construction is implicated in perpetuating social injustices in which the lives of people without political power and material resources are vulnerable and exposed to socio-environmental risks. Grenfell Tower shows how poor people's vulnerability is compounded by neglect and indifference by state and private agents, or what Nadj (2019: 1) describes as 'state violence against populations marked for disposability'. The construction industry ought not to take a neutral stance on this because while rich people can afford high-quality, well-constructed buildings, the converse is the case for poor people, many of whom consume flimsy, poorly constructed buildings prone to failure and collapse. When natural events, such as hurricanes or earthquakes, impact on places, the lives that are lost are, disproportionately, the poor or those who live in substandard places that do not conform to building standards.

The systemic nature of waste in construction is also characterised by the wastefulness of speculative building, in which too many buildings are built that are not needed or used, and too few are built that are needed (see Chapter 4). The same is true with infrastructure, with many examples of things being constructed that are barely used or used too much. The problem is that the rationality of construction is premised on models of supply that fail to identify what is needed, when and where. Commercial buildings, including housing for sale, are constructed as speculative investments or a risk-taking venture based on investors' expectations that high profits will ensue. Speculative building is gambling by another name and encourages a 'build without limits' approach that has little regard for specific, demonstrable needs. It is a 'build for profits' approach premised on generating a never-ending supply of the built environment and is typified by property-led regeneration that dominates urban policy and planning.

One of the more spectacular examples is monumental building projects in China, which have been described as akin to constructing a 'city without a city' (Zhu, 2011: 42). This is part of a process whereby land in China is being urbanised much faster than the population, and the predominant supply is high-end, luxury developments that are barely affordable to most people. Both central and local states in China promote speculative building, irrespective of whether or not there is the demand for it, as part of a politics that conceives the expansion of urban space as the basis of modernity and prosperity. Woodworth (2017: 891) describes this as an anticipatory urbanism that promises 'new development futures'. One example is the city of Kangbashi in Inner Mongolia (see Figure 2.10). Construction began in 2004 but Ishak (2019: 1) notes that by 2019, a city planned to house 1 million people had less than 100,000 and its 'skyscrapers and residential buildings remain as empty as its streets'.

This might lead to the conclusion that the provision of partially occupied space is wasteful, but some suggest that a city without a populace, or a place like Kangbashi with less than its target population, is a viable economy. The development of new cities in China can be productive for investors, and Woodworth and Wallace (2017) note that if one evaluates city building, such as Kangbashi, in economic terms, far from it being 'wasteful', it is, potentially, highly productive for the actors and agents involved in land transactions and real estate. Kangbashi is an investment machine or mechanism that, in giving lucrative building contracts to construction companies, is facilitating wealth creation, or as Woodworth and Wallace (2017: 1279) suggest, it is a 'gigantic absorption of capital in urban built space'. The paradox is that the logic and rationality of creating an economy by investment in speculative

Figure 2.10: A view across Kangbashi, Inner Mongolia

Source: https://upload.wikimedia.org/wikipedia/commons/thumb/2/20/Ordos_city.jpg/
1280px-Ordos_city.jpg

buildings is also, potentially, illogical and irrational through constructing wasteful spaces that may never be occupied and used.

This paradox is part of the contradictory nature of capitalism, whereby whether or not a space that a speculator constructs is occupied may be immaterial to the flow of capital or returns to their investment. Similar situations arise in relation to political and vanity projects that are constructed more for prestige than remuneration. An example is the Ryugyong Hotel in North Korea, a political project commissioned in 1987. The hotel's 3,000 rooms remain empty but its symbolic status in displaying the potency of the nation state offers a powerful, aesthetic statement of a modernising country (Prisco, 2019). Similar projects include the construction of skyscrapers, in which governments compete with one another to build the world's tallest buildings. The buildings have aesthetic and sculptural features that render the top-most parts unusable, or what Frearson (2013: 1) describes as 'vanity height'. For example, 30 per cent of the world's tallest building, the Burj Khalifa in Dubai, falls into this category, as do at least five other towers in the city (Frearson, 2013).

There is irresponsibility attached to the construction of such structures, which use the earth's resources without contributing anything to the welfare of people and the environment. They represent no more than the commodification of buildings and the built environment, and form part of an anti-social urbanism in which the spaces and places constructed are often antithetical to sociability and responding to social need. This is typical of much of the built environment, including suburban sprawl – described by Mumford (1961: 581) as 'space eating with a vengeance' – the billions of pounds spent on widening roads that do not need widening and the construction of proposed rail systems (like HS2 in the UK) that threaten to destroy ancient woodlands (Phillips, 2017). This is not to say that roads, rail and buildings are not needed, but more to challenge and change the systemic processes that underpin the supply of speculative infrastructure and buildings, in which economic criteria outweigh broader social and equity considerations.

Conclusion

The making of the modern world revolves around construction and the design and development of buildings and physical infrastructure. Construction is a ubiquitous activity, and the scale and rate of building continues its inexorable rise, with mixed outcomes. On the one hand, construction and building is intrinsic to species survival and the reproduction of people and human activities. Yet, on the other hand, much of the way that we build and construct has deleterious consequences for the quality of human settlement, ecology and environment. Construction is anti-nature because, as much as it creates and crafts objects, it disturbs and destroys environments, and leaves various forms of despoliation and decay in its wake. Thus, many of the materials that comprise the constructed environment, such as asphalt, cement and concrete, are some of the most polluting substances in use, and they contribute much more to global warming than, for example, the use of fuel in the aviation industry (Rogers, 2018).

While construction has the potential to create a built environment that is responsive to people's needs and those of nature, in practice, the evidence is the propagation of a utilitarian approach to the building process. This is characterised by actors seeking to maximise rewards for investors in buildings by reducing costs to a minimum and disregarding nature. The rationality of building is predisposed towards the efficacy of technology and engineering that, for Kellert et al (2008: 1), has 'fostered the belief that humans can transcend their natural and genetic heritage'. The reality is the reverse, in that far from transcending nature, construction and building are intertwined with it. Yet, the (re)production of the built environment by builders and other actors in the process 'reflect[s] no understanding of ecology or ecological process' (Orr, 1999: 212). The evidence to support Orr is wide-ranging, from the extensive loss of green space and fragile habitats, to the excessive waste of construction rubble and the pollution of air and water.

The dominant paradigm of construction is to 'build without limits', or the production of environments that facilitate the operations of the exchange economy. The culture of construction encourages actors to propagate the continual quantitative growth of building, and less so its quality (see also Chapter 9). An indicator is that the predominance of construction is newbuild, which accounts for 68 per cent of total activity by value in the UK construction sector; the rest is the extension, repair and maintenance of existing stock (see ONS, 2020a). The focus on 'newness' is part of the ideology of building, that is, the pursuit of value enhancement that, coupled with the technical and logistical capabilities of construction companies to build at industrial scales, continues to transform environments into repositories of concrete and an assortment of techno-fossils.

These transformations include the construction of sprawling cities and infrastructure projects, roads filled up with construction traffic, and the non-stop sounds and smells of building work. The growing scale of building work is dominated by speculative investments that do not respond to, or address, the needs of the many. Builders preside over, and contribute to, new forms of socio-spatial inequalities. These range from gentrification to the displacement of people from redevelopment areas marked out for privatisation and the construction of super-rich enclaves. In all of this, most actors in the construction sector remain silent, seemingly apolitical, without conveying any meaningful sense of social responsibility or articulation of ethical standpoints. That construction should be such a dominant part of everyday life relates to its strategic roles in shaping the economy and society, and its interrelationships with the state is crucial here, a theme I turn to in Chapter 3.

3

Building and the
Construction State

Introduction

Building is indivisible from the actions of governments, and there is no construction that is not simultaneously shaped by state policy programmes, particularly relating to the promotion of economic development. Gordillo (2014) recounts the emergence of state-sponsored investments in the Chaco region in Northern Argentina, in which building and construction are characterised by waves of 'disruption by bulldozers' as countless villages are destroyed to make way for new buildings, roads, bridges and towns as part of opening up the region to cattle ranching and agribusiness. For Gordillo (2014), the emergent built environment in Chaco is part of the destruction and spatial obliteration of indigenous communities, a process similar in many other areas. Thus, in Chinese cities like Shanghai, government policy encourages the demolition of traditional *lilong* housing and alleyways as part of the city's modernisation, a process that involves the displacement of people and their removal to often peripheral, semi-suburban estates.

Both examples illustrate the power of construction to transform space and the social fabric of places, while drawing attention to the role of the state in shaping the (re)production of the built environment. Construction is a highly organised, and institutionalised, process involving many actors, and foremost is the state, which has a major stake in ensuring the supply of buildings and infrastructure. In this chapter, I develop the understanding that the political stratagems of states are linked to the proliferation of building and construction. States, and supranational bodies like the World Bank, support a growthist agenda that, while claiming to benefit all, is part of a politicised strategy that encourages 'building without limits'. From the opening up of frontier areas by constructing road and rail networks, to the displacement of local communities in places such as the Three Gorges Dam in China, the policies and programmes of states are a major part of why we are building too much and too badly.

In exploring this theme, I divide the chapter into three sections. First, I consider the interrelationships between building and territoriality, or the propensity for states to deploy construction in the process of securing access to, and control over, territory. From the earliest foundations of empires, construction has been pivotal in providing physical infrastructure to facilitate state governance, and integral to developing territorial presence and ambition. From the establishment of imperial empires, to the political control of insurgent groups threatening internal security, state actors use building and construction not only to secure economic benefits, but also as 'weapons of war' and means to control populations and resources. Construction is also part of the soft power deployed by states seeking to develop their influence over other countries, in which investment in infrastructure, through loans, technical assistance and materials, has become a defining feature of 21st-century geopolitics.[1]

Second, construction is a potent source of social and economic change, and states are dependent on the building industry to develop critical infrastructure that contributes to societal development, including growth in incomes and employment. I develop the understanding that the state is responsible for the well-being of the population by seeking to assure the requisite supply of physical infrastructure to enable life to flourish. This extends to the governance of construction in supporting economic development, and the state, in conjunction with private sector organisations, is part of a political economy of building or the propagation of the monetisation of the built environment. Following McCormack (1995), I develop the notion of the 'construction state' to understand how the state, construction industry and financial institutions interrelate in seeking to shape the mentalities of 'building without limits'.[2]

Such mentalities are often intertwined with corruption and criminality in the building sector, and in the final part of the chapter, I explore the significance of corrupt and criminal practices relating to construction. Crime and corruption are widespread in the construction industry, particularly where public sector contracts are involved (Transparency International, 2017). These often involve vast sums of money and are prone to a variety of illicit practices, including bid rigging, accounting fraud, asset misappropriation and the substitution of high-cost, quality material for low-grade, cheaper varieties. The implications range from the supply of poor-quality buildings to the construction of infrastructure that is unnecessary and unsuitable or not fit for purpose. There is a need to transform the ways that buildings and infrastructure projects are procured, and to overhaul the governance of construction, as part of a process of ensuring the quality of the built environment.

Modernisation and building the nation state

Building and construction is intrinsic to the development of nation states and securing territories and the welfare of populations within them. From the earliest periods of people organising the means of governance, building has been paramount as part of a biopolitics or a political rationality that, in Foucault's (1976: 138) terms, seeks 'to ensure, sustain and multiply life, to put this life in order'. To build is to solidify life into places, to literally concretise it by implanting territory with the physical imprint of human occupation. Building is both a precursor to, and outcome of, human activity, and it reflects a territorial acquisitiveness or the propensity for people to assert their presence in place. This propensity reflects not only the necessity of species survival, or to build to continue living, but also the pursuit of political and economic imperatives relating to territorial expansion and control over, and consumption of, resources.

Some of the earliest building programmes reflect the geopolitical nature of building and construction. For instance, between the early 15th and mid-16th centuries, the Incas constructed 24,000 miles of roads along much of the length of South America as a means of securing their empire and instituting their power (Covey, 2006). Likewise, as alluded to in Chapter 2, the functioning of the Roman Empire was facilitated by the construction of a sophisticated physical infrastructure that enabled ease of territorial control. Roman engineers were skilled in excavating sites and levelling hills, filling in waterlogged places, and transforming the natural landscape to facilitate habitation and the exploitation of resources (Hill, 1996). They constructed over 53,000 miles of paved roads, including bridges and tunnels up to 3.5 miles in length, and, as Staccioli (2003: 5) suggests, the infrastructure was 'rational, well organised, and widespread ... [binding] together all the territories of their sprawling empire'.

The making of the modern world reflects the colonial impulses exhibited by both Inca and Roman expansionism, and the development of systems of political control embedded in networks of building and infrastructure. The enduring images of late 19th- and early 20th-century European colonialism are roads, bridges and railways, or a technopolitical infrastructure to assure colonial powers of control of their territories. The construction of the Baro-Kano railway in Nigeria between 1908 and 1915 created an infrastructure that enabled British colonialists to move tin from the Bauchi tin fields in Northern Nigeria to ports for shipment overseas (Olukoju, 2004). In Ghana, a rail network constructed by the British state absorbed 30 per cent of public expenditure between 1898 and 1931, and, like in Nigeria, connected mining areas to coastal ports and established military control (Jedwab and Moradi, 2016). In both instances, the power of the colonial state was augmented by construction, or what Larkin (2013: 328) calls an 'architecture of circulation' acting as 'the undergirding of modern societies'.

In its more extreme variations, construction can be conceived as a weapon of war, or means by which states subjugate people and assert territorial claims. Kemman (2015), for instance, claims that state-funded dam projects in South-eastern Turkey are less about providing water resources than preventing Kurdish separatist groups gaining a foothold in the region. These 'security dams' have potential to flood hideouts and routes used by separatist groups, while relocating villagers who might otherwise provide them with shelter and resources. Jongerden (2010: 138) refers to the dams as a 'wall of water' and 'instruments in a political struggle'; they are tools to manage populations. In the case of the Ilısu Dam in Mardin Province, once it is fully operational, it will displace over 50,000 Kurdish people in the region, a process that is well under way (see Figure 3.1). Some see this as the ongoing 'Turkification' of Kurdish people by forcing them to move to cities for work and pressurising them to assimilate into Turkish culture (Warner, 2012).

Similar neocolonial building projects are evident across the globe, including the construction of settlements in places such as the West Bank, a disputed territory that is administered, in part, by the Israeli state. Over 3 million Palestinian people live in the West Bank, but since 1967, Israel has controlled much of the territory. The construction of new settlements, and expansion of existing ones, was adopted as Israeli government strategy (Allegra et al, 2017). This has entailed populating the West Bank with people relocating, primarily, from Israel, with the Israeli state sanctioning the construction of buildings and infrastructure as a political means to control this disputed space.[3] By 2012, 250 settlements had been constructed in the West Bank and over 350,000 Israeli people had relocated there, a process illustrative of the use of building as 'a territorial strategy for the creation of a new state space' (Allegra, 2017: 52).

This strategy uses physical infrastructure to extend and solidify Israel's occupation of the West Bank, illustrated most starkly by the steel and concrete West Bank barrier or wall. The wall's construction started in 2002; it measures 440 miles in length and extends into the West Bank (Jones et al, 2016). It encircles some Israeli-occupied settlements, and during its construction, Palestinian farms were destroyed and/or incorporated into territory behind the wall, thus causing further conflict. The wall is justified by the Israeli state as a security measure, while its detractors describe it as evidence of Israel's ongoing land grab and annexation of West Bank territory (Weizman, 2004; Jones et al, 2016). Weizman (2004: 5) notes that the wall is 'a sequence of convoluted boundaries, security apparatus, and internal checkpoints', which serves 'to increase the space, physically and conceptually, between neighbours' (Hallaq, 2003: 1) for people who live in the West Bank.

Figure 3.1: The drowning of Hasankeyf, Turkey

Note: Hasankeyf is a 12,000-year-old settlement and a World Heritage site on the banks of the Tigris River, and the construction of the Ilısu Dam has since led to its evacuation, with much of the place now underwater.

Source: https://upload.wikimedia.org/wikipedia/commons/8/8f/HasankeyfPanorama.jpg

While physical infrastructure constructed in the West Bank shows the potency of building as a technology of closure and control, it can also be a means to conjoin and connect, or open up territories to one another. This takes many forms, and a recent illustration is Russia's disputed annexation of Crimea, taken from Ukraine in 2015, which was followed by the rapid construction of the 12-mile-long Crimean Bridge, completed in 2019 (see Figure 3.2). The bridge has been described by the Russian media as the 'construction of the century', in recognition not only of the engineering feat to construct it, but also of its political significance in the physical conjoining and unification of Crimea and Russia (see Roth, 2018). The bridge provides the only physical point of contact between Crimea and Russia, and its physicality, as a constructed artefact, is also deeply symbolic of Russian nationalism and the state's expansionist, territorial policies.

State policy can also operate in less coercive and direct ways to develop and extend political influence and territorial control. This often includes governments providing countries with economic resources, such as technologies, labour and finance, to support a variety of social and welfare programmes, including building projects. The proliferation of building and construction globally is due, in part, to nation states seeking to develop strategic policy goals by exercising soft power, or what Fan (2008: 2) describes as allegiances with 'virtue and not force'. China is the best example of using soft power, and for the last 30 years or more, the Chinese state has been a

Figure 3.2: The Crimean Bridge

Source: https://upload.wikimedia.org/wikipedia/commons/thumb/e/e3/Крымский_мост_21_декабря_2019_года.jpg/1280px-Крымский_мост_21_декабря_2019_года.jpg

significant investor in building projects globally, especially in Latin America, Asia and Africa (Batabyal, 2019). Thus, China is the largest financier of African infrastructure by funding 20 per cent of building projects, and is directly involved in the construction of 30 per cent of them (Marais and Labuschagne, 2019).

Since 2005, the total value of Chinese investment and construction in Africa is worth over US$2 trillion, and is focused on large-scale projects such as hydropower generation, roads and railways (American Enterprise Institute, 2019). China is in the vanguard of industrialising African nations, which Eisenman and Kurlantzick (2006: 220) interpret as a 'courtship of Africa' or 'a resource grab' of much-needed raw materials for its domestic industries. This translates into building on an unprecedented scale, including well over 2,000 km of new roads in Angola since 2002, as typified by the Mombasa–Nairobi railway, funded, in part, by a Chinese loan of US$3 billion (Herbling and Li, 2019). Huang and Chen (2016: 47) interpret China's role as exporting its own experiences of 'infrastructure-induced industrialisation', in which the economic success of China, and its political stature, is understood by Chinese politicians as dependent on globalisation and the country's insertion into the socio-political structures of other countries.

This is the premise of the 'Belt and Road' policy inaugurated by the Chinese state in 2013, a construction-led initiative in which China is projected to spend trillions of US dollars on railways, energy pipelines and highways across at least 60 nations (see Huang, 2016). While the initiative will be decades in the making, its impacts are evident in Zambia, with the construction of the Copperbelt International Airport, due to open in 2021 (Wood, 2020). The state-owned Aviation Industry Corporation of China constructed the airport at a cost of $600 million, to provide ease of access for investors to mining resources in Zambia, particularly the Chambishi copper mine (Wood, 2020). Other countries, while benefiting from major construction, are indebted to Chinese investors, with the financing of four road projects in Kyrgyzstan, costing US$1.3 billion, being primarily based on loans, leaving the country with an accumulated debt of US$4 billion, of which 45 per cent is owed to the Export–Import Bank of China (Hurley et al, 2019).

Loans on building projects are integral to the geopolitical strategies of the Chinese state, and as a form of ingratiation, they encourage host nations to facilitate China's access to, and control of, their land and resources. This is evident in Tajikistan, which, in 2019, owed Chinese creditors US$1.2 billion, or just under half the country's total debt (Levina, 2019). The money is primarily used on construction-led development, including roads and dams, as well as vanity projects that have included US$40 million on the world's tallest flagpole and US$230 million on government buildings

(Chorshanbiyev, 2017). The payback has included the Tajikistan government signing away land and mining rights, and in 2011, ceding 1,100 km^2 of land near the Afghan border to China (Yu, 2016). While this may be conceived of as a neocolonial venture extending the power of the Chinese state, China's promotion of building in Tajikistan reflects, for Yu (2016), the role of physical interconnectivity in facilitating closer political and economic integration between host countries and China's inland core.

Here, Chinese state sponsorship of property-led regeneration globally is indicative of the potency of modernity and the promise of political prestige and economic power by investing in modernisation projects. This trope is one that many governments have been seduced by, believing that building has the capacity to boost, and augment, state power and be a focal point for the inculcation of particular understandings of national identity. This was to the fore in Germany in the 1930s, where the construction of the autobahns was an explicit state strategy, or desire, to create a permanent monument to the Third Reich, while promoting motoring as a form of modernisation (Zeller, 2007). For Zeller (2007: 62), the autobahns were part of the Reich's political propaganda, presented by the regime as 'uniquely German'; their construction came 'to symbolize power and the conquest of space'.

For the German state, building was a political strategy and a projection of the future, in which 'to build' was at the heart of the liberal ideal of modernisation and societal progress (Bellah, 1968). This idea of building as the kernel of a modern, progressive society became established as part of the ideological apparatus of nation states over the course of the 20th century, facilitating rapid, some would say rampant, property-led development in cities as emblematic of modernisation (Imrie and Thomas, 1999). For the nation state, modernisation, as a political theme and ambition, is premised on what Bellah (1968: 45) refers to as its 'transient' nature, which is 'subversive of every fixed position'. The implication is that modernisation is a restless, never-ending project in which the means of modernising, such as construction, is a continuous process, or a rationality that propagates 'building without limits'.

The political economy of building and the construction state

In seeking to modernise society, states pursue and prioritise economic development, and construction, both as a conduit for the modernisation of society, and for its contributions to economic growth. From contributing to employment, incomes and tax revenues, to providing the buildings and physical infrastructure necessary for the functioning of society, construction is integral to the well-being of a nation's population. The construction sector is diverse, spanning civil-engineering projects, new building and the continuous maintenance and repair of existing infrastructure. Its activities range from mining raw materials to the demolition of buildings and the management and disposal of waste products. These activities extend to the manufacture of bricks, tiles, pipes and thousands of building materials, as well as ancillary, support services such as scaffolding, plastering, plumbing, energy supply and installation, lighting, planning, architecture, and design.

The World Economic Forum (2016) note that the construction industry is the single largest global consumer of resources and raw materials, and in countries such as the UK, it contributed £117 billion to the economy, or 6 per cent of total income in 2018 (see Rhodes, 2019). In the US, the value of the construction industry in 2019 was 4.1 per cent of gross domestic product (GDP), and the sector employed nearly 11 million people (Statista, 2020). In 2018, American construction companies spent more than US$10 trillion on goods and services, and total revenues were US$2 trillion (GoContractor, 2019). Similar figures can be cited for other countries, notably, China and India, where the growth of construction is phenomenal, illustrating its strategic importance in contributing to employment and economic growth. In India, for instance, the construction sector contributes 9 per cent of GDP, employs over 51 million people and is growing at 6 per cent per year (Brown, 2019).[4]

Construction has long been a lever of social and economic development, as well as an important tool of macroeconomic management. For instance, to combat the Great Depression of the 1930s, the US government set up the New Deal to invest public money in the construction of buildings and infrastructure, primarily as a means of job creation. The Public Works Administration (PWA), a government construction agency established in 1933, gave US$6 billion of federal government money to private sector companies between 1933 and 1944 to construct public works such as airports, dams, highways, sewage systems, bridges and schools (Nash, 1999). The PWA provided funds for over 35,000 building projects, including notable schemes such as the Hoover Dam, constructed between 1931 and 1936, and the East River suspension bridge in New York City, completed in 1936 (Nash, 1999) (see Figure 3.3).

The New Deal is one example of many instances of state intervention in building and construction, in which the state is pivotal in influencing the supply of property and infrastructure. The strategic nature of building as the means of life and economic development necessitates intervention in its supply by the state as part of a process that can guarantee the reproduction of the built environment. Such interventions range from the state acting as builders to the use of legal powers, such as planning and building control,

Figure 3.3: East River suspension bridge, New York City

Source: https://en.wikipedia.org/wiki/Triborough_Bridge#/media/File:PWA,_New_York_
"Like_a_modern_Flying_Carpet,_the_Tri-Borough_Bridge_swings_across_the_Sky_with_
'Bagdad_on_the_Subway'..._-_NARA_-_195864.tiff

to regulate the activities of private construction companies. The state sets construction targets, identifies critical infrastructures to be built, regulates the repair and maintenance of the built environment, and provides fiscal and other incentives to private sector companies to engage in the building process. These activities are characterised by complex governance arrangements that are never neutral or apolitical, but, rather, shaped by specific, contextual, socio-economic and political considerations.

Some of the earliest interventions by the state in housing illustrate the political nature of building. In the UK, the development of a social house-building programme from the early 1920s was an ideological riposte to the inability of the market to provide for people on low incomes. The process took off spectacularly after the Second World War, and between 1945 and 1980, the state was responsible for the construction of over 4 million low-cost dwellings (English, 1982). This was mirrored in the US, with the federal state providing fiscal guarantees for people on low incomes to gain access to privately built houses. This encouraged a major expansion of the production of owner-occupied housing and the growth of suburban homes. Levittown is the classic example, comprising seven suburban settlements built by William J. Levitt & Sons between 1947 and 1963. They epitomised mass production by using a 26-step rationalised building method in which 'one house every 16 minutes was being built at the construction's peak' (Marshall, 2015: 1).

The British and American examples illustrate two different ideological approaches to the construction of dwellings, the former using state-controlled building to bypass the market, the latter using banking finance, underpinned by state guarantees against default, to lubricate the housing market. The apogee of state-led construction was reached in the Soviet Union and the communist countries of Eastern Europe between 1953 and 1990. The period witnessed a remarkable take-off in the quantity of construction, presaged by Premier Khrushchev's (2009) speech at the Soviet National Conference of Builders in 1954. Khrushchev (2009: 1) observed 'that conditions exist for the extensive industrialisation of construction', exhorting the state building industry to follow 'the path of using prefabricated reinforced-concrete structures and parts'. His vision was rapid volume construction by using precast concrete and constructing 'a single type of building for the whole country' (Khrushchev, 2009: 1).

This translated into the industrialisation of housing production and the construction of four- and five-storey prefabricated buildings (see Figure 3.4) (Morton, 1980). By 1960, 23 per cent of total capital investment in the Soviet Union was being spent on housing construction, and over 2.2 million

Figure 3.4: Panel Khrushchev house in Tomsk, Russia

Source: https://commons.wikimedia.org/wiki/File:Panel_Khrushchev_house_in_Tomsk.jpg

dwellings per year were built throughout the 1960s and 1970s, with 80 per cent of Moscow's housing built between 1960 and 2000 (Morton, 1980). Towns and cities throughout the Soviet Union were changed beyond all recognition by new building on their fringes, and, for Reid (2006: 227–8), the construction programme 'emphasised modernity', as once-familiar places were 'erased to make way for new urban micro regions'. These regions epitomised the role of state-led, comprehensive planning, with vast quantities of agricultural land appropriated for new construction and, as Hirt (2018: 45) describes, the erection of 'modern buildings arranged in neatly geometric super blocks'.

The dominance of state-led construction, both in the Soviet Union and elsewhere, began to dissipate towards the end of the 20th century, and new, mixed economies of building provision began to emerge, characterised by intricate networks of state and non-state organisations. Construction was influenced, increasingly, by combinations of powerful state actors and individual and corporate interests, including transnational networks of banks, industrialists, landowners, the World Bank, the International Monetary Fund and professional associations of engineers, designers and scientists (Mollenkopf, 1975). This governance of construction was akin to a 'construction state', in which state organisations, with partners, were promoting a developmental logic, or a political economy of construction in which the paramount objective was facilitating ever-increasing amounts of building activity, irrespective of whether or not it was needed.

This describes many state-led approaches to regeneration after 1945, in which a modernisation discourse and developmental model of urban politics were reshaping the spatial structure of cities. One example is Sweden, in which its major cities experienced what Johansson (2011: 412) calls a 'radical destruction and rebuilding programme'. From 1950 to 1970, 50 per cent of the oldest housing stock in inner Stockholm disappeared through demolition and was replaced by a corporate, modernist landscape of retail, offices, new roads and multistorey car parks (Johansson, 2011). Many small firms and residents were displaced by a process facilitated by state-led action that enabled municipalities to acquire private land for assembly and disposal to large development organisations, 'without having to compensate for the higher values that might follow the implementation of their plans' (Johansson, 2011: 413). The legislation imposed restrictions on improvement to buildings in renewal areas as a means of persuading existing building owners to sell up and move out.

The Swedish experience was based on a particular type of construction state in which local municipalities purchased city-centre land and retained control of it by granting site leaseholds to private developers. In the case of the long, drawn-out development of the Lower Norrmalm in Central

Figure 3.5: The Hötorget buildings, Stockholm

Note: The buildings are five high-rise office complexes constructed between 1952 and 1966 in the wake of large-scale demolitions.

Source: https://upload.wikimedia.org/wikipedia/commons/thumb/4/42/Hoghus_1-5_2007a. jpg/1280px-Hoghus_1-5_2007a.jpg

Stockholm between 1953 and 1980, planning was dominated by local politicians, who orchestrated a pro-construction agenda in which the vision for the city centre was its comprehensive redevelopment as part of a new modernist vista (see Figure 3.5). By the mid-1960s, the plans reflected a business-led agenda that, as Johansson (2011: 412) notes, was characterised by the municipality interacting with, and encouraging, 'strong pressure groups formed by big business, including national retail chains, banking and insurance, and the oil–automotive complex'. These groups envisaged, and strongly lobbied for, a motorised city dominated by ring roads and, what has since become, the homogenisation of Central Stockholm into an office and business district (Johansson, 2011).

Pro-growth construction groups were even more to the fore in countries such as the US. Post-war governance in US cities increasingly revolved around state-led coalitions in which creating the conditions for the capture of economic growth was presented by many local politicians as 'an inherent collective good' (Rogers, 2009: 44). This idea was mobilised by states using legal and fiscal powers to intensify the use of land to enable property owners to benefit from a rise in rental land values (see also Chapter 4). The notion of the city as a 'growth machine' was coined by Molotch (1976) to describe this process, whereby local landed elites interacted with state actors to create the conditions conducive to the 'growth and prosperity of private institutions' (Gotham, 2001: 289). The growth machine was ostensibly a pro-growth 'construction lobby', or interests that conceived of high-value construction as the saviour of down-at-heel cities and the means to boost jobs and incomes.

From Detroit to San Francisco, the 1950s and 1960s witnessed state policy in the US fuelling construction booms and pro-building lobbies becoming mainstream in the politics of urban economic development. They were supported by the US federal government, which encouraged privately led building revitalisation through a series of funding streams or, ostensibly, providing subsidies to private sector organisations to encourage urban reinvestment (Gotham, 2001). The Housing Act 1949 gave loans to city governments to clear slums and sell land to private developers, and this encouraged the operations of organisations such as the Kansas City Downtown Redevelopment Corporation (DRC), set up in 1952 (Gotham, 2000). As Gotham (2000: 286) notes, the DRC lobbied for construction-led renewal, and in partnership with local state agencies, it secured commitments to 'bolster downtown property values, including the construction of better shopping facilities, and more office and parking space in the downtown area'.

Similar pro-building coalitions were evident in places such as Japan, where a specific form of the construction state involved powerful corporate networks levering public finance to fund large-scale building projects. Waley (2005: 201) refers to these networks as 'a dominant vortex of forces' coalescing around the state, banks and construction companies to propagate a more or less endless programme of building. Construction was, and remains, the apex of Japan's political economy, and by the mid-1990s, building companies were consuming 40 per cent of the public budget, shaped by a 'system of collusion between politicians, businessmen, and bureaucrats' (Feldhoff, 2002: 34). The system evolved after the Second World War as 'a mutual aid community', in which politicians sanctioned major public investment in construction projects in return for political support from recipient companies, or what Feldhoff (2002: 40) outlines as state actors transferring 'resources to special interest groups [seeking] to capture wealth transfers'.

This system of governance was structurally predisposed towards 'building without limits', in which, for McCormack (2001: 34), constructed artefacts were a by-product, or an 'incidental' element, of a broader process of wealth transfer from public funds to private accounts. The legacy is what Pearce (1997: 1) describes as the world's 'biggest concrete pouring enterprise', producing underused and redundant infrastructure, including cities with many empty public buildings and roads, bridges and airports that are barely used. Jeff Hays' (2012) informative website documents a host of infrastructure that, while adding to public debt, have boosted private profits, in which 'growth and development have become the ends, rather than the means to the ends' (McCormack, 2001: 26). For instance, near the city of Yamagata, there is a US$165 million stretch of road that begins and ends with dirt tracks, while the Aqua-Line, a 15 km tunnel/bridge that runs under Tokyo Bay constructed at a cost of US$13 billion, only had 40 per cent of the originally estimated traffic flows six years after its opening in 1997 (Faiola, 2003).

The developmental rationality of the Japanese construction state is also evident at supranational state levels. An illustration is World Bank involvement in funding the construction of dams as part of its development strategies to modernise economies. Between 1948 and 2007, the World Bank supported more than 550 dam projects around the world. Over US$90 billion was provided in loans and guarantees, with the understanding that such infrastructure was necessary to underpin economic growth (International Rivers Network, 2007). Dams, as grandiose, multimillion-dollar projects, proved lucrative for the host of private construction and investment companies awarded contracts, yet, as commentators note, many schemes were over-engineered, inappropriate to meeting local needs and degraded ecologies and environments (Dunphy, 2018). Dye (2019: 2) refers to the World Bank as perpetuating a 'high modernist ideology' in relation to dam building that, while creating profitable investment channels for private building contractors, often ended with wasted infrastructure that was uneconomic and barely used.

The same might be said for continental-wide, inter-state developments based on the supply of major regional infrastructures. One of the most ambitious is the Initiative for the Integration of South America's Regional Infrastructure (IIRSA), inaugurated in 2000 and involving 12 Latin American countries and corporate and supranational state bodies, such as the World Bank (van Dijck, 2008). This is a massive construction-led development project in which the objective is the integration of roads, railroads, waterways, power grids and telecommunication services across South America as part of a broader process of creating a globally competitive region. In 2009, the IIRSA outlined over 550 projects as part of their initiative, with a budget of US$37.4 billion, with 70 per cent sourced from public funds (Rios, 2009). A controversial project, first outlined in 2007, is the Madeira river dams in Brazil that, while enabling soy to be transported for export, is implicated in what Fearnside (2014: 264) describes as 'population displacement, deforestation, [and] loss of livelihoods from fisheries in Brazil, Bolivia and Peru'.[5]

For critics, the IIRSA is a powerful inter-state cooperation shaped by a construction sector with 'a penchant for, mega projects as well as an increasing *need* for such large-scale projects in order to continue operating as large enterprises' (Bebbington et al, 2018: 185, original emphasis). The IIRSA initiative reflects broader political manoeuvres, particularly by the Brazilian state, to develop roads and related infrastructure so that protected areas can be opened up for exploration and the extraction of minerals and hydrocarbons. This is a global 'land rush' facilitated by reforms of environmental licensing, a rollback of regulations and a slowdown in 'the formal recognition and titling of indigenous lands' (Bebbington et al, 2018: 194). The IIRSA is part of a land grab or neocolonial venture, described by Santi as 'ethnocide against indigenous people' (quoted in Watts, 2014: 1). For indigenous people living near the Xingu River in the northern Brazilian state of Pará, its biggest project, the Belo Monte dam, means the end of a way of life, or, as a spokesperson said, 'when they close the river, it will be like they are destroying our lives' (quoted in Watts, 2014: 1).

The strategies of the IIRSA, such as the Belo Monte dam, mark the ascendency of neoliberalism, or the belief in market reform policies to enable private investors to operate free from restraint, as part of a broader political agenda of wealth creation. For builders, banks and finance companies, this is the green light to pursue speculative building as an investment strategy and source of capital accumulation, aided and abetted by state policies that are supportive of a deregulated environment. By the end of the 20th century, construction, globally, was growing at rates previously not seen, underpinned by governments, investment capital and building companies promoting property-led development as a vital means of boosting economic growth, jobs and incomes. This was occurring at all scales, and more or less everywhere, from large projects such as the redevelopment of London's docklands, to smaller-scale developments such as Battery Park in New York.

London's docklands illustrate the significance of the state in boosting construction, as private construction companies were given carte blanche to redevelop a 2,700-hectare site, free from most planning and bureaucratic controls. Over the lifetime of the area's development from 1980 to 1998, at least £7 billion of public investment subsidised private building costs and provided windfalls to corporate investors (Imrie and Thomas, 1999). The docklands model was premised on removing perceived impediments to investment, such as land that was expensive to develop, and its market-based approach discouraged plan-led development in favour of speculative building prioritising the construction of high-end, profitable development. The state was reconceived as 'entrepreneurial' by seeking to facilitate a business-led agenda in which private interests were given every encouragement by state actors to pursue a developmental model.

The docklands model has since become an orthodox approach to the redevelopment of towns and cities worldwide. What has taken centre stage is the idea that building is *the* panacea to economic decline and a major means of urban revitalisation (Imrie and Thomas, 1999). While this echoes early periods of building activity, a difference is that investment in land and infrastructure has become 'supercharged', and the 21st century has seen the unleashing of further laissez faire construction, with state actors at the fulcrum of facilitating major waves of property-led building. In the UK, since 2010, governments have encouraged the dismantling of planning controls to make it easier for builders to build, including particular classes of development being able to proceed without the need for planning permission (Lord and Tewdwr-Jones, 2018). In Turkey, Tansel (2018) describes how state-led commodification of land and property is part of an emergent authoritarian politics to remove institutional and regulatory barriers that inhibit privatisation and incentivise building and construction.

This chimes with the rise of urbanisation in countries like India and China, where the state deregulation of planning and provision of fiscal and other incentives to build are key to understanding investments in building and infrastructure. The relaxation in central state controls in China by decanting more power to the local level has encouraged locality-wide entrepreneurship, with state organisations mimicking the market, or seeking to replicate the behaviour of private sector, profit-seeking firms (He and Wu, 2007). He and Wu (2007: 196) describe Shanghai's pursuit of 'profitable real estate development' as motivated by the need to offset financial deficits and create a solvent local state. Land has been rezoned and the means of access to develop it has been made easier. The local state has provided incentives to developers, such as part exemption from paying land leasing costs and administrative charges, as part of a Chinese-wide movement to facilitate building through 'state-sponsored property development' (He and Wu, 2007: 196).

The effect has been a rapid take-up and development of land and property. The process is characterised, primarily, by the demolition of dwellings in city-centre neighbourhoods and their replacement by 'commoditised development', typified by the construction of upmarket housing and office and retail use (see Chapter 4). A speculative urbanism has taken hold, resulting in gentrified spaces of skyscrapers, new transport systems, major sports facilities and gated communities (see Figure 3.6). These developments are indicative of the financialisation of Chinese urban renewal, in which construction is the major focus for, and stimulus of, state and private sector investment, attracting capital flows from banks, wealthy individuals and corporate organisations. The process is enabling state agencies, with partners, to transform land and property into valuable financial assets by leasing land and property to wealthy investors as part of investment portfolios (Shin, 2013).

Figure 3.6: Shanghai skyline

Source: https://en.wikipedia.org/wiki/Shanghai#/media/File:Shanghai_skyline_from_the_
bund.jpg

In most countries, state policy encourages a commodification of construction in which building is conceived as an end in itself, or a tradable commodity, what Tricario and Sol (2016: 53) refer to as 'an asset class' (see also Chapter 4). States are implicated in creating whole streams of asset classes for investors in construction, and in the UK, changes in how government procures public sector infrastructure led to the Private Finance Initiative (PFI) in 1992. Instead of the state paying for buildings and infrastructure from taxes and other public receipts, the PFI enabled private sector organisations to pay the upfront construction costs and to charge public authorities, usually over a 30-year period, for access to, and use of, whatever is built. While private companies benefit from a long-term, lucrative asset stream, public debt is incurred, as payback is usually many times greater than the original costs of construction and more than if state agencies had borrowed money from the private market (Asenova and Beck, 2010).

Whether through PFI, the dismantling of planning controls or subsidising private development costs, the state is intertwined with, and supportive of, a construction culture hard-wired to propagating building activity. The financialisation of real estate serves to (re)produce a political economy of construction characterised by land value capture and the production of buildings as investments or monetised objects. This is supported by governance akin to a 'mercantile system', whereby private groups lobby state agents for the rights of access to public goods and services.[6] From growth coalitions to state urban renewal agencies and PFI-style contracts, the governance of construction both enables and empowers organisations seeking to capture trillions of US dollars pouring into the building industry. The question of how propriety can be assured in relation to the appropriate use of such resources, including mitigating corruption, is a topic to which I now turn.

Construction and the criminality of building cultures

State power is interlinked with corruption and criminality, and this is particularly so in relation to the rapid growth of building activity. From illegal land grabs in places such as India and Peru, to local politicians ignoring legal regulations, construction is influenced by interests that often operate at the margins of the law and, in many instances, well beyond it. While it is difficult to generate data that show how much of the built environment is constructed without recourse to law and legal practice, there is evidence that building regulations are regularly flouted by builders and prone to lax interpretation and enforcement by state officials (Shan et al, 2020). Developers often ignore planning laws, and many buildings and infrastructure are constructed that are the product of malpractice and criminality (Shan et al, 2020). There are, therefore, questions to be raised about the culture of the building industry and the systemic weaknesses in the governance of construction that enable criminality and corruption to occur.

This matters because to permit a culture of corruption in building is to condone the supply of a poor-quality built environment and/or the construction of unwanted and unnecessary infrastructure and buildings. Corruption in construction encourages not only the 'building more' mentality, but also the building of substandard and inferior infrastructure that has the capacity to undermine the quality and integrity of human and non-human ecologies and environments (Green, 2005). The construction industry is particularly open to corruption and crime because of its lack of transparency and the complexity of its processes, which make it difficult to police (Locatelli et al, 2017). Transaction chains are complex and the fragmentation of the industry into numerous trades can enable illicit practices to be concealed. It is relatively easy for short cuts to be taken in workmanship and systems of governance, such as public tendering and planning and building control, which are not watertight and provide opportunities for bribery.

Corruption and criminal practice is more common than is thought, and it is estimated that between 10 and 30 per cent of the value of global construction is lost due to corrupt and/or illegal practices (De Jong et al, 2009). The attraction is the vast amount of finance flowing through the building sector, with the global construction industry worth US$13 trillion in 2019, a figure likely to grow by 85 per cent to US$15.5 trillion worldwide by 2030 (Robinson et al, 2015). A survey of actors involved in the UK construction industry found that embedded cultural practices and attitudes in the building sector encourage corruption, with 49 per cent of respondents suggesting that corruption is commonplace (Chartered Institute of Building, 2013: 1). A third of respondents had been offered a bribe and had witnessed cartel activity and 'sharp' practices. A notorious case was the bridge-building firm Mabey and Johnson, which, in 2009, admitted that they had paid substantial bribes to politicians and civil servants in Jamaica, Ghana and Iraq to secure £60 million in construction contracts (Leigh and Evans, 2009).

Laver (2014: 3) suggests that most countries 'are afflicted with systemic corruption', where corrupt behaviour is often accepted as 'a way of life'. In Thailand, for example, construction is controlled by political elites, or what Elinoff (2017: 595) describes as 'close-knit circles' characterised by 'occluded entanglements between the state, capital and development'. There is little public scrutiny of building and construction, and the administration of land transactions is, allegedly, the most corrupt part of government bureaucracy (GAN Integrity, 2020). Public dissent and comment on state projects is stifled by 'legal constrictions on speech', making it difficult for citizens to expose and oppose corruption relating to building projects (Elinoff, 2017: 589). In 2011, over US$32 billion was lost to corruption in construction in Thailand, a loss that translated into what Elinoff (2017: 595) describes as landscapes of 'overbuilt buildings, cracks in sidewalks and abandoned projects'.

The concrete pillars of the failed Hopewell rail project in Bangkok are testimony to corruption and malpractice in Thailand (see Figure 3.7). Proposed in the late 1980s, the project was abandoned in 1998 after sections of infrastructure had been constructed. The project was approved without feasibility studies relating to the financial and technical challenges, and there was no evaluation of 'value for money' (see Elinoff, 2017). The project was beset by malpractice, technical hitches, cost overruns and, by the mid-1990s, an economic downturn that led to the cessation of construction in 1998. The main contractor, Hopewell Holdings, went bankrupt and sued the project's sponsor, the State Railway of Thailand (SRT), which, they claimed, failed to deliver land parcels that made the project unrealisable. Hopewell was awarded US$370 million of public funds in 2019 in recognition of contractual failings by SRT, and the legacy is public debt, abandoned infrastructure and the despoliation of local environments where construction of the rail occurred (Fredrickson, 2012; *Reuters*, 2019).

Corruption is also endemic in Japanese construction, and Choi (2007: 930) notes that it is 'systematically perpetrated, legitimately sustained, and

Figure 3.7: The Hopewell pillars, Bangkok

Source: https://commons.wikimedia.org/wiki/File:Hopewell_pillars_2,_Bangkok,_2009-01-21.jpg

structurally embedded at a high level of administration'. The nature of the construction state in Japan, alluded to in the previous section, is networks that are exclusive and closed, providing politicians and business elites, including criminal groups, with scope to interact beyond public scrutiny (Steele, 2017). Price fixing is endemic under the '*dango* system', in which construction firms collude to predetermine the winner of a project bid and, in doing so, ensure bid prices are kept high and worth much more than the costs of delivering the project (Black, 2004). The winning company distributes profits to colluding partners, including granting favours to politicians who may have been part of the process. Beyond the dubious ethical nature of the *dango* system, research shows that it is inefficient as a delivery system for projects and 'inflates the costs of construction by between 30 percent to 50 percent' (Choi, 2007: 936).

The clientelism of the *dango* system encourages construction firms to lobby public authorities to expand the number of capital projects beyond what is needed, and this has left a legacy in Japan of the overproduction of buildings and infrastructure, and the perpetuation of concrete and despoiled environments (Harding, 2016). The system is wasteful because, as a prerequisite for profiteering, it encourages new building projects and the neglect of existing infrastructure that might otherwise be serviceable and usable. It also pushes up levels of public debt; in one case, the Maeda Road Construction Company and seven road-paving material companies colluded to bid up the price of asphalt, with the implication of inflating the cost of public spending on roads. The practice had been occurring for a number of years, and investigations by Japan's antitrust watchdog subsequently led to a US$536 million fine being imposed on the companies in 2019 (Ae et al, 2020).

Corrupt relationships between politicians, bureaucrats and construction companies have also shaped rapid urban growth in Europe. In Spain, a building boom since the late 1970s has been intense, with the size of built-up areas doubling between 1987 and 2005 (Fernández Muñoz and Collado Cuerto, 2017). The process has been shaped by 'real estate blocks', or political groupings of property interests, including building companies, local politicians and planning officials (Fernández Muñoz and Collado Cuerto, 2017: 210). Fernández Muñoz and Collado Cuerto (2017) outline housing development in the town of Torrelodone that was facilitated by politicians and officials taking bribes from landowners and real estate interests to reclassify undevelopable land to developable and, in doing so, to increase its market value and make it attractive for property-led construction. A consequence was that speculative building was rife in Torrelodone throughout the 2000s. It degraded the local environment, and after the financial crash of 2008, a collapse in the local property market led to an increase in empty and abandoned housing.

The Spanish example is illustrative of weak governance in a context of fragmented government, in which the absence of checks and controls on individuals with vested interests in real estate development has life-threatening consequences. For instance, Green (2005: 528) describes deaths and injuries after two earthquakes in Turkey in August and November 1999 as 'disaster by design' and human rights violations. For Green (2005: 529), the earthquakes did not cause the human tragedies; rather, they were the consequence of 'government and industry corruption, gross negligence and state links to organised crime'. In the rush to economic development from the mid-1980s, Turkey's politicians encouraged unregulated construction in which planning and building regulations were regularly ignored and dwellings were constructed on sites prone to environmental risks. In one of the places badly affected by an earthquake, Marmara, Green (2005) quotes an advisor to the mayor who stated that officials accepted bribes from builders as a quid pro quo to sidestep building codes and inspections.

This building culture reflects a populist clientelism whereby local politicians generate support from business interests by ignoring rules and regulations, and permitting the construction of poor-quality, often illegal, buildings. This lies behind the human tragedy of the Marmara earthquake on 17 August

1999, in which 18,000 people died and 20,000 buildings collapsed. In the quake's aftermath, Turkey's Interior Minister at the time, Saddetin Tantan, commented that 'the contractors who built those buildings and those who issued permits committed murder' (quoted in Bohlen, 1999: 1). In some instances, building permits were not issued, and this reflects a broader problem in Turkey, and elsewhere, where illegal and shoddy construction is able to proliferate. It is estimated that 65 per cent of Istanbul's housing has been erected without permits, and many more have been constructed throughout the country in flood plains, landslip zones and other areas of environmental hazard and risk (Bohlen, 1999).

Construction is also propagated by less overt forms of corrupt and/ or questionable practice that Flyvbjerg and Molloy (2011: 88) refer to as 'delusional optimism' and 'deliberate strategic deception'. They discuss major infrastructure projects across the globe and ask why is it that, time and again, they underperform in terms of cost overruns and benefit shortfalls. One answer, they suggest, is the use of forecasting techniques, such as predict and provide, which extrapolate present trends into future scenarios and are usually overly optimistic by overestimating demand. There is also deliberate deception, whereby planners, builders and others involved in projects create 'scenarios that highlight success and disguise the potential for failure' (Flyvbjerg and Molloy, 2011: 90). As Flyvbjerg and Molloy (2011: 90) conclude, strong incentives and financial benefits to different parties, including enhanced status for politicians, can be part of the rationale for strategic misrepresentations of the costs and benefits of proposed projects.

While it is difficult to show how delusional optimism and strategic deception interact to influence the rate and scale of construction, Flyvbjerg and Molloy's (2011) study shows that consultants advising on the delivery of project proposals will emphasise benefits and de-emphasise risks and costs. As one of their interviewees, a project manager, said: 'it is in line with their need to make a profit' (Flyvbjerg and Molloy, 2011: 92). This is apparent with the proposals for HS2, a high-speed rail line in the UK, in which the state's use of a cost–benefit analysis has been criticised for its 'optimism bias' that has underestimated increases in the forecasted costs of the project (Atkins et al, 2017). This optimism is shaped, in part, by an HS2-commissioned report, produced by the private sector consultants KPMG (2013), which estimated £15 billion in additional benefits to the UK from the project, a number derided as made up and comprising deceptively disarming data that show the project in best light (Dudley and Banister, 2014).

The HS2 case is illustrative of the problem with the supply of infrastructure, where the prevalent econometric approach by politicians, officials and industry actors is to use seemingly objective models to construct cases in favour of construction as part of a broader political economy of building

(Atkins et al, 2017). This dynamic underlies the 'building more' culture that we imbibe, in which the scope for malpractice and unethical activity in construction is manifold (Locatelli et al, 2017). The question is how to confront and undermine corrupt governance, or systems that perpetuate activities that range widely from land grabs to bid rigging and the flouting of planning regulations (see also Chapter 10). There is complexity in these varying contexts that goes to the heart of what governance ought to be, and, in particular, how state–industry actors can be disposed towards judicious actions that ensure ethical practice is paramount in construction.

This focus on ethics is important as it raises fundamental questions about who and what building is for, and what ought to be provided that is commensurate with meeting the necessities of life. While corruption, as dishonest or fraudulent conduct, cannot be purged entirely from state–industry relations, or from life itself, I concur with Sanchez (2016) that corrupt behaviour is not a sideshow that occurs at the margins of society, but rather endemic and enmeshed within socio-political organisation. Corruption is, to paraphrase Sanchez (2016: 1), a symptom of the social and governance structures of society, including building and construction, and the technology that supports them. This is not to say that all building activity in all places will entail corrupt behaviour. The propensity for corruption to occur is situational, with the likelihood of it occurring dependent on the combination of a complexity of socio-economic, political, cultural and legal factors, including state regulations and controls.

Nonetheless, the building sector is recognised as the most corrupt in the world, and until effective measures to combat it are put in place, the construction of poor-quality, often unsafe, buildings and infrastructure will continue (De Jong et al, 2009). While tinkering with the procedural and process parts of the governance of construction can help to mitigate some of the problems, if corruption in construction is systemic, as evidence shows, then radical actions are required to overcome corrupt practice (Laver, 2014). Such actions ought to ensure that the supply of buildings and infrastructure is commensurate with responding to the needs of both people and the non-human world rather than, as in many instances, being a product of a combination of profiteering, the monopoly powers of politicians and state officials, and illicit and/or unethical, even criminal, corporate practices.

The challenge of confronting, and reducing incidences of, corruption relate, in part, to overturning the actions of rent-seeking elites propagating building as part of their financial and investment portfolios. Here, the liberalisation of construction activity since the 1980s, including the weakening of state capacities, has unleashed the potency of building as a significant form of asset accumulation, and with it, the potential, indeed probability, that various, often dubious, actors and activities will be attracted to the sector. At a systemic level, it follows that a fundamental way to reduce corruption in construction is to break its financialisation, that is, to socialise land and property markets in ways whereby whatever is constructed is no longer a monetised object with exchange value (see Chapter 10). Rather, the production of the built environment ought to be based on what is needed, or its use value, and produced in ways whereby the associations between investment, assets and buildings are broken.

Conclusion

The proliferation of building and construction is related to the activities of the state, which has the responsibility to secure the lives and well-being of its population. Given that building and infrastructure are important to the welfare of people, and significant to social and economic development, the state, as part of the governing apparatus, has a pivotal role in shaping the rates and scales of construction in society. From the provision of public finance to the planning and development of strategic infrastructure, the state provides an array of material and administrative resources to stimulate and encourage building activity, including organising and orchestrating the legal and regulatory frameworks that govern it. These activities extend to the geopolitical strategies of nation states and their territorial ambitions, in which building and construction are integral in seeking to, militarily and politically, secure territories and open them up to economic development.

From state-sponsored land grabs to neo-colonial ventures led by powerful supranational organisations and nation states, state organisations are deeply implicated in propagating building and construction as development strategies or means to liberalise flows of goods and services. This chimes with the global liberalisation of property markets, in which the capacity for companies to invest in new construction has proliferated in a context whereby states are encouraging land development strategies by creating the conditions for unfettered building activity. These conditions include various state funds for building projects, tax incentives and the dismantling of land-use planning and environmental regulations. Despite COVID-19, this appears to be translating into the biggest construction boom in human history, in which speculative investment and building, particularly in mega-projects such as rail and airport infrastructure, as well as high-end office, retail and residential uses, continues to escalate (see, for example, Al-Kodmany, 2020).

The different ways in which land and property are brought forward for development, including new construction, depends on a complex of state–industry linkages that is akin to a 'construction state', or a symbiosis between political and administrative officials and actors in the private sector building industry. The rise of property-led development and the hyper-marketisation of construction activity are both features of contemporary times, and are redolent of building based on 'crony' capitalism, or strong interrelationships between a business and political class. While deregulation and the liberalisation of markets are suggestive of the withdrawal of states from shaping private actions, I concur with Mazumdar (2008: 1) that they are facilitating ever-closer linkages between, or 'an enhanced degree of state capture' by, corporate and other powerful groups involved in the production of the built environment.

Such capture opens up possibilities for corruption and criminality in construction, and a significant supply of buildings and infrastructure appears to be derived from illicit and illegal activities. This is not surprising given the lucrative nature of construction, and the trillions of dollars flowing through the sector (Statista, 2019). However, as evidence in this chapter suggests, the weak and/or corrupt governance of much construction activity encourages incursion into fragile environments, illegal mining and the extraction of minerals such as sand and gravel, and it propagates the supply of poor-quality and often unwanted and underused infrastructure. It also contributes to, and exacerbates, one of the major challenges of our times, that is, speculation in land and property markets and the perpetuation of places as pure investment spaces.

4

Speculation and Building Booms

Introduction

Speculation is a dominant feature of contemporary land and property markets and is significant in fuelling the rise in building and construction activity. It is most obvious in the changing vistas of major cities that, since the late 20th century, have spawned numerous tall or vertical buildings, often replacing land uses that command low rental values (Graham, 2016). Goldman (2011) suggests that we are living in an era of speculative urbanism, in which an objective of politicians is to transform land deemed to be of marginal use into lucrative real estate, primarily by attracting flows of global investment to fund the construction of new buildings and infrastructure. From the skylines of Shanghai and Mumbai to those of Lahore and London, the evidence of speculative construction consists of ever-escalating rates of urban development, shaped by the core logic of capitalist urbanisation in which the appropriation and redevelopment of land is intrinsic to the (re)production of economic value.

Speculation is not only the staple diet of capitalist land and property markets, and the driving force behind the building booms of the early 21st century, but also an enduring feature of human society. Investors looking to make lucrative gains from the purchase of land will take a risk on its development, with the expectation that, over the course of time, its market value will increase. Such developments are described by Shin (2013) as 'pre-emptive', or part of an anticipatory mode of acting in which actors tend to supply more than 'can be consumed and with the expectation that demand will follow'. This is a recipe for overbuilding, providing much more than is needed. In this chapter, I develop the argument that speculation is fundamental in shaping the contemporary crisis of construction. This entails the overproduction of buildings and infrastructure, and a regressive urbanism in which the benefits of construction projects do not accrue to the most disadvantaged, while the ecological integrity of the environment is undermined.

I divide the chapter into three sections and begin by outlining what speculative construction is and entails, placing it in its historical context as an enduring and systemic part of building activity. From the Greek city-states to major Roman cities, speculation was a feature of early urbanisation, and is significant in shaping the supply, quality and cost of buildings, particularly dwellings. Speculation was at the heart of industrial urbanism from the late 18th century, and was instrumental in shaping the social geographies of urban expansion from the early 20th century (Mumford, 1961). Since the late 20th century, speculative development has increased significantly, becoming a core part of a broader process of corporate capital seeking value-enhancing outlets for investment. Such outlets range from the construction of spectacular and monumental buildings, such as the Petronas Towers in Kuala Lumpur, Malaysia, to the construction of industrial infrastructure, such as Electronic City in Bangalore (Stallmeyer, 2011).

In a second section, I discuss and evaluate a particular type of speculative building that has come to dominate land uptake and development in major cities around the globe. This is the construction of dwellings for investors seeking to protect and realise income by investing in buildings, which they regard as akin to depositing money into savings and investment banks (Atkinson, 2020a). Here, the rationality of construction is the propagation of speculative spaces in the service of profiteers concerned less with the social or human fabric of places, and more with the physical and technical functioning of the built environment, in which the realisation of monetised value is the paramount objective (Skeggs, 2014). I relate the discussion to building for rent and sale, and the construction of housing aimed at wealthy purchasers. As data suggest, much of this property remains unsold or, if purchased, is often left empty, contributing to the creation of lifeless places, or what Atkinson (2019: 2) describes as 'dead residential space or necrotecture'.

I conclude the chapter by considering the alternatives to speculative construction, in which what is built ought to be shaped by socio-ecological needs, and a politics that reflects, and develops, a progressive urban agenda. The starting point is to challenge, at a systemic level, the *raison d'être* of speculation, in which building ought not to be an exercise in pure consumption and profiteering, or the deployment of construction as the means to respond to, and bolster, share prices. Instead, construction ought to be a process of nurturing people and the environment, including the (re)production of places that provide for the necessities of life, without threatening finite planetary resources. Speculative building is a threat to ecological integrity because it is hard-wired to build without limits, as well as socially divisive in seeking to construct for the greatest monetary returns, or pandering to those with the ability to pay for whatever is built. In both respects, speculative building should be consigned to the past.

Speculator capitalism and the crafting of urban space

Speculation in land and property markets is stimulating the proliferation of buildings and infrastructure, encouraged by state actors, private equity companies and other investors with a stake in cultivating wealth creation and personal enrichment. From the large-scale acquisition of territory by speculators and foreign investors in the Cerrado savanna of Brazil, to what Levien (2012: 934) describes as the state's forcible transfer of farmers' land to private companies in India to facilitate 'privatised infrastructure development', liberalised real estate markets are fuelling significant investment in land speculation and development across the globe (Levien, 2018). In the Cerrado savannah, agribusinesses have been investing heavily in soybean production, and the rapid escalation in land values since the early 2000s has attracted even more investment in land as a financial asset. Conant (2018: 1) refers to this phenomenon as land 'functioning as a stock option'.

The same can be said about the designation of special economic zones (SEZs) in India, which Levien (2012: 933) describes as providing investors with the 'opportunity for windfall real estate gains'. The SEZs are a development tool avowedly committed to promoting economic growth by attracting speculative global capital, often to farming areas or places deemed to be 'low value'. By providing tax breaks and various state subsidies for commercial and residential developments, SEZs promote real estate development over other, alternative, types of land uses (Shiva et al, 2011). An ongoing project is Electronics City in Kochi, which, while ostensibly an industrial complex of electronics and information technology (IT) software production, is a mixed-use development comprising a shopping mall, an international convention centre and upscale residential apartments. For Levien (2018: 48), the SEZs are 'outlets for speculative real estate capital', with housing developers taking advantage of cheap land at the urban periphery.

The examples of the Cerrado and Kochi highlight how investors, attracted by the combination of state subsidies, low land values and the prospects of high profits, commit to constructing buildings and infrastructure without necessarily securing a purchaser. The expectation is that, over time, purchases will transpire that, along with upward movements in land and property values, will lead to windfall gains or at least significant profits. Speculation is the epitome of a growth-oriented system and chimes with capitalism, with its predilection for securing rapid appreciations in economic value. It takes different forms, from the disastrous sub-prime mortgage crisis of the 2000s, when banks and financial institutions poured money into housing speculation by lending to people who subsequently defaulted on payments, to the construction of millions of housing units, many remaining unoccupied, on the edges of Chinese cities (Poon, 2019).[1]

There are mixed views about speculation, ranging from those, such as Ryan (1902), who regard it as unethical, to others, such as Pennington (2000), who conceive of it as a rational, economically efficient process. For Ryan (1902: 346), speculation 'feeds the passion of avarice, strengthens the ignoble desire to profit by the losses of his fellows', whereas for Pennington (2000: 45), speculation encourages 'competitive decision making' that enables land to be allocated 'to its most productive uses'. These contrasting views reflect a broader equivocation about the roles and impacts of speculation in society, in which the more negative comments regard speculators' actions as contributing to the inflation of land values and adding volatility to market transactions (Pettifor, 2018) Other observers, in a positive vein, note that speculation may increase economic output and enhance job growth by, for instance, bringing underutilised land back into productive use (Ely, 1920).

Whatever the problems with, or merits of, speculation, it is not a new process or confined to capitalism. Its roots are evident in early urbanisation, and it was significant in Roman and Greek cultures. Craver (2010: 153) describes the emergence of a strong real estate market in the 2nd century BC in Rome, in which the speculative building of 'domus', or villas occupied by the wealthy, was prominent. Stambaugh (1988: 358) notes the 'intense real estate speculation' in Rome during the 1st century BC, in which building contractors usually fixed the price of dwellings before their construction but often increased it by well over 50 per cent prior to completion (Yavetz, 1958: 513). Most construction was of 'insulae', or cheap residential buildings built to house major influxes of migrants to Rome (see Figure 4.1). Powerful landowners, such as the Roman statesman Cicero, were in the vanguard of speculative building, usually by acquiring land cheaply and constructing poor-quality buildings prone to collapse and failure (Yavetz, 1958).

Speculative urban development was also a feature in medieval Britain. Platt (1976: 32) describes urban extensions to Cheltenham in the 13th century that involved laying out house plots that were subsequently not 'taken up immediately by the builders', being left unoccupied for two decades before being built on. Bell et al (2019: 604), having compiled a unique data set of freehold land and property transactions in medieval England, show that 'a rising number of people were involved in multiple transactions'. They suggest that people of a particular stature and financial means, such as merchants and legal professionals, were 'able to accumulate sufficient capital to engage in property speculation' (Bell et al, 2019: 604). By the mid-14th century,

Figure 4.1: Insula dell'Ara Coeli, Rome

Note: The Insula dell'Ara Coeli is a 2nd-century Roman dwelling that is five storeys in height and typical of most dwellings in Rome during that period.

Source: https://upload.wikimedia.org/wikipedia/commons/thumb/c/c0/Campitelli_-_Insula_romana_1907.JPG/1280px-Campitelli_-_Insula_romana_1907.JPG

the rise of property as a commercial asset had taken root, characterised by investors, usually from outside the locales that they were investing in, buying multiple properties and promoting property speculation, or the 'purchase for means other than consumption' (Bell et al, 2019: 604).

Land and property speculation was not confined to European and Western societies, and the development of urban settlement in the Middle East, particularly in the 8th and 9th centuries, provides some evidence of speculative building activity. Lapidus (1973) refers to the emergence of administrative settlements in Iran that were the headquarters for government administrators and military personnel. Large populations of labourers, merchants and soldiers settled in such places, and a practice was for army officers to gain access to building plots, or *Khitta*, and engage in 'speculations in housing and market construction' (Lapidus, 1973: 25). Likewise, Bulliet (2009: 132) refers to speculative development related to the boom in cotton production in 10th-century Iran, a period of 'exuberant growth in the size of Iran's cities'. This stimulated a demand for local housing and services that was met, in part, from the cotton industry, which provided its owners, local wealthy elites, with the 'money for urban construction and land speculation' (Bulliet, 2009: 132).

The growth of early medieval Iranian cities is indicative of the ubiquitous nature of speculation in land and property, and throughout the period of the Renaissance into the European Industrial Revolution, and beyond, the potential financial rewards from speculation continued to foment major building and construction programmes. Goldthwaite (1982) notes that speculation in the early-modern period was a feature in the growing capital cities of Europe, and much of London's reconstruction after the Great Fire of 1666 was aimed at the middle and upper classes moving to the city. There was an early form of gentrification in which property speculators bought up tracts of land and developed housing projects with the expectation that financial returns would accrue from rental income. An illustration is Abraham Arlidge, a property developer responsible for a speculative project in Holborn between 1659 and 1694, in which 372 leasehold properties were constructed for merchants 'who wanted to live in the quieter suburbs and near the surrounding fields but still close to the City' (Stone, 2020: 1).

The Great Fire was significant in London's development by providing builders with the opportunity not only for catering for wealthy elites, but also, and more lucratively, for constructing housing en masse to respond to the 100,000 people left homeless by the event. The situation led to the rise of large-scale speculative builders, with most dwellings 'built to a standard plan' (Parsons, 2012: 62).[2] Mumford (1961: 477) quotes an observer of the time, Roger North, who noted the 'method of building by casting of ground into streets and small houses ... [that] had made ground rents high' (see also Millard, 2000: 124).[3] North was alluding to the rationality of speculation, whereby the denser the occupation of dwellings, 'the higher the income [and] the capitalisation value of the land' (Mumford, 1961: 477). This rationality was, for Mumford (1961: 477), perverse, as it propagated the 'anti-social exploitation of land', including the construction of 'clotted tenements' and building practices whereby 'the worse the dwelling, the higher the total rent of the property'.

By the mid-19th century, speculation was rampant across the Western world, with Jameson (1998: 163) describing the plundering nature of land speculation in the US, including the 'seizure of native American lands ... the acquisition of immense tracts by the railroads [and] in the development of suburban areas'. In European cities, such as Paris, Antwerp and Berlin, real estate speculation was at unprecedented levels, stimulated by banks and finance capital that, in the Parisian context, lent vast sums to newly formed joint-stock companies set up purposely to pursue speculative building. This was indicative of the rapid financialisaton of the real estate market in Paris, in which architecture and construction were no more than 'financial tools' in the hands of financiers and bankers. The supply of plentiful credit dedicated to building enabled the opening up of new markets and productive outlets, with architects operating as 'architect-financiers', or purveyors of what Yates (2015: 15) calls the 'mastery of increasingly compressed space'.

This involved the demolition of Parisian neighbourhoods in the latter part of the 19th century and the construction of thousands of apartment buildings, a reflection of investors 'seeing the city primarily as an assemblage of exchange values' (Glotzer, 2019: 719). A rentier class emerged to manage a new asset class of rental buildings, with critics, such as Lemercier (quoted in Yates, 2011: 9), describing the speculators as constructing 'thoughtlessly ... without studying the aspects and needs of each neighborhood'. Others, such as architectural critic Emile Rivoalen (1882), outlined how the low-cost economies of speculation were reflected in the poor quality of newly constructed, monotonous buildings. For Rivoalen (1882, quoted in Yates, 2011: 14), speculative buildings were constructed whether or not they were needed, or, as he observed, 'the builders of these striking districts don't seem to have agreed in advance on the need to build ... life is completely lacking in these symmetrical heaps of stones'.

Speculation was not confined to parts of cities, but also occurred on a grander scale, often in conjunction with major infrastructure works to catalyse development. The construction of the new town of Heliopolis or New Cairo in the early 20th century was part of what Adham (2004: 138) describes as a 'real estate explosion' in Cairo, characterised by the influx of foreign 'speculators, real estate developers and architects'. Heliopolis was conceived in a context of a major building boom in Egypt at the turn of the 19th century in which numerous foreign land and building companies were formed and, as discussed by Abu-Lughod (1971: 153), operated as pure speculators by purchasing land and waiting 'for an increase in value, and then sell'. This was part of a process that saw a significant increase in the suburbanisation of Cairo, facilitated by new transport infrastructure provided, primarily, by overseas real estate organisations, including the Cairo Electric Railways and Heliopolis Oases Company.

This company acquired a 25 km^2 site north-east of Cairo in 1905, and over the following years, tramway and rail links and numerous dwellings and public buildings were constructed. The company's directors were seeking to replicate the experiences of the southern Cairo suburb of Helwan, which was connected to Cairo with a rail link in the early 1900s. This precipitated frenzied speculation in and around Helwan, and 'land prices soared as people rushed to buy and speculate on lots along the Nile' (Dobrowolski and Dobrowolski, 2006: 42). Heliopolis was the second-largest foreign investment in Egypt after the Suez Canal, and for Édouard Empain, the instigator of the project, it was 'no more than a capitalist venture, a real estate development' (quoted in Adham, 2004: 147). What transpired was a place for elite groups, including wealthy colonialists, with Heliopolis described by Russell (2004: 34) 'as a suburb for British officials and a health resort'.

The suburbanisation of Cairo, along radial transportation routes, was to be repeated in many places worldwide throughout the 20th century as speculative city building became one of the defining features of rapid urbanisation. A large literature describes the role of speculation in facilitating the suburbanisation of US cities, including Clawson (1962: 102), who notes that the rapid uptake of undeveloped suburban sites reflected their 'value from the expectation of ... later development as urban land'. For Mumford (1961: 475), the US suburbs were the epitome of speculative development, in which builders sparked housing demand by purchasing agricultural land in volume at cheap prices and made money by minimising construction costs, usually by utilising formulaic, standardised designs and house types. Mumford (1961: 580) condemned the speculatively formed suburbs of the mid-20th century, stating that they were antithetical to the 'good life' and were destroying 'the living tissue of the city'.

These characterisations were indicative of a discontent with the rise of the volume builder and with what appeared to be a disregard for aesthetic and environmental quality. The sheer volume of speculative building can overwhelm a place and transform its aesthetic qualities and character, a view to the fore in South Korea in relation to the process of 'apart-isation'. Over the last 20 years, South Korea's cities have been transformed by the volume production of thousands of residential apartment blocks, the aesthetics of which have been described by Harlan (2013: 1) as redolent of a 'militant geometry' (see Figure 4.2). The blocks can be 60 storeys in height and extend for kilometres, obscuring views and creating an overwhelming presence. The mayor of Seoul in 2013, Park Won-soon, said that because of 'our obsession with quantitative supply, uniform apartment blocks have standardized our lives, damaging our unique urban scenery' (quoted in Jackson, 2017: 1).

The volumetric production of the built environment also extends to other, non-residential uses, particularly retail and offices, and the making of major cities, such as New York, Hong Kong and Tokyo, is closely interlinked with the supply of speculative vertical space, or the high-rise building (Graham, 2016). For developers, the vertical building is efficient at maximising the volume of constructed floorspace and potential rental incomes, and cities worldwide are experiencing a 'verticality boom'. This translates into the perennial problem associated with speculation: an oversupply of space in which cities are awash with underused and empty buildings. In 2009, over 10 million square feet of office space in London was empty, and recent reports suggest that this figure is now greater and likely to be impacted by COVID-19 with the decline of the office environment (Glowacz, 2020).[4]

Figure 4.2: Garak, Seoul

Source: https://commons.wikimedia.org/wiki/File:Seoul_garak_APT.jpg

The emptiness of such spaces does not mean that they lack value for speculators or do not accrue wealth for investors. In a world where many people are homeless or without access to decent, liveable spaces, speculators often keep buildings empty as an 'investment strategy'. An example is Centre Point in London, a 34-storey building that was constructed as offices in 1966 but stood empty for almost ten years (see Figure 4.3).[5] For Harry Hyams, the developer, the rationale was to wait for an appropriate, single-use tenant and to benefit from the appreciation in London land values. Between 1966 and 1974, the value of Centre Point increased from £10 million to £60 million and the increase in land values offset the ongoing charges of maintaining the building (Weiler, 2013). The building became a cause célèbre, with Peter Walker (1972: col 1094), former Secretary of State for the Environment, describing 'the scandal of developers who ... have constructed office blocks and deliberately left them empty to enhance their capital gains'.[6]

Such exhortations have rarely translated into meaningful actions against speculators, and, if anything, the scale of contemporary speculation is greater than ever. The property industry continues to reproduce Centre Point-type developments all over the world, encouraged by the activities of city governments, who utilise a range of fiscal and other incentives to encourage mobile finance capital to invest in the built environment. Goldman (2011)

Figure 4.3: Centre Point, London

Source: https://commons.wikimedia.org/wiki/File:Centre_Point_-_New_Oxford_Street,_Holborn.jpg

refers to the process as 'speculative urbanism', or the development of land into lucrative real estate. Goldman's (2011) influential article, based on research in Bangalore, India, documented the city's transformation into a centre for IT, aided by the rapid uptake and development of semi-urban and rural land. For Goldman (2011), speculation in the city was indicative of new forms of speculative government and economy, in which citizenship rights were curtailed to enable the ease of land appropriation and the displacement of anyone, or any activity, that might prevent it from being converted into profitable real estate.

The ascendency of speculative urbanism, particularly in Asian cities, is characterised by Ong (2011: 209) as 'hyper-building', in which the objective of local city politicians is not only to attract global flows of investment into real estate, but 'also about an intense political desire for world recognition' (see also Shin, 2013; Shin and Kim, 2016). Hyper-building is a way to create 'world city' status, and the means to unlock it is to ensure a more or less unlimited supply of land and to enable its development, particularly for landmark buildings. Evidence of this process is etched into the skylines of major cities, and Ong (2011: 205) refers to 'Beijing's cluster of Olympic landmarks, Shanghai's TV tower, Hong Kong's forest of corporate towers, Singapore's Marina Sands complex, and super-tall Burj Khalifa in Dubai' as leading exemplars.

The outcome is what Ong (2011: 206) describes as a global 'building frenzy' characterised by the construction of many buildings that fail to respond to local needs, have little in common with vernacular or cultural mores, and rarely command sufficient demand by international investors. Some of the spectacular examples of such speculative development are in places such as Dubai. Dubai's governments have been described as encouraging a 'build it and they will come' development model that, since the 1980s, has led to the city becoming an international tourism destination and a haven for second-homeowners buying high-end residences (Bolleter, 2019). The city is also a repository for the highest volume of speculative real estate in the world, and Dahl (2011: 49) describes developers as 'running wild', with cranes and assorted building equipment on the outskirts of the city that resemble 'a kind of mechanical primeval forest'.

The speculative urbanism exhibited in Dubai and elsewhere is implicated in a culture of building that appears to occur with impunity and without limits. The logic of speculation, that is, to supply without any end user secured, is, at best, risky and, at worst, reckless and a waste of resources. Its rationality is anathema to creating an environment that provides for need at the point of demand, and it leads to a mixture of empty and abandoned spaces, as well as the stalling or postponement of half-finished infrastructure projects. Speculative urbanism is also seeing the emergence of a new generation of landlords, such as private equity companies, that have little interest in the quality of habitation and lived space, beyond it providing a rental income. The underlying rationality is highlighted by Almacantar (2020), a property investment and development company that owns Centre Point in London, which declares on its website that 'our strategy is to transform assets into prime products with sustained value'.

What is striking about this observation is how devoid it is of references to the people who are likely to inhabit the environments that Almacantar creates. The statement, like others on Almacantar's website, indicates an accounting mentality in which the built environment, including its public spaces, parks and recreational areas, is no more than an investment opportunity, or the means to accrue assets and wealth. This reflects Harvey's (2006: 347) understanding concerning the trading of land, and buildings upon it, 'according to the rent' that is yielded, and it draws attention to what appears to be an increasing interdependence between financial and real estate markets. For van Loon and Aalbers (2017: 222), institutional investors in building and construction are transforming elements of the built environment 'into tradable financial assets such as shares, bonds and securities'. The implication is, as Mörtenböck and Mooshammer (2018: 109) note, that building and construction are no more than 'the lubrication of financial trade'.

Speculative real estate and the (re)production of investment portfolios

Speculative behaviour is particularly pronounced in relation to housing, which, while integral to domesticity and homemaking, has become a significant part of both individual and corporate investment portfolios. Housing is much more than a home, and for many people, it represents a valuable and appreciating asset that has significant wealth vested within it. While housing is, ostensibly, shelter or the means to provide people with a safe and secure environment, it has developed into what Weaver (2018: 1) describes as 'the single largest asset class in the UK', which has 'a total value of £6.2 trillion'. Speculation in housing ranges widely, from individual homeowners commissioning a builder to extend their house, with the expectation that financial value will be added to it, to private equity companies investing in the construction of high-end residences aimed at super-rich investors. In both instances, housing is primarily conceived as an economic asset and only then as a 'place to live' (Young, quoted in Hannah, 2016: 1).

This rationality has spawned a series of speculative building booms in housing and witnessed the rise of the built environment as proffering a wide range of investment securities or tradable assets. In the UK, one of the main areas of growth is the rental market, specifically, 'build-for-rent'. In a context of increasing controls on access to mortgage finance, homeownership has become much more difficult in recent years, and this has increased the demand for renting. Major institutional investors, including private equity companies and hedge funds, have responded by constructing multi-unit residences of purpose-built rental housing (PBRH). Investors retain ownership, and developments are managed as financial assets, accruing income through rents and capital gains. Laming (2018) has described build-for-rent as a new 'mainstream asset class', and between 2019 and 2020, construction of PBRH grew by 12 per cent, with 157,152 homes being built or at planning stage across the UK (British Property Federation, 2020).

The increase in supply has not dampened rents, and in the UK's private rented sector, they reached record highs in 2019 (ONS, 2020b). Much PBRH is aimed at people on high incomes, and the portfolio of PBRH properties include many high-end residences with weekly rents well in excess of £5,000. T. White (2018) notes that newbuild rentals charge 11 per cent more than older properties in the same neighbourhoods, and concludes that the PBRH market is, primarily, 'for affluent young professionals'. Likewise, Da Silva (2019) outlines research by the flat-sharing agency Ideal Flatmate, which notes that the cost of renting a room in a build-for-rent development is 15 per cent higher than the cost of renting in the buy-to-let market. This reflects, ostensibly, the higher quality of build-for-rent properties, including the provision of gyms, workspaces and concierges, and is indicative of a sector seeking to create 'added value' as part of the development of its asset-class status.

The emergence, and development, of build-for-rent as an asset class is encouraging new construction and spawning a range of dwelling types, including an increasingly lucrative student market with the growth in construction of purpose-built student accommodation (PBSA). In 2018, global investment in PBSA was US$16.3 billion, and the sector was described as 'the most standout performers for investors' (Lane, 2019: 1; see also Knight Frank, 2019). What was once a social and welfare service owned and controlled by universities, has been transformed into 'a global asset class', with ownership primarily vested in corporate institutional investors (Knight Frank, 2019: 5). A typical illustration is a £18.2 million, 207-bed development under way at Stirling University (Maven, 2018). It is owned by two private equity and real estate companies, Maven Capital Partners and IP Investment Management. The latter outlines its activities as seeking 'to generate attractive risk-adjusted returns by investing and proactively managing assets' (IPIM, 2020: 1).

A range of investment portfolios related to PBSA, including 'buy-to-let', is available to investors. This, combined with market projections of high growth rates in student numbers, has led to what Jessel (2020: 1) describes as 'over-built university towns', with examples of unfilled PBSA 'flipped' to other uses. Jessel (2020: 1) cites the example of how student accommodation constructed in Cardiff in 2018 filled 65 per cent of its capacity and was subsequently 'converted into an aparthotel'. In other places, there is high demand, and market analysts note that there is scope for major expansion in the construction of PBSA (Metcalf, 2018). However, research by Kinton et al (2016) shows that PBSA can 'hollow out' established student neighbourhoods by diverting students away from pre-existing dwellings and places, and creating new swathes of empty properties. For Kinton et al (2016: 1633), PBSA is not a coherent or efficient way 'to meet increasing social demands for housing'.

The construction of student accommodation as 'an investment' is the tip of a much broader trend in which housing more generally is promoted as a means of making money. This was a defining feature of the context of the pre-2008 global financial crash, where cheap and easy credit was flooding mortgage markets, enabling people on average to low incomes to gain access to housing. The trend was encouraged by a mixture of financial and building interests, and was instrumental in fuelling extensive building that, in the wake of the 2008 crash, led to a glut of properties, many of which, even to this day, remain empty. In some countries, development was excessive. Spain experienced a threefold increase in the number of new dwellings constructed between 1995 and 2008, far in excess of the growth in population (Martin et al, 2019). The excess supply did not prevent house prices more than doubling in Spain over the same period, and this, coupled with the post-2008 downturn, meant more empty and unoccupied dwellings than in any other part of Europe.

By 2017, Spain had the fourth-largest number of empty homes, after Malta, Greece and Mexico, with 3,443,365 unoccupied residential properties, equivalent to nearly 14 per cent of the country's total housing stock (Glover, 2017). Entire towns and villages have properties left unoccupied, and one of the more notable examples is the Residencial Francisco Hernando project in Seseña, a small town 40 km south of Madrid. The proposed development by the property company Onde was to construct 13,500 apartments as part of a plan to develop Seseña as a satellite or commuter settlement for people working in Madrid. The project commenced in 2003, but by 2008, the developer, having built 5,000 apartments, stopped construction with over 80 per cent of the properties left empty. By 2017, while there were signs of revival and evidence of increased uptake of property by people seeking to escape high house prices in Madrid, much of the development remained empty and apartment prices were half those of 2008 (Barry, 2017).

The evidence from elsewhere is similarly stark in documenting high levels of newly constructed dwellings that lie empty. Shi et al's (2020) study of new construction in China estimates that there are 1,048 ghost neighbourhoods in the country, occupying a land area of 353.64 km^2, with the dwelling capacity to accommodate 13.6 million people. These are remarkable figures in which well over 3,500 new settlements have been constructed since 2000 in places where there is no obvious demand for them (see Stahl, 2014). At a different scale but with similar consequences, the building company Sarot Group began construction in 2014 of chateau-style villas in Turkey's Bolu province, with the intended market being investors from the Gulf states (see Koc, 2018). The complex includes a hotel and a mosque, as well as the villas, of which 587 of the planned 732 units were completed. While 350 villas were sold for up to US$530,000, the rest remain empty and the project incomplete, with demand having dissipated and the developer filing for bankruptcy.

These illustrations of an oversupply of newly built property draw attention to the illogicality of a system that condones the construction of buildings on the basis of what Korcheck (2015: 93) describes as a 'fantasyland of the future'. Korcheck (2015) has assembled a series of evocative photographic images of empty and abandoned places in Spain to highlight the contradictions of speculation, which while premised on contributing to the modernisation and development of society, appears to do anything but this. Korcheck (2015: 92) conceives of places such as Seseña as 'speculative ruins', or vacant structures with 'a future that never came'. This is a recurring theme about empty housing projects, in which the notion of the ruin is evoked to critique modernity's conception of progress, while reflecting 'on the fragility of the contemporary world' (Marí, 2016: 1, quoted in Gual, 2019: 53). Such fragility is characterised by the indebtedness of failed property companies and homeowners trapped in negative equity and living in places that barely function as liveable environments.

Despite well-documented supply issues, the proliferation of housing as an asset class continues to spawn a range of 'products' and attract a multitude of providers from the financial sector (Knight Frank, 2019). From the construction of care homes to the supply of age-friendly housing and the provision of buy-to-let properties, corporate and individual investors are investing record sums of finance in residential property globally (Campbell, 2019). In Sweden, for instance, 2019 was a record year for investment, with €4.81 billion being transacted in residential property in 'the first nine months of the year', and with 40 per cent of investment derived from foreign investors (Wiman and Zuckerman, 2019: 1). These patterns are evident across the globe, and in the UK, the real estate consultancy firm Knight Frank (2019) suggest that the value of residential investment will increase by 68 per cent by 2025, with the total value of the sector worth £146 billion.

A significant tranche of investment relates to residential property as 'safe deposit boxes', or secure places for investors to place money with the knowledge that they are buying into an asset likely to appreciate in value. Here, dwellings are less to be lived in than procured as financial assets, otherwise known as a 'buy-to-leave' investment (Toynbee, 2017). This phenomenon is an integral part of redevelopment projects in cities worldwide, with places such as London, Sydney and New York undergoing 'safe deposit box' construction programmes (Atkinson, 2020b). Much of the demand is from overseas, and Booth (2014) notes that in the early 2010s, there were 30,000 newly constructed dwellings on redevelopment sites in London that were owned by just ten investors, primarily from Hong Kong, China, Malaysia, Australia, Singapore and Sweden.

The influx of money from overseas, particularly Asia, has precipitated a surge in the numbers of homes being constructed in the UK, a trend that was well under way by the end of the 1990s and has since accelerated to become a defining feature of land and property markets. A report by PricewaterhouseCoopers (2020: 10) reaffirms the trend by suggesting that much of London's population growth emanates from the 'overspill of the new wealthy in, and from, emerging markets, seeking a luxury home in Europe'. The new wealthy are a transnational grouping of super-rich purchasers, described by Pow (2017: 56) as people seeking to grow their 'wealth beyond the traditional confines of national boundaries'. Real estate in places such as London and New York provides the potential for high and sustained growth in secure environments in which property offers high liquidity, or ease of sale if access to cash is required.

This demand from a super-rich clientele is manifest in the burgeoning construction of luxury housing that sells for prices well beyond the reach of most people (Atkinson, 2020a). In London, there are many high-profile development projects recently completed or under way in which dwellings are being constructed, specifically, for a super-rich market (see Atkinson, 2020a, 2020b). Prices range from £1 million to £160 million, with the latter sum paid in 2018 for an apartment in One Hyde Park (see Figure 4.4). This apartment was bought by two offshore companies, PHB London Holdings Ltd and PHB London Dormant Ltd, secured with a loan from the financial services company Credit Suisse. Similar types of expensively priced real estate include Park Modern, a £450 million mixed-use development located in Queensway. On completion in 2021, it will include retail and 57 flats, the cheapest of which will market at £2 million and the most expensive at £30 million (Neate, 2018a).

Many of the new developments in London are tall buildings that enable developers to maximise the supply of space and rental income. The most notable completion is the Shard, London's tallest building, constructed in 2012. It has ten luxury apartments, yet by 2017, most of these, with a £50 million price tag, were unsold, and there has been no contrary information since then to suggest that the situation has changed (Neate, 2017). The supply of such speculative property continues unabated, and

Figure 4.4: One Hyde Park, London

Source: Rob Imrie

a survey by New London Architecture (2019) indicates that 541 high-rise developments have been granted planning permission, with many of these under construction. An example is One Blackfriars, a 50-storey building containing 274 dwellings, described by CBRE (2020: 1) as 'one of London's most iconic and truly unique residences'. Part of the development's uniqueness, albeit shared with other, similar projects in London, is the outlandish and, for most people, unaffordable prices of its properties, with penthouse apartments on the market for £23 million in 2016 (White, 2016).

Atkinson (2020b: 1) estimates that 42,000 dwellings, including newbuild, have been bought by super-rich investors in London. Some lie empty and are used to store cash; as estate agent Lulu Egerton, of property agents Lane Fox, suggests, 'the super-rich acquire property in the same way as they buy fine art or fine wine – it almost turns into a kind of international collection' (quoted in Bar-Hillel, 2007: 1). As a safe deposit box, there is limited incentive for purchasers to occupy their properties, and in the 14-storey Bezier development in Shoreditch, completed in 2010, only 75 of the 127 apartments are listed as having occupants registered for council tax. Many newbuild developments are also struggling to sell due to oversupply, and Neate (2018a) notes that in 2017, there were over 15,000 luxury flats unsold, with Pryor, a property-buying agent, commenting that the market is 'already overstuffed but we're just building more of them' (quoted in Moss and Co, 2019: 1).

Such sentiments have relevance to one of the highest-profile schemes in London, the Nine Elms project, located on a 560-acre site spanning the boroughs of Lambeth and Wandsworth. It is a £15 billion development with a target of 20,000 new dwellings, including the refurbishment and rebuild of one of London's landmark buildings, Battersea Power Station. The Nine Elms development has been facilitated and supported by local government, keen to capture major private sector investment, a process that began in 2008 when Nine Elms was identified and designated as an 'opportunity area' by the Greater London Authority (2008). This designation described Nine Elms as having 'significant capacity for development', and it gave a green light to property companies and their affiliates to pursue speculative real estate investments. Since 2010, the area has been Europe's biggest building site, with the completion, to date, of approximately 5,000 dwellings and a piece of public space called Linear Park.

The process has been helped by the extension of London's underground system into the area, enhancing transport links, as well as by the strategic relocation of the American Embassy to Nine Elms in 2018 and technology company Apple looking to open a tech campus at Battersea Power Station in 2021. Both signify confidence that Nine Elms is a 'place on the up', with the real estate service company Jones Lang LaSalle (2020: 1) noting that the area 'will very soon take on the mantle of a vibrant and exciting locale'. What is emerging in Nine Elms is the development of a vertical city and an exclusive, privatised environment that is highly secure, exhibiting a style of militarised architecture in which gates and surveillance equipment pervade the landscape. It is classic safe deposit box terrain typified by its tallest building, St George Wharf Tower, a 50-storey tower block that contains 223 apartments, including a top-floor penthouse suite that sold for £51 million in 2014 (see Figure 4.5).[7]

Speculation in Nine Elms is illustrated by investors buying properties off-plan, then selling them on prior to their construction and capitalising on rapid upward movements in prices. West (2013) notes that the 866 flats in Battersea Power Station were sold long before they were built and primarily to overseas investors. Rahman (2014) recounts an example of speculator behaviour in which a studio apartment bought for £1 million in Battersea Power Station was sold for £1.5 million six months later, well before construction started. It was, in the words of one observer, redolent of a buyer taking a 'financial position rather than buying a property' (quoted in Hodges, 2015: 1). Nine Elms is the epitome of speculative capitalism, or, as an industry insider argued, 'buying off-plan was the ultimate option play for a lot of the buyers ... you only need to put down 10% and then see how the market goes' (quoted in Hodges, 2015: 1).

Figure 4.5: St George Wharf Tower, Nine Elms, London

Source: Rob Imrie

The market fixation of the builders and agents supplying the buildings, as well as the people purchasing the properties, belies that fact that Nine Elms is, ostensibly, a place to live. However, while much of Nine Elms has been bought up by investors, it remains a quiet and relatively empty place, seemingly bereft of people. While visiting the area, I noted in my research diary that 'there are few people walking and there's no sense of a destination, or places to visit; it feels lonely and hardly part of a bustling city'.[8] The rows of tower block buildings felt austere and unwelcoming, and when I approached the entrance to St George Wharf Tower, I was quickly ushered on my way by a security guard dressed in a smart black suit with tie. As I recorded in my diary: 'I was made to feel out of place and not welcome, and I was wondering "Is this the way we should be building a place, one that turns in on itself, and has little feeling of sociability, of friendship, of reaching out?"'

The aesthetic character of Nine Elms seems to reflect a lot of high-end speculative building, or, as I recorded at the time, 'an inoffensive, but bland, international style of architecture with little standout character, no sense of the vernacular, and a semi-detachedness or a disconnection between buildings and other objects within the built environment'. My thoughts were how this was part of the way to secure investment by 'avoiding design that's too racy or likely to offend or be culturally insensitive and be off-putting to certain groups of overseas investors'. The standout impression I had, however, was the privatised and highly securitised nature of the environment, 'probably inimical to public gatherings'. What public space there is seemed orchestrated or organised, programmatic even, and not likely to encourage people to be part of a collective, public presence. While walking around a public park, I noted in my diary the feeling of being 'in a place that doesn't seem to welcome strangers, and I don't feel that I can hang around the area for too long'.

These feelings of being 'out of place' in a locale constructed purely as a functional piece of real estate are captured by Atkinson's (2019: 2) writings about the spaces of super-prime real estate, in which he refers to them as 'lifeless places' and 'dead residential space or necrotecture'. For Atkinson (2019: 4), London's super-rich enclaves, such as Nine Elms, are characteristically a 'landscape of empty residential units' and the evisceration of the public realm (Jacobs, 1961). Here, Atkinson draws attention to the important matter that it is not only about *how much* is constructed, but also about *what is* constructed and for whom, and how this shapes liveability and public life in our cities. In Nine Elms, I observed 'an absence of places to meet up, or for people to hang out, as though any public space is no longer that, but only a series of places to pass through, it's as though the place has been constructed without any sense of how people populate it'. Atkinson (2019: 6) captures my unease about the 'apparent waste and emptiness' of Nine Elms 'as homes for capital rather than people'.

The speculative spaces of Nine Elms have no place for people on low incomes, or of a social status that is not commensurate with those who can afford to pay millions of pounds for an apartment. Nine Elms is the epitome of Britain's socio-spatial divisions and inequalities, and while not the direct cause of this, property speculation is one of the factors that enables, and reproduces, an unequal, some would say unfair, society. In Nine Elms, the miniscule amount of social housing is hidden out of sight, offsite from the super-rich towers as part of the protective veneer to ensure that there is no dilution of the investment. This is redolent of the speculative 'safe deposit box' model because, for it to work on its own terms, that is, providing lucrative returns to wealthy investors and wealth funds, it requires the (re)production of exclusive spaces, or environs that cater only for the few.

Conclusion

Speculation is the fulcrum of land and property markets, and the dynamic that shapes much of the construction of the built environment. While speculation has always existed in one form or another, its natural bedfellow is the capitalist system, which is predicated on the maximum extraction of wealth from risk-taking investment. Capitalism is indifferent to the social, human and ecological fabric of places, and its proponents regard objects and materials, including the environment, as conduits for wealth creation. This is reflected in the design and construction of the built environment, in which much of what is built is part of a portfolio of commercial assets, or the means to facilitate flows of investment and the accretion of wealth. Wherever one looks, there is the commodification of bricks and mortar and a never-ending supply of speculative building, ranging from incomplete and empty housing estates in Spain, to vertical towers in places such as Nine Elms in London and Central Park in New York.

The rate and scale of speculative building far exceeds what can be consumed, and the quantity of underused and empty buildings in the UK, and elsewhere, is increasing, a trend that seems to support what Alpert (2013) describes as 'the age of oversupply'. The last 30 years or so provide evidence of this, with billions of dollars pouring into a wide range of speculative buildings and infrastructure that people do not need or want. Many are grandiose vanity projects, often orchestrated and sponsored by the state, and in the vanguard of perpetuating an oil-based and fossil-fuel economy anathema to the preservation, even enhancement, of ecology and environment. Speculation is particularly implicated in land grabs and privatisation, and one of its features is the transfer of land from collective or communal ownership to individual proprietorship, in which, as Mumford (1961: 475) suggests, 'moneyed interests progressively [dominate] landed interests' in shaping the built environment.

This, though, is only one side of the multifaceted nature of speculative development. Speculation is implicated in a host of human and ecological outcomes that ought not to be part of any rational system of building provision and consumption. From the oversupply of buildings and infrastructure, to the construction of upscale, expensive real estate that can contribute to inflationary pressures in local housing markets, the deleterious, socially iniquitous effects of speculation require redress. This observation has historical precedent, with Parker (1911: 154), writing about speculation in 19th-century US industry, noting that there is need for 'the adoption of higher standards of social ethics by those who conduct the industrial enterprises of the land'. Parker's (1911) observation draws attention to the ethical and moral bases of people's actions, and, in doing so, rejects any sense of speculation per se as a natural, or neutral, even technical, activity. Rather, it is political, with socially distributive consequences.[9]

This understanding is the basis of many different social movements and actions that, over the course of human history, have sought to influence and resist the activities of property speculators. Over the last 30 years or so, resistance, while often piecemeal and small-scale, has ranged widely, from squatters occupying office blocks left empty, to people in local neighbourhoods organising to prevent building work they believe has no community benefit. In New York, Chen (2020) describes residents in low-rental neighbourhoods stalling redevelopment projects that would otherwise have led to the construction of tall, upmarket residential towers. In the development of Inward, in Upper Manhattan, a Supreme Court judge in 2019 annulled the city's rezoning plan on density and the height of tall buildings, effectively limiting what could be built, while noting that the city's environmental review process was flawed by not assessing 'the risk of racial displacement and the effect of speculative development on local businesses' (Chen, 2020: 1).

Community resistance in Inwood is illustrative of many more, similar movements prompted by the desire to confront the socio-ecological effects of the financialisation of real estate and to offer alternatives to finance-led accumulation by construction. Wijburg (2020) refers to the potential of de-financialising tendencies, in which spatial development ought to be subject to scrutiny and evaluation in relation to how well it is able to address, and fulfil, basic human needs (see Chapter 10). Here, Wijburg (2020: 2) refers to a report by the United Nations (2019) that in recognising access to adequate housing as a universal human right, questions how far this is possible with the hyper-financialisation of real estate. For the United Nations (2019), there is a need to 're-moralise' the values and activities of financiers and others involved in spatial development, and to establish that housing is, first and foremost, a social good and that whatever is built ought to occur within the framework of 'human rights guidelines' (quoted in Wijburg, 2020: 2).

This is a significant observation, though, as Wijburg (2020) notes, it does not tackle how financialisation per se can be rolled back, or how far a socio-legal framework, as espoused by the United Nations, is able to be the basis for a countercultural movement to the dominant building paradigm. Often, attempts to mitigate speculation revolve around crude fiscal measures implemented in anti-speculation zones, or parts of cities that are targets for speculative activity and experiencing shortfalls of affordable housing (Ja-young, 2020). In Seoul, South Korea, 15 zones have been designated to address housing speculation. Development within each is subject to higher levels of capital gains tax and property tax than in the rest of the city (Ja-young, 2020). At the time of writing, rules on lending and tax regulations on corporate bodies owning homes are about to be implemented in the city to control what Kyung-min (2020: 1) describes as 'a frequently used tax avoidance scheme by owners of expensive homes'.

While these measures are welcome, and underpinned by a moral and ethical sense of social and distributive justice, they do not tackle the underlying causes of unjust and unfair outcomes related to spatial development processes. Rather, such measures are interventions in procedural and fiscal mechanisms, such as the tax system, and an attempt to ameliorate some of the worst outcomes and effects of speculation. They are not designed to eradicate speculative behaviour or transform the financialised models and activities of land and property development. How far, then, should one restructure, even dismantle, finance-led spatial development and the systems whereby the impulse is usually to build more at high value, while seeking to ensure that minimum valuations of properties are reached and maintained? Is it sufficient to reregulate how finance is emplaced and enacted within real estate, or, to follow Wijburg's (2020: 14) logic, should one be looking to sidestep this with 'the negation of any form of finance'?

In reality, the latter option is intractable and not a viable choice because social, political and economic systems are deeply enmeshed within, and dependent on, the operations of financial and moneyed relations. Most city authorities in places where speculation is perceived to be a problem have little choice but to follow the Seoul model, and to use planning and other procedural and regulatory means to mitigate the effects of speculators. The alternative is systemic change, but a difficulty is envisaging what this is or might entail, and how it can transpire in ways whereby the negative effects of speculation can be mitigated. It is not possible, or desirable, to be programmatic about any of this. However, given the concern of this book, there is need to control construction and/or to ensure that building is commensurate with what is *needed* for the reproduction of the planet. This includes the (re)shaping of human actions that cannot be anything less than respectful of ecology and people's interdependencies with nature.

This is the beginnings of a value position or statement about how building ought to be disposed towards matters other than personal financial returns, or the cultivation of new rentier classes or means of generating moneyed assets. While I will return to these matters more fully in Chapter 10, the notion of the common good, or that which benefits society as a whole, seems an appropriate and useful idea to consider and develop. Here, 'the common' refers to the interrelations between the human and non-human worlds, and the 'good' relates to people's dispositions and actions to care for, and care about, others, including non-humans and the materials that comprise the natural world. For Williams (1989: 222), the notion of the commons rejects the 'inherent capitalist priority of profit' redolent of the operations of land and property markets. It orients the activities of builders and others involved in the production of the built environment towards responding to *the needs* of both people and ecology, and the development of their capacities.

This is a general framework and only suggestive of ways of rethinking the ongoing commodification of construction in society. Speculation is anathema to the idea of the commons because it is the epitome of self-seeking, individualistic behaviour at odds with broader sensitivities towards, and understanding of, the collectivity of interests that relates to the development of land and property. There is, however, a 'culture in common', and commonality of interest, with the excavation of the earth, the extraction of its materials and its reworking as built form, precisely because it affects everyone and everything (see also Chapter 10). People ought to have the rights, and means, to be able to influence, and change, the hierarchical and elite-based systems that govern the (re)production of the built environment, yet the culture and political economy of construction are all but impervious to this. This is particularly evident in relation to clearing, literally, the ground for construction, and the processes of both displacement and dispossession, which is a theme that I turn to in Chapter 5.

5

Disruption, Displacement and Dispossession

Introduction

Construction is a positive action insofar that it involves the creation of objects, or the crafting of materials to produce an artefact that has value, whether that is a dwelling to enable people to live well, or a road or rail system to facilitate people's ease of mobility and movement. There is, though, a paradox at the heart of all building activity, in that for all that is crafted and created by construction, the process, necessarily, involves disruption to people, places and ecologies. This can range from the excavation and movement of earth to create groundworks for new building, in which local ecologies may be damaged or destroyed, to government officials serving compulsory purchase orders, requiring people to leave where they live to make way for comprehensive rebuilding programmes. In both instances, the building process can be conceived as inherently disruptive and implicated in transforming the nature of habitation and the environment.

One of the more unusual instances of localised disruption to social life is the fad for subterranean excavation to construct residential basements (Baldwin et al, 2019). Baldwin et al (2019) note that between 2008 and 2017, planning applications for the construction of 4,650 basements were granted permission in the seven most affluent boroughs in London. While the majority were one storey, or 3 m, in depth and occupied the footprint of the house, 112 were classified as mega-basements or three storeys in height (Baldwin et al, 2019: 8). Their construction has had problematical effects, with Railton (2016: 1) describing 'leaking gas pipes, malfunctioning sump pumps and collapsing facades', while Bloomfield (2018: 1) refers to the insensitivity of builders 'dumping building materials across pavements, unsafe sites, or carrying out noisy work outside regular working hours'.

While these localised effects of building are significant, they come nowhere near the scale of disruption related to major infrastructure projects, such as dams and road and rail networks, nor do they involve shifts of population, or people's loss of home and habitat. It is estimated that over 80 million people globally have been displaced by dam construction over the course of the 20th century (World Commission on Dams, 2000). The construction of transport networks is also implicated in people losing their homes. In the city of Kochi in Kerala, India, the construction of an international container trans-shipment terminal, including major road and rail facilities, meant that 1,600 people were affected, with most suffering a 'loss of their homes, part of their land or property, or access to livelihoods' (IDMC, 2017: 1). For the Internal Displacement Monitoring Centre (IDMC, 2017: 1), such displacement is often part of purposive plans in the cause of 'development' that tends to 'impoverish and marginalise' those people who are displaced.

I develop this theme in the chapter by exploring the disruptive and displacing nature of building, in which the modernist quest for modernisation and development is part of a constant process of socio-ecological turmoil and upheaval. This is particularly evident in relation to people's acquisition and usage of territory, in which there is never no construction or building activity, with diverse impacts on land and settlement. As previous chapters have outlined, the operations of real estate and property markets are paramount in shaping a continuous process of land acquisition and its social and physical transformation. The process is part of a politics of renewal and development, ranging widely from corporate land grabs to state-organised land clearances, and from major rebuilding programmes to widespread gentrification, all of which are implicated in, and illustrative of, the disruptive and displacing effects of building and construction.

In this chapter, I focus on the social and human dimensions of disruption in relation to displacement by construction. I consider building practice to be a process of unsettlement just as much as it may also be considered to be part of settlement, or establishing the means of life and habitation. Unsettlement, as a process of disruption, can be understood in relation to the production of less-than-liveable environments, or the impact of building and construction in destabilising the conditions required for people's inhabitation of a place (see also Chapter 9). The destabilising characteristics of unsettlement can range from the psychological effects on people having to live with the noise and pollution of building works, or close to major road systems, to the toxicity consumed by people living beside waste dumps, mines and quarries, all of which serve the business of construction. In its most disruptive forms, unsettlement can force people to leave places and be dispossessed of their homes and livelihoods, changing, even rupturing, social ties and networks.

I divide the chapter into three parts. I begin by situating the process of unsettlement in its historical context and show that there is nothing new about the interrelationships between building and the disruption and displacement of communities in the wake of major (re)building projects. Human history is characterised by recurrent episodes of people's appropriation of places, in which building and construction are integral elements in facilitating new and displacing old functions, and changing the social mix and composition of spaces. Changes can be subtle and difficult to detect over short time periods, such as infill housing leading to the gradual gentrification of a neighbourhood. In contrast, other changes, such as major urban renewal projects, can precipitate the rapid, and very visible, decantation of the existing population to make way for incomers. In either instance, the lives of people in existing communities, and their modes of habitation, are threatened and undermined.

Such threats and corresponding modes of displacement can be considered to be part of inherently anti-democratic processes and indicative of construction as a form of violence against people and nature. I develop the understanding that construction, as implicated in displacement and dispossession, is a form of violation that devalues particular categories of people, objects and places, while, correspondingly, ascribing value and worth to others (Skeggs, 2014). This feeds into the making of places in ways whereby socio-spatial inequalities are reinforced and extended, as witnessed with gentrification. I discuss these themes in the second part of the chapter in relation to a case study of the displacement of elderly people living in sheltered accommodation in a small town in suburban London. The site they lived on was acquired by a house builder and rebuilt as a low-density, affluent neighbourhood, and the elderly population were decanted from the area.

The case illustrates a form of social cleansing, or eradication of specific social groups, in which displacement was simultaneously the diminution of public, social housing and the construction of private, individualised dwellings. This was the supplanting of the public by the private, or the social by specific niches of individual demand, including the creation of an exclusive, demarcated space. I conclude the chapter by reflecting on the unsettling nature of construction. I refer to some examples of people's resistance to the displacing and disruptive effects of building, in which what is paramount is the attempt to foster and sustain heterarchy and plurality in places, or the cultivation of spaces of inclusion. Part of the process is to ensure that building is deployed not as a weapon of violation, or means of erasure of particular people and ecologies, but, rather, as a positive way to enhance lives while ensuring the sustainability of the planet.

Unsettling settlement and the disruptive and displacing nature of building

The history of humanity is intertwined with settlement and its disruption, or a process of unsettlement, including the displacement and movement of people from one place to another. While we tend to live with what Magnus (1978: 190) refers to as the 'illusion of permanence', the reality is the destabilisation and impermanence of life, with people constantly on the move, ranging from major migrations caused by war and conflict, to many small-scale movements, varying from relocating to a new house in search of a job, to daily commutes between home and workplace. Amid all of this is the role of building and construction in shaping the patterns and dynamics of settlement, and its corollary, unsettlement. Much of what is built, while seeming to provide the basis for longevity of habitation, is often ephemeral and part of a chimera that is undermined by a broader series of political and ecological relations.

This is evident in relation to environmental change and the increasingly unstable nature of the climate and biophysical processes in undermining settlement patterns. From the increasing incidences of the flooding of cities, such as the devastation of New Orleans by the floods caused by Hurricane Katrina in 2005, to major wildfires burning down neighbourhoods in suburban areas, there is evidence that much of the built environment is poorly designed and constructed, and does not ensure a stability of settlement. D. White (2018) describes urban wildfires as the 'new normal' in California, with the encroachment of construction into the edges of wild areas. Rapid population growth, coupled with the lack of appropriate control of construction in potential fire zones, has facilitated what Pyne (2001) describes as a process of 'built to burn' developments in California, in which 'homes continue to be constructed with [flammable] wooden shake roofs' (Rielage, 2017: 1).

The use of construction materials prone to failure and the siting of buildings in areas of environmental risk are particularly evident in many of the global mega-cities, such as Dhaka in Bangladesh. Here, it is the combination of poverty, inequality and poor building design that creates hazardous living conditions. Over 4 million people live in substandard buildings located on low-lying land close to water (Ahmed, 2014). In periods of flooding, which occur on a regular basis, people 'abandon their settlements and seek shelter on roadsides, schools or mosques' (Ahmed, 2014: 748). Such displacement is compounded by other risks, and Ahmed (2014) notes that one of the biggest threats to habitation is fire related to flammable materials used in buildings, such as timber and bamboo. Davis (2019: 1) describes a fire in Dhaka in August 2019 that left over 10,000 people homeless, with their homes having been designed as a fire risk by comprising 'thin sheet metal, wood and plastic'.

The Dhaka example is illustrative of a common problem in which social and political pressures to build can lead to disregarding the quality of construction and habitation. One of the major risks relates to construction in flood plains, and despite knowledge of the problems that can occur, there is evidence of continual building in such places, with consequences for the people who live there (Fielding, 2018). In the UK, there is political pressure to increase the quantity of house building, and in a context of land shortfalls, planning permissions have been given for construction in flood-prone areas (see Chapter 7). In February 2020, rainfall in the UK led to major flooding and many people lost their possessions and were temporarily displaced and made homeless. Some people who had been flooded on more than one occasion over the years said that they would never return to their home, with one person, Sharon Williams, noting: 'I'm going to move. I have had enough. I can't do this again' (quoted in BBC, 2020: 1).

The floods in the UK, like elsewhere, are more than a climate change event; rather, they show the problems of inappropriately designed and sited building. One example was the devastation caused by the 2005 New Orleans floods, in which a million people were displaced in the Gulf Coast region of the US. Over 90,000 people have never returned to New Orleans, including 33 per cent of former black residents. The flooding was exacerbated by deficient building practices and political decisions, including what Lopez (2015: 1) calls 'bad engineering', in which the levees, constructed to keep water out of the city, were 'inconsistent in quality, materials, and design'. Their failure was compounded by many years of excessive construction of dwellings in the areas most vulnerable to flooding, many of which were below sea level. This process was facilitated by a political decision to provide government flood insurance policy to households. This encouraged building programmes in risky areas over a period of years, or places where insurance would ordinarily have been withheld (Lopez, 2015).

The history of construction is replete with similar instances in which the human impacts of environmental, biophysical events are always mediated by a complexity of socio-political and technical relations, including the state of building technology, knowledge and application. The Romans were never able to make the river Tiber, flowing through Rome, safe, and regular floods were a significant source of building failures and displacement of local populations. Aldrete's (2006) discussion of the floods of the Tiber in Ancient Rome refer to written accounts at the time, which note that construction techniques contributed to building failure, including the collapse of structures. There was a social class dimension in which monumental buildings, such as the Circus Maximus, and the villas of the wealthy survived, while those that perished were the insula, or speculative housing 'constructed out of the flimsiest materials, made with poor workmanship, or possessing intrinsic flaws in engineering' (see Figure 5.1) (Aldrete, 2006: 105).

Similar observations are apt in relation to the Great Fire of Rome in AD 64, in which hundreds of thousands of people lost their homes and were left destitute. The fire burnt for over six days and destroyed most of the city (Walsh, J., 2019). Integral to it taking hold was the poor quality of the buildings, or, as J. Walsh (2019: 6) describes it, 'the nature of their placement, construction, and materials'. Most buildings were densely packed together and constructed from timber and flammable materials. In the fire's aftermath, the displacement of people continued, with the rebuilding of the city leading to gentrification (Newbold, 1974).[1] Poor people were either forced into overcrowded conditions to minimise rental payments or relocated to the margins of the city to find affordable accommodation (Newbold, 1974). Rebuilt areas had wider streets, common walls between buildings and the use of timber were prohibited, and building heights were restricted. Consequently, building densities were lowered, land costs became more exorbitant and higher rents were charged for new buildings.

J. Walsh (2019: 102) refers to the aftermath of the Great Fire of Rome as 'one of history's greatest ever urban regeneration projects'. The city centre became, increasingly, the place of the wealthy, and there was an excess in Rome's reconstruction, with Emperor Nero commissioning grandiose buildings and what Stambaugh (1988: 70) describes as the 'prodigal use of open space in the middle of a crowded city'. This included straight, wide avenues such as the Sacra Via, and a new building code guided the design of 'colonnades and shops laid out according to a regular and rational plan' (Stambaugh, 1988: 71). The process stimulated the emergence of a lucrative real estate market and a pattern of city building that was to become commonplace over the centuries. This was property-led regeneration, or the upgrade and modernisation of the built environment, in which new construction was a process of social upheaval and unsettlement, or the destabilisation of communities, including the decantation and dispersal of populations.

One of the more controversial, and debated, episodes of urban regeneration was the reconstruction of 19th-century Paris, a state-led modernisation of the city organised by the city's Prefect, Georges-Eugène Haussmann. The project was ambitious and included the demolition of much of medieval Paris, which was an act of vandalism for some commentators and the making of the modern city for others (Jordan, 1992). In his memoires, Haussmann

Figure 5.1: Circus Maximus, Rome

Note: The Circus Maximus was a public event venue constructed in the 6th century BC that held up to 300,000 people.

Source: Petar Milošević, https://en.wikipedia.org/wiki/Circus_Maximus#/media/File:Circus_Maximus_in_Rome.jpg

recounts his antipathy to the medieval streets of Paris. On crossing the Pont Saint-Michel, he writes: 'I had to cross the miserable little square where, like a sewer, the waters flowed out of the rue de la Harpe' (quoted in Jordan, 1992: 99). For Jordan (1992: 99), this reflected the 'authentic Haussmann', who 'had little affection for old Paris' and sought to impose a modernist space of rational, geometric proportions, clean lines, and broad, linear avenues.

Among the many outcomes from the reconstruction of 19th-century Paris was the role of the building process in destabilising and dispersing populations in the city. Over 20,000 buildings were demolished between 1854 and 1870, and 350,000 people were displaced from neighbourhoods in Central Paris (Evenson, 1979). For Frederick Engels (1975 [1954]: 71), commenting on the aftermath of the reconstruction, it was a classic case of embourgeoisement, or 'making breaches in the working class neighbourhoods … to the accompaniment of lavish self-glorification by the bourgeoisie'. The widespread demolitions, and dispersal of, primarily, poor people from Central Paris to the outer suburbs chimed with Haussmann's vision, and McAuliffe (2020: 81) notes that he was 'hostile to the idea of workers' housing' and did not want any rebuilt in the city. What ensued was a form of modernist destruction, or what Herscher (2008: 38) describes as 'a war by other means', in which the weaponry was a panoply of construction technologies.

This weaponry, ranging from wagons to shovels and picks, was deployed as part of a process described by Benjamin (1969: 171) as the 'strategic beautification' of Paris, or an aesthetic apparel of grand buildings and tree-lined streets masquerading as a progressive rebuilding of the city. For Benjamin (1969), the reality was the heightening of class antagonism and the deployment of a purposive building strategy to separate rich from poor areas. Jordan (1992: 102) describes how Haussmann transformed the old centre of Paris, including the Ile de la Cite and adjacent neighbourhoods, from 'teeming neighbourhoods' into isolated public buildings, such as the Louvre and the Tuileries. Neighbourhoods that had previously been relatively low cost, low rental and densely packed with people became, post-Haussmann, freed from the 'dangerous classes' and changed into what Jordan (1992: 102) describes as a 'deserted quartier'.

Haussmann's reconstruction of Paris presaged the coming of an urban age of unsettlement and the role of demolition, building and construction in propagating dispossession, or decanting those that, in his vision for the new city, had no place there (see Chapter 6). Haussmann's vision was to create a showcase city that exemplified the best of urban living, and to do this, he deployed the full armoury of state, legal and planning instruments. This was not an armed or military repossession of the city, but a forceful appropriation of Parisian territory. By using planning ordinances and taxes to 'persuade' particular categories of people to leave the city, Haussmann was able to accomplish what Jordan (1992: 100) describes as the 'gutting' of Paris. For Haussmann, his vision had no place for 'dirty industries', such as railway depots, engineering and 'backstreet' manufacturing, and his deployment of excise duties on building and other raw materials entering the city forced 'undesirable land users outside city limits' (Wagenaar, 2010: 345).

Haussmann's techniques were a subtle form of non-physical violence and a violation of people's rights to inhabit space, a process that has since come to characterise the (re)building of cities. Till (2012: 3) refers to the wounding of cities in which the (re)construction of neighbourhoods is often marked by 'structures of violence and exclusion' and the production of spaces 'steeped in oppression'. Till (2012) cites the example of the construction of a new public park in Central Bogota between 2000 and 2005, the Parque Tercer Mileno, which Berney (2017: 85) describes as a vanity project and 'prestige park' that, in its making, involved the social cleansing of an area renowned for its informal economies, prostitution and drugs (see Figure 5.2). Up to 12,000 people, mostly poor, were displaced, without compensation, around Bogota, and the park was subsequently constructed 'to catalyse the market and pride in the city' (Berney, 2017: 86).

Figure 5.2: Parque Tercer Mileno, Bogota

Source: https://upload.wikimedia.org/wikipedia/commons/thumb/d/df/2017_Bogotá_
Cerros_Orientales_desde_el_Parque_Tercer_Milenio.jpg/1280px-2017_Bogotá_Cerros_
Orientales_desde_el_Parque_Tercer_Milenio.jpg

The rationale for the construction of Parque Tercer Mileno was not dissimilar to the plans by Haussmann in seeking to create safer, secure spaces and to cleanse parts of the city of social threats. Both projects, albeit at different scales, reflected the ideology of comprehensive urban renewal, or the attempt to sweep away the old social order and replace it with a vision for a better society. This idea was associated with the tabula rasa and its implication that 'the good city' could ensue by changing the mix and types of buildings, and eliminating, often by dispersal, certain categories of people inhabiting them (Mehan, 2017). The tabula rasa was the archetypal, modernist concept in seeking to propagate a new beginning and to deploy techniques of erasure to facilitate a clean break with the past. This idea has appealed to generations of architects and politicians with a desire for the eradication of existing socio-spatial patterns and the reconstruction of a new society.

One of the keenest proponents of the tabula rasa as a guide for city building was the French architect Le Corbusier, who, in a letter to the Italian government in 1936, suggested a plan for the reconstruction of Addis Ababa in Abyssinia (Woudstra, 2014). As Woudstra (2014: 1) notes, Le Corbusier's plans chimed with colonial mentalities in conceiving of the city's rebuilding as a tabula rasa in which the intent was to clear 'the land of all signs of humanity and centuries of urban culture'. For Le Corbusier, both Addis Ababa and Abyssinia were empty places, or, as he said, spaces 'without time, and therefore, without history', and a perfect laboratory for imposing, through design and construction, the Italian colonial order.[2] This (re)ordering of the city was later left to Italian architects who followed Le Corbusier's conception that Addis Ababa's history had little of value worth preserving. Instead, the political directive was a racialised building programme that by dispersing indigenous people to the physical margins of the city, sought to render them invisible.

These ideas, and related building practices, were redolent of autocratic modernism, in which the organisation of many major building projects throughout the 20th century was rarely a democratic process, or sensitised to the needs of a diverse citizenry. Rather, city building, particularly after the 1940s, was imposed from above by cadres of administrators and politicians intent on pursuing comprehensive urban renewal, in which the destruction of places was seen as the corollary for the (re)construction of better environs and lives. This was particularly evident in the US, and the country's history of urban renewal from the 1950s to the late 1980s bears testimony to the displacement of large numbers of people from their neighbourhoods, usually in the name of 'progression' and 'improvement'. The reality was a little different for those people displaced, and a litany of projects came to define the period as a brutal culture of clearance (see also Chapter 6).

This is illustrated with the coming of the motor vehicle and the construction of intra-urban road systems that shattered, and displaced, many communities. Such systems were presented by many politicians and policymakers as technical and progressive instruments, integral to a country's economic system and requiring the adaptation of urban spaces. The planning orthodoxy in the US from the 1940s to the 1970s regarded the construction of urban highways as an opportunity to eradicate social problems by removing, primarily, black people from areas labelled as 'slums'. Shelton (2010) describes the language of the day as both 'racist' and demeaning of the poor and poverty. In 1944, Robert Moses, a leading exponent of comprehensive renewal, proposed sweeping plans to demolish the homes of 19,000 people living in a black neighbourhood in West Baltimore to make way for a freeway, noting that by doing so, 'the healthier Baltimore will be in the long run' (quoted in Mohl, 2004: 693).[3]

Such characterisations were commonplace, and one of the leading advocates of road building, Lawrence Hewes, a Public Roads official based in California, conceived of federal highways construction as a technical, engineering solution to urban blight and poor housing. For Hewes, road construction was not only a means to enhance the mobility of the population, but also the panacea for overturning the problems of 'obsolete buildings and lowered property values' (quoted in Shelton, 2010: 331). What was required, so Hewes and others advocated, was the eradication of the source of the problem, that is, the population, and one of the means to facilitate this was to construct major freeways through, predominantly, black neighbourhoods. In doing so, the population could be dispersed and areas opened up to new investment opportunities, becoming a focal point for renewed real estate activity. Fullilove (2004: 64) describes this process as racially motivated by city business leaders propagating a programme to 'clear blight and clear blacks'.

Population dispersal due to road building was so widespread in the US that at its height during the 1960s, it was destroying '62,000 units of housing per year' (Mohl, 2004: 679). The US House Committee on Public Works noted that over 32,000 families were displaced each year throughout the 1960s, an outcome described by the committee in 1965 as 'astoundingly large' (quoted in Mohl, 1993: 101). An example was a freeway building project in Harlem Park in West Baltimore in the mid-1970s, the Interstate 170, or what Walker (2015: 1) describes as 'a six-lane ditch of a highway'. The highway is less than 2 miles in length and was a connection between two other freeways (see Figure 5.3). The construction was not completed and the connection between the freeways was never made. The road is a barely used monument to the failures of a building policy insensitive to the needs of local communities; its construction led to the loss of 971 homes and 62 businesses, and 1,500 people were displaced from the area (Walker, 2015).

Figure 5.3: View east along US Route 40 (former Interstate 170), Baltimore

Source: https://upload.wikimedia.org/wikipedia/commons/thumb/6/6b/2016-05-11_09_
44_11_View_east_along_U.S._Route_40_%28former_Interstate_170%29_from_the_overpass_
for_U.S._Route_1_northbound_%28North_Fulton_Avenue%29_in_Baltimore_City%2C_
Maryland.jpg/1280px-thumbnail.jpg

The proliferation of construction since the end of the 20th century has continued to disrupt and unsettle communities, and, if anything, the scale of the displacement of people has increased in the wake of the rapid urbanisation and regeneration of cities, particularly in South-east and Eastern Asia. Shatkin (2008) describes urban developments in Manila that involve major land clearances and the construction of high-end retail, offices and residential uses. Such spaces are connected by elevated transport systems to link them together, which enable people to bypass the streets below them, a system that Shatkin (2008: 388) refers to as 'bypass implant urbanism'. The process is not only the production of elite, gentrified spaces, but also the erasure of the ordinary city, in which, as Shatkin (2008) estimates, over 31,000 people, primarily living in shanty settlements, had been evicted from their neighbourhoods by 2008. This situation has been compounded by a recently constructed rail system in Manila that Choi (2016) estimates displaced 35,000 people.

Such displacements are often part of a process of development-induced movement in which governments will present the outcomes as improving the life opportunities of people who have been relocated from their neighbourhood to make way for new building activity.[4] This is a feature in Luanda, Angola, a city that Black (2015: 1) describes as having 'been invaded by western office buildings, luxury hotels, and beachfront nightclubs'. Some of the most expensive real estate in the world has been constructed in the city, and the price has been paid by its poorest inhabitants. An example is the displacement in the early 2000s of 50,000 residents from central districts of Luanda to a new town called Zango, a purpose-built settlement 20 km outside the city. As Black (2015) recounts, while relocated residents have new, sturdy, concrete dwellings connected to water and electricity supplies, infrastructure construction is incomplete and many of the dwellings in the development are unliveable.

Like former residents of West Baltimore and countless other places affected by major rebuilding projects, people living in Zango lost their chosen place of residence. They were decanted to a place far from where they had established social ties, and they were distanced from the main sources of work and life opportunities in Luanda. Their removal was an undemocratic fait accompli and a prerequisite for the (re)valuation of space in downtown Luanda as part of a process to catalyse local land markets and convert prime real estate to enrich elites. Zango is not untypical and is illustrative of a contradiction at the heart of development-induced displacements in which while an objective proffered by politicians is to provide a better life, the reverse outcome is too often the result. It also highlights the ascription of worth and value in relation to building, and brings to the fore the question of what is, or ought, to be valued in the physical reconstruction of places, a theme I develop in the next section.

Building as the devaluation and displacement of communities

The construction of places is part of a process that often leads to significant harm to people by threatening, and undermining, the stability and quality of their habitation. All over the world, there are ongoing disputes between local residents and state and corporate construction interests intent on reconstructing land and property as part of a revaluation of real estate markets. The main manifestation of this is gentrification, or a process whereby the rebuilding of the urban fabric leads to an upward pressure on land values and an escalation in property rents and/or prices. A consequence is that the inflation of land values and rents is likely to be less affordable to pre-existing residents, particularly those in rental properties, and is part of a process that sees them displaced and replaced by wealthier people. This trend is well established across most major cities globally, and the upscaling of rents by changing the type and mix of land uses also attracts state developers intent on clearing areas to benefit from the potential accretion of wealth that can ensue.

Not surprisingly, the operations of the construction industry tend to revolve around the search for locales with sites and buildings ripe for 'upscaling', and then to clear them of any obstacles to their conversion to highly profitable land uses. The obstacles can be significant and reflect struggles between residents and builders about who and what has the right to a place, or what Nguyen (2017: 651) calls, in relation to China, 'construction conflicts'. These conflicts reflect rapid urbanisation in China, where millions of people have been displaced from their homes, often through violent evictions, and land converted to make way for the rise of a new middle class. There has been much resistance characterised by what Nguyen (2017: 650) describes as 'site fights', or attempts by local people to 'slow development and construction time down to a trickle'. It is evocatively captured by the 'nail houses', in which households refuse to move and try to either get greater compensation or thwart the development process (see Figure 5.4).[5]

The resistance by owners of nail houses is part of a broader, global phenomenon of people continually struggling to assert their rights to be present in places, often in the face of insurmountable and irresistible forces.

Figure 5.4: Nail house near Shenzhenbei Railway Station, Shenzhen, China

Note: This seven-storey nail house was originally identified for demolition in 2010 but the owner held out for seven years. It was acquired and demolished in mid-2017, and the site will become part of the development of Shenzhen North Railway Station.

Source: https://upload.wikimedia.org/wikipedia/commons/0/0b/Nail_house_near_
Shenzhenbei_Railway_Station_%2820160812144108%29.jpg

This is a struggle about the relative values, and valuations, that different actors ascribe to land and buildings, and about how best to build upon, and nurture and manage, the environment. For owners of nail houses, the objective is to slow down construction to make builders think about the multiple rhythms and temporalities of a place. For Nguyen (2017), a problem is that construction revolves around the value of speed and the time economy, or a process in which for builders to unlock economic value, a linear, progress-oriented time of construction, planning and development predominates. This process has little time for sensitising itself to the fine grain of a locale, or seeking to understand the daily, local rhythms of life, nor for adjusting to different, and diverse, values and valuations of a place.

The rationalities of the building process, as alluded to in previous chapters, appear to value profit-seeking behaviour, and what is most of value is monetary returns on investment. Discourses on urban regeneration are replete with references to values, valuation and the worth of things, ranging from the contribution of projects to uplifting land values, to the effects of investment in infrastructure and buildings in enhancing the competitive performance of urban economies. There is a normalising of construction and building as conduits for the acquisition of wealth, and media present them as intrinsic to the rational development of places. The property pages in mainstream media celebrate the waves of upmarket residential development by heralding the release of new property onto the market as akin to a film premiere or the opening night of a gala. Ascribing value and worth appears to attach itself to specific types of people, inhabiting particular forms of development, namely, the wealthy living in upmarket residences.

There is no inevitability in these representations, or the outcomes that occur, despite their dominance in media and popular discourse. As the example of the nail houses implies, building and construction activity is a contested field of values that reflects moral and ethical standpoints about what is worthy and valuable in relation to the make-up of cities. Part of the process is the struggle to define what is of value, and valuable, for inclusion in place making. This understanding relates to the unsettling nature of construction activity, in which who and what is defined as having value can have a bearing on the make-up of a place and people's life opportunities. Here, the dominance of market fundamentalism in construction is significant. It is premised, primarily, on a calculus in which 'objects, things and people' are allocated a (monetary) value and valued in ways whereby only particular objects, things and people will be included as permissible parts of development projects (see Skeggs, 2014: 4).

This has a bearing on the social fabric of places, and contemporary building projects are deeply implicated in the (re)production of socio-spatial inequalities through the use of valuation practices, or means of ascribing value and worth to particular categories of objects and people. In the rest of this section, I consider an example of how valuation, as method and process, is intertwined with the clearance of a site and the dispersal of an elderly group of long-standing residents. The process exemplifies how a category of people were decanted from an environment that provided a host of locational benefits, including ease of access to the local high street, containing shops, health care and public transport links, to a residential setting that included large gardens and on-site services such as a concierge. In discussing the case material, I refer to a mixture of documentary, research diary and interview data that were generated from a project conducted between 2014 and 2016.[6]

The research setting is a place called Esher, a small town located at the fringes of south-western suburban London. It is stockbroker belt and one of the richest parts of the UK. Average house prices in Esher in June 2020 were £946,666, well above the UK average of £247,000 (Rightmove, 2020). The focus of the research was a 1.7 hectare site, named Wootton Place, located within the gated community of Esher Park Avenue, where the average house price in June 2020 was £1,328,833, though this masks significant variations, with many properties in Esher Park Avenue selling for well above £5 million. Esher Park Avenue has been a focal point for significant rebuilding projects over the last 20 years, and the trend has been the construction of a mixture of blocks of upscale apartments and very large, single dwellings, most of which have exceeded £6 million in sales value (see Figure 5.5). It is part of a trend of the area's conversion to a rich, elite enclave and a locale that does not contain a diverse population.

This process was well under way by the early 2000s, and by 2009, the owner of Wootton Place, Elmbridge Housing Trust (EHT), an offshoot of Elmbridge Borough Council (EBC), was looking to develop it as in keeping with the ongoing privatisation of Esher Park Avenue. This was far from straightforward for EHT because the site had previously been owned by a local resident, Lady Carr, who left it to EBC in her will on the understanding that it would be used to house elderly people needing care. On receipt of the site from Lady Carr, EBC subsequently converted it into sheltered housing to accommodate elderly people. The site comprised one large main building and a bungalow, and it had extensive open grounds that functioned as a garden (see Figure 5.6). There were 36 units on the site at its time of closure in 2008, including 25 bedsits, nine one-bed flats, one two-bed flat and the bungalow. A maximum of 42 people lived on the site at any one time, and they had easy access to Esher town centre that was only 200 m away.

Figure 5.5: Esher Park Avenue, Esher

Source: Rob Imrie

Figure 5.6: The original Wootton Place, Esher

Source: Rob Imrie

The sheltered housing worked well for its residents because of its central location. In interview, a long-term resident of Esher described the site as dominated by:

'Massive grounds and people could walk everywhere from there … so elderly people living on the Wootton site just had everything they could want on their doorsteps … they could go to church, they could go to the chemist, they could go to the betting shop, they could go horse racing at Sandown Park [down the road].'

This person amplified by describing the character of the place, "how it was a sociable and lively place to walk by", and that "In the local streets, you would meet people from the Wootton, and many a time I'd have a chit and chat with them." Another interviewee, a local planner at EBC at the time of Wootton's closure, commented on the community feel and nature of the environment, or, as he said, "I've always liked it because it was open, you had some green space. It was public, you could see into it."

The publicness of Wootton Place was a unique, and disappearing, part of the locale, as most of the surrounding environment had been transformed into privatised, gated estates. This was the context for the ensuing development pressures, in which land in the area was highly prized and a valuable financial asset, and where there was increasing pressure on EHT to sell the Wootton site in order to enable them to 'cash in' and, subsequently, use receipts from the sale to fund and manage their wider portfolio of social housing throughout the borough. In interview, a manager from EHT explained the background to the subsequent sale of the site. He noted that when they acquired the site, the accommodation was "in need of modernisation and most units lacked basic facilities … there was no lift in the main building, and for some units, people had to use shared bathrooms". It was felt by EHT officers that "people did not want to live in such poor facilities and the site was underoccupied".

For EHT, the choice was either to sell the site located on prime residential land, or redevelop it by updating the existing buildings and adding new units. As the EHT officer said, "It would have cost too much to redevelop and refurbish the site as social housing … it made good business sense for us to sell it on and reinvest the receipts into affordable housing elsewhere in our operating area." This rationale, however, was never tested or subject to critical scrutiny, and as a local planner said, "It would have been more than viable to keep the site for sheltered housing." Instead, EHT's approach was a fait accompli, reflecting a pro-market stance and the development of a strategy to enhance the financial valuation of the site. The approach was shaped by a one-dimensional fiscal model seeking to use the development of the Wootton site as a tool to generate income to feed into the EHT's investments and enhance its assets.

This reflected a financialised rationality, or value set, and as an officer for EHT said, "We're overseen by government and this is the main way of practising, which is how to increase the value of developable assets to achieve targets and outcomes." For EHT, maximising the monetary value of Wootton Place had always been its longer-term game plan. Throughout the 2000s, up to the premise's closure in 2008, this objective shaped the EHT's strategy of underinvestment in Wootton Place, with the onset of blight. Residents were gradually moved out to other housing schemes around the borough, and any vacant premises that became available at Wootton were not advertised or filled, nor were they maintained or kept in a habitable condition. As a local planner said, "The approach by EHT was self-fulfilling because by withholding investment from the site, not maintaining it, it became much less of a going concern as sheltered property, and much more attractive as a site for private development."

By 2009, EHT had formed a partnership with a house builder, Octagon Developments Ltd, with a view to selling the site to them for a luxury housing scheme. A snag was the local planning framework, which was premised on maintaining Wootton Place as sheltered housing, thus, ostensibly, preventing any further, alternative development of the site. A planning officer outlined the local plan policy: "There was a presumption of on-site affordable housing, the primary driver to that was inclusive communities to ensure that we didn't have just large houses and everything shipped off somewhere else." By 2009, EHT, with Octagon, decided to challenge the presumption of the local plan, and after the submission of a planning application in mid-2009 that was subsequently withdrawn, they submitted another by May 2010 that, despite recommendations by planning officers for it to be rejected, was approved by the EBC planning committee in September 2010.

The approved planning application was for the construction of 13 large, detached and private dwellings, with no affordable or social housing to be built on site. Instead, the developer, Octagon, promised to part-fund EHT's investments in affordable properties in other parts of the borough. This outcome was a flagrant breach of the local planning framework; as a local planner involved in the decision said, "We messed up as the authority and that scheme is wrong for so many reasons." He amplified by noting that "A site of that scale should have delivered on-site affordable housing by virtue of the scale of it", and it did not address the "issue of ensuring inclusive and sustainable mixed communities". The decision also breached the trust that Lady Carr placed in EBC to preserve and develop the site for vulnerable, older people, and the means by which it came about illustrates a devaluation of the efficacy of 'the social' and 'the collective' in contributing to Esher's community.

The process was aided and abetted by the local social milieu of Esher Park Avenue. Local residents opposed to the retention of Wootton Place as sheltered housing were vocal advocates of EHT's planning application. Residents' letters of support for the application, and other forms of lobbying, were part of the 'devaluation' process, or means to create an aura that was disparaging of social housing provision. There was a class politics at play in which, as described by a local planner, "Esher Park Avenue, typically, in terms of affordable housing, is as remote as it can be from that world." For local residents, the application was part of a struggle to ensure the (re)production of elite, wealthy spaces, and to keep at bay anything that would dilute the exclusivity of the neighbourhood. As the local planner recalled, "Every clichéd objection popularised by people who read the *Daily Mail* was made: antisocial behaviour, single-parent families. So, all of the worst things that people imagine affordable housing to be was set in the minds of many people who lived in Esher Park Avenue."

This was a systematic process of disparagement of a particular type of housing and, by implication, a particular type of person not perceived to be in keeping with the neighbourhood. As a local resident said in interview: "People living in Esher Park Avenue saw social housing as a threat to their property values and sense of security, and they lobbied local councillors to make sure that it would never happen." By 2010, this outcome had transpired, and as one of the local planners said in interview: "By handing over Wootton Place to Octagon, EHT was effectively creating a millionaire's ghetto, that's what they were creating, and they were contributing to an ongoing trend and just making it worse." The ghetto effect was exacerbated by Octagon sidestepping a legal obligation to construct on-site social housing and, instead, as part of the £8.5 million they paid EHT for Wootton Place, contributing to EHT's broader portfolio of building around the borough.

One of the developments is Mayfield Close in Walton-on-Thames, and compared to Wootton Park, it is a remote location, far from shops and other facilities. As a local planning officer said: "The people that left Wootton Place after it closed went to less-central locations and lost access to amenities. There's nothing wrong with Mayfield Close, but it's cut-off, well over a mile from the town centre." He amplified by noting that EHT's properties are "considered to be in poorer areas of the borough", and that the dispersal of remaining residents from Wootton Place to other locations "felt like second-class treatment, a bit like social cleansing and getting rid of social housing residents from Esher". A local resident concurred by suggesting that the dispersal of people from Wootton Place was about "lifting the values of the surrounding properties". It was, she said, the antithesis of inclusivity and reflected a locale that is "not community-minded, and containing the sorts of people who are very self-contained, very sure of themselves, and don't want to mix".

The Esher case is a microcosm of a much wider trend of orchestrated and systematic devaluation of particular social groups or types of people in which building and construction is a tool not only of creating new physical infrastructure, but also for transforming the social mix or milieu of places. The process in Esher was facilitated by a local class politics opposed to anything other than the perpetuation of elitist spaces, and it is illustrative of a politics of denigration in which to preserve and/or create value, you need to devalue something else. In this case, not only did elderly people living at Wootton Place see their homes devalued – first blighted, then demolished – but as 'social tenants', their social status and standing were also brought into question as 'not appropriate' for residence in Esher. Here, the dominant definition of worth and, by implication, the right to occupy space was propagated by a self-serving elite described by a local resident as "opposed to anything that's not in their image".

By 2014, Octagon had completed the construction of 13 new dwellings, and were marketing them to wealthy clients at international fairs (see Figure 5.7). The development has intensified the homogeneous nature of the locality and exacerbated socio-spatial inequalities through Octagon seeking the highest market return from their investment and involvement in decanting people on low incomes from the locale. The reconstruction of Wootton Place illustrates the potency of building in transforming

Figure 5.7: The new Wootton Place, Esher

Source: Rob Imrie

places, and core to the process was dispersing a vulnerable population that was dispossessed of means to stay within the locale and had little voice to thwart the machinery and machinations of local politics. Specific interests, including those of Octagon and the residents of Esher Park Avenue, were able to use the building process not only to defend property values, but also to fashion the local social structure as in keeping with the dominant views, circulating locally, about what types of people ought to be living in the locale.

While the case is only a single instance of dispersal and dispossession, it provides insight into the role of building cultures in reshaping the socio-spatial structure of places. The construction of Wootton Place as an elite enclave is the antithesis of an inclusive social agenda, and highlights that the dispersal of people is integral to much of the building process, particularly where the objective is the upscaling of neighbourhoods. In this instance, the process reinforced, and perpetuated, socio-spatial homogeneity, and denied a certain category of person ease of access to the emerging environment. If one judges that the exclusion of people from space is a form of social injustice, the case raises the important question of what can be done to ensure that a larger proportion of society is defined as valuable in building projects, and what kinds of institutions and sociocultural practices can be put in place to foster and sustain heterarchy and plurality.

Conclusion

The design and construction of the built environment have the potential not only to create the means for settlement by contributing to the stabilisation and routinisation of everyday life, but also the obverse, that is, unsettlement and destabilisation of human habitation and the daily rhythms of life. For many people, the built environment is experienced as a source of delight and contentment, but for others, it represents the struggle to gain access to affordable housing, to remain in place in a context of rising rents and land values, and to manage a host of external threats, including proximity to noise and air pollution, and environmental hazards such as flooding and fire risk. In this chapter, I have focused on the phenomenon of people's dispersal and dispossession from places, in which one of the facets of how construction affects people and nature is to despoil and displace, including the destruction of specific forms of habitation.

From the 48,000 miles of state highways constructed in the US during the 1950s–70s, in which whole neighbourhoods were dismantled and destroyed, to the dispersal of communities to make way for upscale property-led development, such as the case of Esher Park Avenue, construction is implicated in disruptive, often radical, transformations in the social and physical character of space. The scale of population displacement related to construction is quite staggering, with an estimation that between 1992 and 1999, over 1 million people were evicted from their homes in Central Shanghai to make way for property-led development (Short, 2018: 27). This figure was exceeded by the building of the Olympic Games stadia and infrastructure for the 2008 Beijing Games, in which 1.5 million people were displaced by construction (Short, 2018). In both Shanghai and Beijing, the outcome has been gentrification and the displacement of lower-earning middle classes to the edges of the city to make way for a new affluent middle class.

The displacement and dispersal of people in China, and elsewhere, is often violent, traumatic and undemocratic, with people losing their homes, livelihoods and social networks. Campanella (2008: 167) describes an instance of a resident in Old Beijing being told to leave their 400-year-old courtyard home with a day's notice, despite having lived there for over 50 years. Lees and White (2019) describe similar outcomes in a different context, that is, council tenants forced from their homes in Central London as part of the privatisation of public housing. Here, many people have been dispossessed of their homes to make way for an upscaling process, and for affected residents, the experience is, as described by Lees and White (2019: 8), akin to a 'slow violence'. They quote a resident giving up on the upkeep of their flat when they heard it was going to be demolished: 'it changed things for me, I didn't feel as inspired to decorate and to keep the place. I let it go' (quoted in Lees and White, 2019: 9).

How might building be done otherwise in ways whereby the objective is to ensure settlement, or the stabilisation of building form and patterns, including the right for people, irrespective of income and culture, to inhabit places, without threat or fear of expulsion or denial of access to space? How might this occur whereby settlement is sensitised to the sociocultural relations of a place and embedded into its histories and traditions? How might any form of settlement, which, by implication, will always unsettle the earth, work with, and through, nature in ways whereby construction can be respectful to the interfaces and interactions between buildings and natural environmental processes? Given this, what are the possibilities for people to provide counterpoints to the dominant, deeply embedded development politics of building in which econometric criteria and a balance sheet rationality tend to define what is of worth and value in relation to the construction of the built environment?

These questions, while far-reaching, are core to the whole *raison d'être* of settlement, or the (re)production of places in ways that can guarantee not only the biological reproduction of species, both human and non-human, but also the flourishing of people and nature. Unsettlement is the antithesis of this, and in relation to dispersal by development, there are some interesting insights into what alternative scenarios can be. Returning to Nguyen's (2017) notion of slow time is insightful because the site fights by occupants of nail houses that she refers to offer an alternative, different value and valuation of time by seeking to slow down the temporalities of construction and to compel 'developers, investors, and even construction workers' to conceive of the spaces of development not as 'tabula rasa plots of land, or simply fixed capital investments, but as places embedded and implicated in longer histories and personal trajectories' (Nguyen, 2017: 659).

For Nguyen (2017), there is a need to oppose the anti-vernacularism of construction and its ahistorical readings of place and environment, as though all that counts is a blueprint, or the implementation of a templated, drawing-board conception of the built environment. This is, potentially, an emasculation of the nuances, the details and the specificities of a place, and one of the possibilities for 'slow construction' is to help one to apprehend and appreciate the diversity and complexity of places in order to avoid the erasure of their vitalities. Therefore, as Nguyen (2017: 660) notes, while builders are busy building a new place, slow construction in Chinese cities is a form of resistance to the developmental model of building. As she recounts, it means that builders and others involved in construction 'are forced to reckon with the afternoon nap schedule of Mr Zhou, the demands of Mr Duan, as well as the daily round of other old city residents'. Slow construction will not prevent corporate building practices, but it is a sociocultural tool necessary to reimagine what settlement is or ought to be.

In requiring builders to recognise and work with the rhythms and specificities of a place, slow construction can, potentially, cultivate the multiple hierarchies of worth and value embedded into the fabric of spaces. However, much more needs to be done to prevent the displacement of people and nature by construction, and this will require political strategies, often localised in origin, that can operate outside of, and in opposition to, the technocratic discourses and cost–benefit calculus of the building industry (see also Chapter 10). This is to prevent the reduction of building work to the narrow pursuit of economic value because this is a recipe for emasculating alternative ways of valuing, and giving value to, people and place making. Part of the process needs to challenge some of the seemingly untouchable cornerstones of the building industry, particularly its propensity to demolish and destroy physical objects, and, with it, to undermine the sociocultural fabric of places, or what I refer to as the 'demolition paradigm'.

Demolition: Wasting the City and Teardown Building

Introduction

On a Sunday morning in May 2016, 5 Norfolk Court, high-rise social housing located in the Gorbals, one of Glasgow's inner-city neighbourhoods, was blown up. It was the last demolition in a neighbourhood that, over the years, had become synonymous with poverty and poor housing, and its destruction seemed symbolic of the dismantling of a community's social fabric. The demolition of Norfolk Court can be viewed in many different ways. For some local residents, it was the welcome clearance of buildings that had failed to provide basic amenities, which were delipidated and where the wind whistled through cracks in the facades (*Daily Record*, 2013: 1). The poor quality of construction, and the lack of maintenance by the council, meant that the buildings suffered from chronic dampness, and the breakdown of facilities such as lifts was commonplace. As a member of the Gallagher family said, 'the buildings were old, and had a lot of problems. It was for the best that they come down' (quoted in New Gorbals Housing Association, 2016: 1).

Other residents were less happy, as they saw the destruction of Norfolk Court as the loss of social ties in their local community and the onset of an uncertain future. As one local resident, Katrin Reedik, recalled just before the demolition of number 66 Norfolk Court in 2013: 'I just wish that they would refurbish the blocks instead of destroying them.… If they were well-maintained and in good order, I would happily stay. I don't want to go' (*Daily Record*, 2013: 1). Another resident, Betty Olsen, felt unhappy about having to leave and lose close contact with neighbours and friends: 'We all looked out for each other. It's a bit different now and a lot of the people we knew have died. There are drugs and problems but we loved it then and we still love it now. We feel terrible, we don't want to go' (*Daily Record*, 2013: 1).

This view was echoed by Neil Freel, a long-standing resident, who said: 'it will be sad when they're gone. I would like to see them refurbished. If they are looked after properly they can be great' (*Daily Record*, 2013: 1).

This episode is one of many in which demolition is encouraged by governments as part of the renewal and reconstruction of the built environment. It is presented by some government officials as integral to upgrading buildings and infrastructure to meet changing user demands and needs (Cleveland City Council and Gaylord Consulting, 2012; Glasgow Housing Association, 2020). This understanding conceives of demolition and construction as symbiotic, intertwined and essential to one another, in which the demolition of particular types of environments is a necessary and positive action, or a civilising act integral to the modernisation of society (Liss, 2000). This discourse is at the forefront of propagating the naturalisation of demolition as an activity beyond question. As the Norfolk Court example shows, people's experiences of demolition do not necessarily accord with this view, and for some, it may be experienced as an act of vandalism, the rupture of place-based social ties and the degradation and despoliation of local environments.

While there is equivocation and debate about the role and effects of demolition in society, in this chapter, I develop the proposition that construction is dominated by, and in thrall to, a demolition paradigm in which the propensity to demolish and rebuild is a primary stimulus of activity in the building industry. This has been so, with some intensity, since the end of the 19th century, and while it is difficult, if not impossible, to generate aggregate, global figures relating to the scale and incidence of demolition, there are single studies of construction that provide insights into its prevalence (Öktem, 2019; Xu et al, 2019; Akers et al, 2020). Xu et al (2019: 1) note that vast quantities of the urban fabric in China have been 'demolished while still serviceable', while Öktem (2019: 295, 313) describes the 'populist urban growth machine' in Turkey as propagating a process of 'erasure and effacement' by demolition, including the 'destruction of urban heterogeneity'.

Such studies point towards the politically charged nature of demolition, and its use as a technocratic tool of managing 'problem' people and spaces by seeking to upgrade, and revalue, the built environment. Here, demolition is an instrument of social engineering by removing particular people and uses from demolished areas, while seeking to create the basis for new investment opportunities and profits for the building industry. In places such as Cleveland, Ohio, there is a 'demolition-first' approach to the problems of urban decline, and between 2007 and 2016, over 8,000 dwellings were demolished (Rosenman and Walker, 2016). They were abandoned after the collapse of speculative finance in 2007–08, in which households that were unable to service mortgage debt were forced to leave their properties. Instead of seeking to solve the roots of the crisis, relating to housing affordability, Cleveland City embarked on mass demolitions, intent on pursuing a policy described by Rosenman and Walker (2016: 275) as 'salvaging property values' instead of 'addressing lingering housing needs'.

In exploring the rationales and *raison d'être* of demolition, I divide the chapter into three parts. First, I define and characterise what demolition is, and show its changing scale, character and prevalence, both historically and in contemporary times. I develop the notion of the 'demolition paradigm' to convey the dominance of destruction in the building process (Hackworth, 2016). This paradigm conceives of demolishing the built environment as integral to social and economic progress, and demolition as intrinsic to the rational operations of the building industry by enabling a rapid turnover of, and changes to, its assets and investment portfolios. The paradigm propagates the notion of 'creative destruction' to support its operations, though there is often little that is creative about the process (Komlos, 2017). The term tends to act as a smokescreen, or to deflect attention from, the political, and contested, nature of demolition, particularly where it is deployed as a tool that erases and eradicates places, and perpetuates obsolescence.

Second, with a focus on teardown, or the demolition and replacement of a dwelling, I evaluate the social and environmental impacts of demolishing buildings. Significant to these impacts is the centrality of waste and disposability that demolition incurs as a building practice. This disposability relates to both humans and the environment. With regards to the latter, the demolition industry is one of the world's biggest polluters, being wasteful of materials and implicated in despoiling environments. In relation to the former, demolition is a policy tool used to clear sites for renewal and re-engineer the socio-economic structures of cities. Its use by state officials is highly controversial, and a plethora of research shows how demolition is a blunt policy approach that is instrumental in (re)shaping, often in violent and insensitive ways, the socio-spatial structure of places (Akers et al, 2020). People and places are often laid to waste, with the demolition process implicated in what Harvey (1975: 124) describes as the 'perpetual perishing' of space.

Third, I explore rehabilitation and the possibilities of constructing for disassembly, not demolition. I suggest that, in many instances, demolition is neither necessary nor desirable, but a product of a building culture that fails to value or promote longevity in the design and construction of the built environment. This is not to argue that there is no place for demolition in the recrafting of environments, but rather to suggest that it needs to be used appropriately in respecting, and responding to, people's habitation and the rhythms of ecology and the environment. Demolition is the default position taken by those working in the building industry, often because of technical and practical issues of renovating and retrofitting the built environment. There is a need to rethink the totality of the construction process in relation to how buildings are put together in ways whereby their disassembly, and reassembly, can be achieved.

The demolition paradigm

A prominent feature of construction activity is demolition, or the dismantling and destruction of the built environment that signifies the end of life of a building and infrastructure. Urban landscapes are peppered with semi-derelict and demolished buildings, and demolition activity is omnipresent in cities, ranging from the visibility of excavators and concrete-crushing machines, to rubble dust and dirt pervading and polluting the atmosphere. Vacant sites around cities are one of the key visual indicators that demolition has occurred, and in places like Buffalo in New York State, its population halved between 1950 and 2000, leaving a legacy of empty and abandoned buildings that were subsequently demolished. This includes the Buffalo Memorial Auditorium, a former sporting and entertainments venue that was closed in 1996 and demolished in 2009, with most of the site, to this day, remaining underoccupied and unused (see Figure 6.1).

Figure 6.1: The site of the demolished Buffalo Memorial Auditorium

Note: The photograph shows the site of the former auditorium, an image redolent of many post-industrial cities, with little take-up and reuse of space.

Source: Rob Imrie

In shrinking cities, such as Buffalo, building activity is more likely to be dominated by demolition than the construction of new buildings, reflecting, in part, the legacy of industrial decline in the city and abandonment of the built environment. In other places, such as Delhi and Tokyo, demolition is prompted by a different set of social and political considerations, highlighting the variety of contexts in which demolition transpires. Tokyo is the most demolished city in the world, and housing in Japan has an average life of less than 30 years before it is bulldozed and replaced (Berg, 2017). This means that most of Tokyo's housing has been built since 1985, and while there is much demolition, Beech (2019: 1) notes that 'the net increase in homes is still much larger than the UK – about 600,000 homes are added to Japan's dwelling stock every year'. Berg (2017) refers to the 'scrap-and-build approach' to housing in Japan, in which there is barely a second-hand, resale market, with consumers preferring to purchase newbuild properties constructed to the latest seismic standards and building codes.

This means that older properties in Japan lose their value over time, and are not an investable proposition. Demolition and rebuild is the default option, a process that reflects sociocultural attitudes that regard building structures as ephemeral and part of the impermanency of life itself. In contrast, in Delhi, comprehensive urban renewal is the stimulus for what Mehra and Batra (2006: 182) term the 'onslaught on the spaces of the urban poor'. Referring to the district of Pushta, located along the banks of the main river in Delhi, the Yamuna, Mehra and Batra (2006) note that by 2004, well over 100,000 residents, many of whom had been living in the area for 40 years or more, had been forced out and their homes demolished. The demolitions were part of a city plan to rid the area of a population deemed to be harbingers of crime, disease and other social ills, and to replace them with a beautification programme, including new road systems, upscale housing and commercial development.

These illustrations of Buffalo, Delhi and Tokyo show contrasting contexts in which demolition occurs, and for different reasons. They are illustrative of the rise of demolition as, primarily, a post-19th-century phenomenon associated with the advent of the industrial city and mass urbanisation. Mallach (2011) suggests that most demolition prior to the early 19th century was related to warfare and environmental events, such as earthquakes, fires and floods. The former reflected the invasion and conquest of territory, and the use of the demolition and destruction of buildings as warcraft, or means to subdue and control populations. The latter has been, and remains, an existential threat, and numerous settlements throughout history have been destroyed by precipitous, environmental events, including, in Italy, the Messina earthquake in 1908, in which most of the town was levelled and destroyed (see Figure 6.2).

Figure 6.2: Ruins of Messina

Note: The photograph shows people clearing away some of the ruins of Messina after the earthquake that occurred on 28 December 1908.

Source: https://upload.wikimedia.org/wikipedia/commons/1/1c/Clearing_away_the_ruins_on_route_to_Catania_-_Sicily_%28after_earthquake%29.jpg

While Mallach's (2011) observation about the scarcity of demolition not related to conflict and environmental events seems to accord with the available evidence, there is some, albeit limited, documentation of demolition projects in the Roman Empire that were part of purposive policies and city-building programmes. Lanciani (1899) notes that at the beginning of the reign of Augustus in 63 BC, the demolition of numerous temples and houses occurred in Republican Rome, with the Emperor, following on from the clearance of spaces by his predecessor Julius Caesar, ordering the widening of streets and thoroughfares to facilitate the construction of the theatre of Marcellus. For Lanciani (1899: 10), this was the beginning of 'the destruction of Rome', or the use of demolition as a tool of embourgeoisement and

Figure 6.3: St Pancras Station, London, under construction, 1868

Note: The construction of St Pancras Station displaced a poor community in Agar Town, demolished in 1866 to make way for warehousing and railway sidings servicing the station.

Source: https://en.wikipedia.org/wiki/St_Pancras_railway_station#/media/File:St_Pancras_station_train_shed_under_construction_in_1868_(cropped).jpg

the crafting of the imperial city. Later, in the 3rd and 4th centuries, the construction of the great public baths, or thermae, occurred in Rome where numerous houses or insulae, temples, and shrines existed, which, according to Lanciani (1899: 22), 'were destroyed to the foundations'.

Such purposive demolition activity becomes commonplace with the emergence of the modern city, in which the intricate, often medieval, street patterns constrained urban development. Mumford (1961: 472) notes that for capitalism 'to have a free field for its typical interests' required a different spatial order, and for this purpose, 'urban demolition and replacement became one of the chief marks of the new economy'. Demolition was deployed to create new modes of mobility, and the spatial reorganisation of 19th-century London was influenced by the construction of transport infrastructure. The construction of London's docks and railways led to the demolition of vast swathes of slum housing, with Dyos (1967: 37) describing how railway tracks 'burrowed their way into the centre and swept aside whole neighbourhoods of densely packed houses' (see Figure 6.3). By 1900, railway construction in London had absorbed 800 acres of land occupied, primarily, by working-class housing, and upwards of 120,000 people were displaced by demolition (Kellett, 1969).

This was a common process in which demolition was used as an instrument of strategic planning policy in the reconstruction of the 19th-century city. One of the paramount objectives at the time was the creation of public, open spaces and the decongestion, by demolition, of overcrowded areas. The creation of Central Park in New York City in 1873 reflected such aspirations, and its city governors sought to create a pastoral public space redolent of formal parks found in France and Italy (Rosenzweig and Blackmar, 1992). While the plans for Central Park hinted at a democratic space and a place for an inclusive public presence, the park was a project of beautification and, as Rosenzweig and Blackmar (1992: 7) suggest, 'rooted in the interests of New York's wealthiest citizens'. These interests were the enhancement of real estate values and part of a class politics that also shaped the acquisition of the site for the park, in which demolition was deployed as an instrument to eradicate a local settlement populated by an African-American and Irish population.

The settlement was called Seneca, and by the mid-1850s, it was a community of 50 houses, three churches and a school. A 'demolition rhetoric' emerged to demonise the local population, and they were the subject of scurrilous comments from a host of officials, news reporters and local citizens (Rosenzweig and Blackmar, 1992). The park's first engineer, Egbert Viele, belittled the neighbourhood by describing it as a 'refuge of about five thousand squatters, dwelling in rude huts of their own construction' (quoted in Rosenzweig and Blackmar, 1992: 64). Racist slurs and language were common, with a local news reporter describing residents as 'principally Irish families living in rickety ... little one storie shanties' (quoted in Rosenzweig and Blackmar, 1992: 64). This demonising discourse was part of a politics to create a fait accompli, or the removal of both the people and their homes from the site, a task that was accomplished by 1857.

By the end of the 19th century, demolition had become widespread and an integral part of the governance of cities. This was the beginnings of a policy trajectory that took hold by the early 20th century, and later became the orthodoxy of urban renewal worldwide (see Carmon, 1999). This included the removal of poor-quality, usually working-class, housing as part of a process to address health, welfare and social problems, and, more significantly, to create the vacant spaces for new building and the stimulation of land and property markets. In London, the demolition process was piecemeal yet extensive, and between 1902 and 1913, Wohl (1977: 302) notes that 70,000 working-class dwellings were destroyed. These were not replaced and most of the demolished space was appropriated for commercial uses, which, as Wohl (1977: 303) suggests, led to 'the remaining population to be crowded to a greater degree than before'.

By the early 20th century, a demolition paradigm was emerging that has since become an integral part of the (de)construction of the built environment. This paradigm dominates most building cultures and serves to propagate the attitude that knocking down buildings and infrastructure is a panacea for many of the social and economic problems found in cities. It regards demolition as a natural and normal process of building, in which there can be little or no construction without the dismantling and destruction of the pre-existing built environment. Thomsen et al (2011: 329) suggest that demolition can be regarded 'as a normal process to regenerate building stocks over longer periods'. This understanding does not interrogate what 'normal' is or might entail, nor does it proffer the possibilities of alternatives, or ways of interacting with, and acting on, the built environment that do not involve its destruction. The normality of demolition is only because building culture deems it so.

The elision between demolition and normality serves to depoliticise the destruction of the built environment, or at least render it a neutral action. This is a core facet of the demolition paradigm, in which demolition is presented as a technical, value-free activity, a tool or instrument in the service of progressing change. Part of this ideology is the co-option of Schumpeter's (1943) notion of 'creative destruction': that the birth of something new is dependent on the destruction of what previously existed. Here, demolition can be conceived as a creative act that, in its destruction of the built environment, brings forth a renewed socio-spatial order that is better than what preceded it. This is a powerful, self-serving conception of demolition that conceives of it as a positive action, part of a linear, sequential process in the service of modernisation and the betterment of the built environment. This conception leaves little room for critique of, or reflection on, the potential downsides to demolition.

Planning policy and urban renewal after the Second World War were closely intertwined with the demolition paradigm, and by the early 1950s, a 'demolition-first' approach had taken centre-stage, with the wrecking ball a symbol of a modernist makeover and facelift for ailing cities. The logic of demolition was an econometric rationality in which the objective was, first, to eliminate blight and places of poverty and poor housing, and, second, to reactivate local land markets by the transfer of real estate to private property companies. The understanding was that as long as places were blighted and characterised by dilapidated and vacant buildings, the values of properties would fall and a spiral of degeneration of places would take hold. For proponents of the demolition paradigm, the solution was the deployment of demolition as an efficient, cost-effective approach able to remove the sources of blight quickly and provide the impetus for renewal.

This logic was to the fore throughout the middle to the end of the 20th century, and few cities escaped comprehensive demolition projects. In the 1950s and 1960s, much of America's urban renewal was a demolition-led process of knocking down poor-quality housing in, primarily, African-American and Hispanic neighbourhoods (Hackworth, 2016). Highsmith (2009) recounts the demolition of housing in the St John's neighbourhood of the city of Flint in Michigan, a poor black area that lacked basic amenities and services. Between 1960 and 1977, most housing in St John's was demolished and the black population was removed to make way for new commercial uses and housing that was subsequently occupied by white, higher-income residents. Highsmith (2009: 349) describes St John's demolition as state-sponsored racial politics characterised by 'a combination of public policies and private racism' that, through demolition, created new market opportunities for house builders and real estate organisations.

These patterns were commonplace across the US, and the scale of demolition was staggering. It is estimated that nearly a million housing units were demolished from the mid-1940s to the late 1960s (National Commission for Urban Problems, 1969). Encouraged by the availability of billions of dollars of federal funds, city governors in the US embarked on a 'demolition spree', typified by the approach in New Haven in Connecticut. Throughout the 1960s, New Haven received more federal funding for urban renewal than anywhere in the US, and its mayor, Richard Lee, sanctioned major demolition programmes that often created 'dead space' or vacant sites, which even to this day, remain as parking lots (see Rae, 2003). Over 3,000 buildings were torn down between 1957 and 1980, and over 20 per cent of the city's population were relocated (Ammon, 2016: 164). For Ammon (2016), the demolitions broke up dense social networks, and once people left the neighbourhoods, local businesses lost custom, with the process exacerbating economic decline.

Other studies corroborate Ammon's (2016) observations and challenge the core assumption of the demolition paradigm: that the demolition of buildings in areas of socio-economic decline is likely to enhance recovery and reverse spirals of decline. Talen's (2014) study of the demolition of housing units in the US between 1940 and 2000 shows that socio-economic conditions did not improve in areas of high demolition, and that much of what was demolished was not substandard. Talen (2014: 248) also undertook a comprehensive visual inspection of aerial photographs of pre- and post-demolished sites, and the data confirm a view that 'mid 20th century demolition replaced the finer grained texture of the 19th century city with larger-scale projects, complexes, and infrastructure'. For Talen (2014: 248), what was being lost was a community vitality and a smaller-scale urbanism of 'localized networks of social and economic interaction'.

This was the irony: demolition as a tool of economic revitalisation often did not achieve this objective, yet by the beginning of the 21st century, the demolition paradigm, as a planning rationality, was in the ascendency.

It has become an orthodox planning tool across America's shrinking cities, where population losses have led to thousands of properties lying empty. In Detroit alone, 10,000 houses were demolished between 2014 and 2016, prompting the mayor at the time, Mike Duggan, to claim that 'every time one of these houses goes down, we raise the quality of life for everyone else in the neighbourhood' (quoted in Hackworth, 2016: 1). For Hackworth (2016: 1), Duggan's claim is core to the ideology of the demolition paradigm yet comes with little or no evidence to support it. Nonetheless, it holds a power over city politicians, and it is the basis for continuing large-scale demolitions, as witnessed by the city of Buffalo adopting an 'accelerated demolition' plan in 2007 to demolish upwards of 10,000 vacant properties (see Yin and Silverman, 2015).

While the scale of demolitions in the US has lessened compared to the mid- to latter part of the 20th century, on a global basis, demolition activity has proliferated since the early 21st century, and in some countries, like Russia and China, it has been occurring at unprecedented levels (Shepard, 2015a).[1] In Russia, the largest demolition project ever undertaken, globally, is under way in Moscow to demolish 8,000 apartments built during the 1950s, which will affect 1.6 million people (Steiner, 2017). Despite opposition from local residents, Steiner (2017) notes that 'demolitions have been occurring throughout the city in waves', and since 2000, over 12 million m² of housing has been demolished. The announcement in February 2017 of a scaling up of this demolition programme has led some commentators, such as former MP Dmitry Gudkov, to claim that the demolitions are 'in the interests of the construction lobby' (quoted in Luhn, 2017: 1). For Luhn (2017), some vacant sites where demolished blocks once stood are being appropriated by building companies and being built on as part of a broader process of gentrification in Moscow.

Similar processes are evident in China, and on a more extensive scale than in Russia. The modernisation of Chinese cities is predicated on demolition, and Shepard (2015b) notes that 40 per cent of China's developable land is created by demolishing older buildings. Laoximen in Shanghai is an example of an old, established, lane neighbourhood with vernacular, low-rise buildings, yet 300,000 m² was demolished in 2019, and less than 20 per cent of its original inhabitants remain (Walsh, M., 2019). It is illustrative of a teardown culture that appears largely impervious to history and heritage, and, instead, is propagating a rapid erasure and turnover of buildings. It is estimated that over 50 per cent of China's housing stock will be demolished and rebuilt by 2030 (Shepard, 2015b). This is despite much of the stock being built less than 20 years ago. Its destruction reflects the poor quality of construction and a disposable culture described by Li Dexiang as encouraging the 'blind demolition of relatively new buildings' (quoted in Yanfeng, 2010: 1).

Figure 6.4: Cabrini Green, Chicago, 1999

Note: The tower blocks of Cabrini Green have since been demolished and replaced by low-rise housing, selling, primarily, for market rents and prices.

Source: https://upload.wikimedia.org/wikipedia/commons/thumb/8/8b/Cabrini_Green_Housing_Project.jpg/1280px-Cabrini_Green_Housing_Project.jpg

This disposability is part of the rationality of the demolition paradigm to escalate land values, and in the 21st century, this logic is central to urban economic development, with gentrification to the fore. An example is the destruction of Cabrini Green in Chicago, a public housing scheme that was constructed over a 20-year period between 1942 and 1962 (see Figure 6.4). It comprised 3,600 units in a series of high-rise blocks and low-rise, row housing. By the 1980s, the estate was characterised by gang violence, drugs and other social problems; yet, as Vale (2012: 1) recounts, for residents, Cabrini Green 'was a community with problems, but not a "problem community" or a "slum"'. Despite this, Chicago Housing Authority (CHA) began demolishing Cabrini-Green in 2000, with the last tower block demolished in 2011. Many residents were relocated some distance from the area, and others moved to mixed-income communities in the Near North Side, a few blocks from Cabrini Green.

The demolition of Cabrini Green was never negotiated with residents, but imposed, and, as Austen (2018) implies, CHA opted for demolition rather than seeking to preserve, and enhance, the local community. For Austen (2018), erasure enacted by demolition in Cabrini Green could have been avoided by funding estate regeneration to maintain the buildings and provide local services and amenities. Instead, the imperative of the demolition paradigm to eradicate a 'problem place' by demolition held sway, and the vacated sites of Cabrini Green are now part of a broader upscaling process in Chicago on some of the city's most valuable real estate. Mortice (2016: 1) estimates that areas adjacent to Cabrini Green are worth US$9.8 million per acre, and private sector-led real estate development is seeking to take advantage of the rise in land values since the demolitions occurred. An example is a recent 88-unit townhouse development with the price of apartments upwards of US$500,000, well beyond what people on low incomes can afford (see Koziarz, 2018).

Such post-demolition developments are inexorable, with few political challenges to, or trenchant critiques of, the rationality of the demolition paradigm and the continuous nature of demolition in the building and construction of places. The evidence suggests that demolition remains central to state strategies of urban renewal, and an integral part of the demolition paradigm is state actors providing funding and legal authorisation for the destruction of buildings and infrastructure. In many countries, there is a presumption in favour of demolition, as against renovation and building upkeep. In the UK, there is no value added tax to pay on new construction materials, whereas for renovation and maintenance, anything between 5 per cent and 20 per cent is levied. In March 2020, the Prime Minister, Boris Johnson (2020), in his 'Build, build, build' speech, also gave a green light to demolition by announcing the extension of permitted development rights to allow empty buildings to be demolished and replaced by housing without the need for planning permission.

This approach to building seems counterintuitive in a context whereby the social and environmental costs of demolition and new construction are often high, and the Royal Institution of Chartered Surveyors (RICS, 2020) and the Royal Institute of British Architects (RIBA) (Lowe and Gardiner, 2020) have criticised the UK government's approach as an anti-green agenda that encourages carbon emissions (see Chapter 9). This chimes with others who conceive of demolition, when deployed as a tool of urban renewal, as the antithesis to progress (Sinclair, 2011). Sinclair (2011: 9) notes that the demolition of part of East London to provide for the Olympic Games in 2012 was a 'long march towards a theme park without a theme', with social costs borne by local businesses that were forced out and gentrification set in motion. While demolition was not *the* causal mechanism, it was implicated in, and constitutive of, a regressive urbanism, highlighting the partiality of the demolition paradigm in deploying the wrecking ball as a singular instrument in influencing the (re)production of space.

Teardown and the consequences of demolition

While much attention on demolition focuses on the spectacular event, such as the explosive destruction of buildings, a significant proportion of demolition occurs by 'teardown', or a process of wilful dismantling of a structure that is 'functional, well-maintained, and valued by the community' (CMAP, 2008: 3). The teardown process typically involves a one-to-one replacement of a dwelling in good structural condition that, once demolished, is usually replaced by a larger version, or the 'mansionisation' phenomenon (Nasar et al, 2007). Teardown is the epitome of the demolition paradigm in seeking to find new ways of extracting value from real estate, in which demolition is used as a tool to create investment flows and opportunities. Hickey (quoted in Corley, 2006: 1) notes that teardown reflects the appreciation of land values and the depreciation in the value of a house, creating a 'value-in soil-scenario' in which there is economic sense in demolishing domestic structures and rebuilding them.

In this part of the chapter, I focus on the teardown phenomenon as an illustration of the demolition paradigm encouraging an irrational action, that is, the destruction of perfectly habitable buildings and the stimulation of construction activity that is not needed. Teardown is most evident in older, well-established suburban neighbourhoods that are affluent and seen as highly desirable as places to live. Developers target houses that are dated, lack modern features and amenities, and are unable to realise their full market potential. This potential can be realised by tearing them down and replacing them with a larger, modern, state-of-the-art property. The activity is not without controversy, and it is implicated in wasteful and harmful outcomes, ranging from the loss of local ecologies, to the production of high levels of carbon emissions and rubble waste dumped in landfill sites. By demolishing functional and, sometimes, historically valuable buildings, teardown may undermine the aesthetic qualities of a place, and it has implications for housing affordability by substituting lower- for higher-value properties.

In developing these, and related, observations, I refer to examples of teardown in a range of different countries, including Canada, Australia and the US, where the teardown trend is endemic. I also outline and discuss research data that I generated from a small-scale study of teardown building in the suburban town of Esher in South-west London.[2] Here, there has been a continuous stream of demolition and rebuilding since the late 1990s, in which builders, not only in Esher, but throughout the UK, have been encouraged by successive governments to build infill housing, including teardown construction, on brownfield sites as part of a process to create compact, dense settlements (Bibby et al, 2018). The process has become particularly pronounced in the south-east of England and around the affluent suburbs of London, with evidence suggesting that, in some neighbourhoods, it has changed the social and aesthetic character of places (Bibby et al, 2018).

The teardown trend was barely noticeable in countries like the UK and US until the mid-1980s, but by the early 2000s, it had become an observable, and established, part of building and construction activity (CMAP, 2008). Scott-Fine and Lindberg (2002: 1) note that teardown had reached epidemic proportions in historic areas in the US by 2000, and in some instances, it was compromising the architectural integrity of neighbourhoods. They describe how in two neighbourhoods in Dallas, more than 1,000 character dwellings built in the early 20th century were demolished by builders in 2001 and replaced by the construction of large, luxury homes up to 10,000 square feet in size. In Denver, a similar process was under way at the same time, with 200 dwellings constructed in the 1920s torn down and replaced 'with stucco-clad houses three times their size' (Scott-Fine and Lindberg, 2002: 1).

Teardown has continued apace in the US, and Charles' (2014) research in Chicago, investigating the period between 2000 and 2010, describes one neighbourhood in which 12.8 per cent of single family homes, or 65 units, were demolished and replaced by new dwellings. A measure of teardown is the number of demolition permits to demolish single-family homes or duplexes, and Gelardi (2019) notes that in Denver, over 400 permits were issued in 2018. Likewise, in Dallas, 6,530 demolition permits were granted by the City Building Department between 2012 and 2018 (Goodman, 2019). Similar experiences were occurring in Seattle, and Rosenberg (2016: 1) outlines that in 2016, one house every day was torn down to make way for newly constructed property, or what he describes as small houses being 'replaced by large, boxlike houses that on average cost about three times as much'.

Teardown activity is also prominent and well documented in Canada and Australia. St Denis (2018: 1) notes that in Vancouver, 'more than 20,000 single-family homes in the city were demolished' between 1985 and 2014, and continuous increases in land values are leading to an intensification of the process. O'Brien (2018: 1) describes rapidly rising land values in North Vancouver, where sites with old townhouses are 'selling for up to $10 million an acre' and 'the majority of residential land deals lead to demolition of existing homes'. Vancouver is also beset by a 'teardown cycle' in which newly constructed homes that have replaced demolished structures are themselves torn down shortly after construction to make way for a new wave of rebuilding in the wake of land price inflation in the city that, for some analysts, is reaching unprecedented levels (see McElroy, 2016).

Sydney in Australia has been undergoing a similar series of processes, albeit at a scale well below what is occurring in the US and Canada. Recent data are hard to source, but studies prior to 2015 are indicative of trends. For instance, Pinnegar et al (2010) note that teardown rebuild activity constituted approximately 30 per cent of total new housing starts in the six years up to 2008 in New South Wales, with the majority occurring in Sydney. Research by Legacy et al (2013) identified 6,800 applications for the demolition of houses in Sydney in the study period of 2004 to 2008, representing 1.4 per cent of the total stock of detached houses. Unlike experiences in the US and Canada, where teardown typically involves a homeowner selling to a developer and moving out, in Sydney, Legacy et al (2013: 121), in surveying 1,200 homeowners involved in teardown, found that many were using demolition and rebuilding as an 'in situ reinvestment', or a means 'to improve the physical condition of their homes'.

In the UK, there are few, detailed studies of the teardown trend per se, though there are a number of important studies about compact cities, urban densification and infill (see, for example, Whitehand and Larkham, 1991; Bibby et al, 2018). To complement these studies, and as pointed out in Chapter 5, I have been conducting my own, small-scale, walkabout study in an area of teardown since 2003. This is in the affluent neighbourhood of Esher, and my first inklings of the process occurred in early March 2003, when a planning application notice was pinned to a tree near to my house, notifying the public of the intent to demolish a single, detached, Victorian-era dwelling and replace it with four town houses. In distinction to the teardown trend in the US, this planning application was responding to government directives to intensify the use of space by rebuilding to higher density on brownfield sites (DETR, 1997).

Residents in the neighbourhood were upset by the proposal, as it involved not only the demolition of a beautiful Victorian house, but also the orchard that surrounded it. Here was a history dating back to the mid-1850s about to be eradicated with the loss of a period building and its open space. The replacement was a formless, modern block, far removed in style and aesthetic terms from the Victorian streetscape and the design character of the street. It was, in the words of a neighbour, "a complete travesty of design that has no place in the neighbourhood". Residents formally objected to the planning application and it was turned down by the local planning authority, only to be approved on appeal by the central government minister responsible for planning matters. A year later, the Victorian dwelling had been demolished and the new buildings were erected (see Figure 6.5).

Figure 6.5: The construction of town houses, Esher

Source: Rob Imrie

The demolition and rebuilding process was insensitive to the wishes of local residents, and it was indifferent and contrary to the design qualities of the street. The process was a quantitative exercise of seeking to maximise numbers of housing units on a site, shaped by central government guidelines to encourage newbuild dwellings. It did not account for, or value, the existential qualities of the local environment, and, as I wrote in my research diary at the time, 'my walk past the old house is spoilt by the loss of the view over the wall into the orchard, and instead what we have is a nondescript building that has taken away valuable open space, of gardens, plants and places for nature to be nurtured'. Such feelings were shared by neighbours, with one local resident lamenting the construction of an "out-of-scale" and "out-of-character" structure that did not fit well in the neighbourhood. As she said: "The mass of the building dwarfs the street, and it looks like it belongs in a different place; it has no place here."

The loss of the Victorian building and its orchard is a single, small-scale example of the erasure of a historic structure and a rupture with the past, or the period of time that the building reflects. This is one of the common criticisms of the teardown trend: that it undermines the heritage and historic values of a neighbourhood. Newman and Saginor (2014) suggest that by the late 2000s, teardown was endemic in at least 500 places across the US, and note that a common objection by residents in areas affected was the failure of new dwellings to blend in, or complement, the aesthetic character of the neighbourhood. One neighbourhood in Toronto, Forest Hill, was established in 1923, but by 2008, 30 per cent of its historic dwellings, designed by once-prominent architects, had been torn down and replaced (Alberga, 2017). Nasmith, a local architect, commented that demolition activity was targeting '10 of 22 homes in the area by Eden Smith, one of Toronto's most sought-after designers during the late 19th and early 20th centuries. It's a complete disaster' (quoted in Lorinc, 2006: 1).

Loss of historic value in neighbourhoods is paralleled by the environmental effects of teardown, with the production of different types of waste. Foremost is the waste of serviceable, habitable structures that provide the basis of good-quality accommodation. Figure 6.6 is an example of a dwelling in Esher that was demolished in the late 2000s that, while of limited architectural value, was nonetheless well built and did not need to be knocked down because of structural defects or physical faults. Its presence was an impediment to realising high-value returns to the builder, who, in this context, was intent on demolishing and replacing it with the construction of a 'vanity' building, or a structure responding to the latest fads and fashions of property ownership. As recorded in my research diary: 'You can see the yellow-coloured planning notice on the tree, outlining an application for its demolition, but the

Figure 6.6: A house awaiting demolition and rebuild, Esher

Source: Rob Imrie

house is solid, well made and a good family size, and it might need some modernisation or update, but this is nothing that can't be achieved by minor works of renovation.'

The Esher experience has, however, eschewed renovation in favour of demolition, and since the end of the 2000s, the general trend in the richer neighbourhoods has been the adoption of the 'McMansion approach', with builders targeting older, less valuable properties for demolition and replacing them with much larger dwellings (Nasar et al, 2007). Figure 6.7 is a montage of McMansion-style dwellings constructed in Esher in the early to mid-2010s after replacing smaller-sized properties. The new buildings are bulky and two to three times the size of their predecessors, with large driveways and often ancillary, secondary dwellings attached to them. This aesthetic is redolent of conspicuous consumption, and it reflects a 'crude display of ill-mastered luxury' (Bourdieu, 1984: 31). The buildings are characterised by a defensive, securitised and privatised design, featuring high walls and gates, where previously, pre-demolition, they had open gardens and were outward-facing and an integral part of the public realm.

The aesthetics of one of the teardown streets in Esher, Esher Park Avenue, reflects a homogenising tendency, with the construction of a similarity of house types, design styles and frontages. The public areas are characterised by formulaic planting and manicured lawns, and, as I recorded in my research diary, 'There's no individuality or character here, and the place feels sanitised and bereft of any spark of life, as though everything has been designed by reference to a tightly prescribed rule book.' The absence of aesthetic variation, coupled with what appears to be identikit features, such as high walls and entry gates, begs the question, raised by Coward (2009), about identifying, and engaging with, the forces that seek to homogenise and control the urban environment. For critics of teardown, this observation resonates because, as Murphy (2015: 1) points out, the process is a withering of cultural capital in which the demolition of the diversity of historic, and unique, house types leads to a loss of vitality and 'crucial traces of the past'.

This is akin to a process that Coward (2009) refers to as 'urbicide', or violence against the city. For Coward (2009), urbicide is the dissolution of heterogeneity through the purposive actions of destroying buildings, in which shared spaces, and the connective infrastructure that bind people together, are threatened, even dismantled. While he relates the term to precipitous events, such as the destruction of cities by warfare, it has resonance in understanding the dynamics shaping teardown neighbourhoods in locales like Esher. Here, like other places undergoing teardown, there is a de-differentiating effect in which teardown is simultaneously about the creation of social exclusivity, of seeking to cultivate a prestigious environment as part of a process of monetary and cultural value enhancement. This includes the

Figure 6.7: McMansion-style dwellings in Esher

Source: Rob Imrie

re-aestheticisation of teardown locales as part of their reinvention as exclusive private spaces, with streets increasingly gated and displaying signs that seek to discourage a public presence.

This is redolent of an anti-social urbanism that is reinforced by a range of deleterious environment effects related to teardown and demolition more generally. One of the more authoritative reports, by Dahmen et al (2018: 95), of teardowns in Vancouver estimates that new single-family home construction 'will result in 1.3 to 2.8 million tonnes of additional carbon dioxide equivalent emissions between 2017 and 2050'. They note that it will take 168 years for a demolished and rebuilt dwelling to pay back what has been expended in carbon emissions during the process of its teardown and rebuild. Teardown is an irrational action and antithetical to a green, ecological agenda insofar that 'the environmental benefits of tearing down and replacing even very poorly performing buildings are dubious at best in Vancouver' (Dahmen et al, 2018: 100).

Teardown, as a specific manifestation of demolition, highlights some of the broader issues about the efficacy of destroying buildings and related infrastructure. Much of the process is gratuitous and unnecessary, and it is no more than the invention of another asset class, or means for builders and real estate actors to generate additional revenue streams. Teardown responds to upward movements in land values, and those propagating the process have no concern for whether or not a new dwelling is needed. To tear down, and reconstruct, is motivated by price signals, and it is impervious to the social and cultural contexts of places, and to the histories that have made them. Teardown, like demolition more generally, is a form of erasure, of people and places, and is redolent of a culture of practice seemingly indifferent towards, and disrespectful of, ecology and environment. How, then, might it be possible to change the rationale and rationality of demolition, and its role within the construction of the built environment?

Rehabilitation and constructing for disassembly and reuse

I have argued that a demolition paradigm dominates building cultures and practices, and that it propagates the destruction of the built environment as a prerequisite to its reconstruction and recomposition. Here, demolition and construction are indelibly intertwined and are conceived as two sides of the same coin, with one inoperable without the other. There is a disarming, and persuasive, logic to this rationality, but it is one that is flawed and fails to identify, or critique, the role of demolition in the despoliation of the environment, waste of materials and perpetuation of a 'building without limits' mentality. How can demolition be put to use in ways that mitigate its impacts, and how might one craft and construct our built environments in ways where there is less need to dismantle and destroy the materials that comprise it? Such questions point towards the role of renovation and refurbishment in the building process, including the development of techniques of disassembly and reassembly.

These ideas are important in a context where there is an increasing emphasis by governments on sustainable construction practices, including reducing the impact of building activity on carbon emissions. Designing for disassembly is one idea that is gaining some traction; the objective is to enable the ease of taking buildings apart so that their individual materials can be reassembled and reused. This has the potential to create value in the end of life of a structure by maximising the salvage and usage of materials that would otherwise be discarded. However, practitioners in the design and building industries rarely consider the lifecycle of the built environment, and most builders do not build for ease of disassembly and reassembly. Buildings and infrastructure are, literally, set in concrete as in situ and immovable objects, and their structures and layouts are rarely adaptable, moveable or amenable to a structural reconfiguration without demolition and rebuilding activity.

This contrasts with building and construction practices in different historical periods and cultural contexts, and there are insights to be gleaned about how to craft flexible, moveable and reusable building parts and materials (see also Chapter 10). In some cultures, by the nature of their lifestyles and economies, a static or permanent architecture is anathema, and, instead, building materials are part of a vernacular tradition, locally sourced, crafted and constructed, in which little energy is expended in the construction of a structure or its disassembly. Nomadic building cultures are an exemplar of where the lifestyle depends on the ease of assembly and disassembly of building materials and their reuse (Carlisle, 2006) (see Figure 6.8). Such cultures eschew a concept of place in which, in Demissie's (1997: 398) terms, 'time, boundaries, routes, directions are fixed', and, instead, operate in a fluid way, whereby space is occupied, and worked on, in a 'provisional manner'.

The idea of life as provisional and contingent is to the fore in shaping the culture of building in places such as Japan, where the influence of Buddhism is important in emphasising the impermanence of matter and materials, as well as non-attachment. Sinclair (2017: 838) notes that, in distinction to Western cultures, in Japan, building structures are regarded as ephemeral and reflect a belief system in 'the inevitability of change' or a 'lightness of existence'. While these ideas stimulate a high volume of demolition and rebuilding in Japan, they also have a counter-effect or influence in shaping the design and functionality of traditional Japanese housing. Such houses, in using *tatami* mats and *shoji* screens, enable flexibility, or what Sinclair

Figure 6.8: Yurt, Turkestan, late 19th century

Note: This photograph is from the 'Turkestan album', a visual survey of Central Asia
undertaken after Imperial Russia took control of the area in the 1860s.

Source: www.loc.gov/rr/print/coll/287_turkestan.html

https://upload.wikimedia.org/wikipedia/commons/4/47/Syr_Darya_Oblast._Kyrgyz_Yurt_
WDL10968.png

(2017: 833) describes as 'infinite degrees of mutability, plasticity, and change'
(see Figure 6.9). Walls can be moved, and the functionality of a place can
be easily changed, with 'fluctuations in needs, intention and experience'
accommodated without the need for demolition and rebuilding (Sinclair,
2017: 833).

Such illustrations provide insights into what is possible, but the question
is how far the embedded practices of builders in non-nomadic, Western
cultures are amenable to change. It is anathema to the Western culture
of architecture and design to think about a building's finitude, and the
architectural profession, in particular, is wedded to the notion of a building
that, once built, is a complete, and completed, object. At its extreme are the
views of certain architects, such as Le Corbusier and FLW, who conceived
of their buildings as a finality, and their designs as non-negotiable, or a fait
accompli that should in no way be tampered with or changed by a building's
users or any other party. Here, the building is conceived as inviolate and

Figure 6.9: Kusakabe House, built in 1879, Takayama, Gifu Prefecture, Japan

Source: https://en.wikipedia.org/wiki/Housing_in_Japan#/media/File:Maison_Kusakabe.jpg

immovable, or part of the fabric of its environment, and built to last as a timeless object. To renovate or change the style or design of the building is tantamount to the transgression of the artistic conception embedded in the object.

The reality is that no building is able to last, or escape societal demands to cater for changes in the ways people interact with(in) their environments. However, the power of the ideology of 'building as fixity' has not encouraged the development of a renovation and rehabilitative culture, or the ease of means to rescue and reuse the materiality of a building. Rather, the demolition paradigm continues to shape building practice in the world's major countries, with demolition remaining one of the world's growing industries (*Ibis World*, 2020). For instance, in the US, the market size of the demolition sector has grown 2.9 per cent per year between 2015 and 2020, and in 2020, its value was US$7.7 billion (*Ibis World*, 2020). In the UK, the average industry growth rates for demolition in the period 2014–19 were spectacular, at 17.4 per cent (*Ibis World*, 2019). How, then, can a rehabilitative, non-demolition approach to building begin to make greater inroads into the culture of construction, and be part of a transformative agenda for the crafting of the built environment?

This is a difficult question to answer, as there are many cross-cutting variables that influence the decisions about which approaches to adopt in any particular building context. For some commentators, it is less about a broader culture shift, though this is important, and more about the creation of a viable economy in which rehabilitative approaches to building make economic sense for builders. In relation to housing, Power (2010) notes that demolition is costly, not only in terms of the direct costs of demolishing a building, but also in terms of the total costs embedded into the process. These include the costs of acquiring a site, preparing a building for demolition and 'delays in reusing the land, the loss of housing capacity and the infrastructure cost of new housing' (Power, 2010: 212). Other, societal costs also have to be borne, ranging from the loss of non-renewable materials embedded into buildings, to impacts on landfill sites, and for Power (2010: 212), rehabilitation and refurbishment is 'cheaper and less damaging to the local and wider environment than demolition or new build'.

A rehabilitative approach is, potentially, respectful of a building and its setting, and it is premised on the preservation and protection of resources, and their reintegration into a building cycle. The process is much less energy-intensive than demolition, less disruptive to neighbours and stops needless construction. For a rehabilitative culture to take root will require builders to adopt different construction techniques, and materials, to enable the construction of buildings amenable to disassembly, such as the Triodos Bank office located near Utrecht in the Netherlands. The building is constructed primarily from wood, using 165,312 screws, which enables the ease of demounting and reassembling it, and to change its spatial layout and configuration (see Figure 6.10). The architects who designed the building describe it as 'circular' to indicate that the building is remountable without losing the value of the materials, so that they never have to be considered as waste and can be reused (see RAU Architects, 2020).

While these are laudable aims, a problem with the logic of circularity is that it is still premised on the production and consumption of objects. In the context of building, it does not preclude demolition, if in a less disruptive style, as the prerequisite for yet more construction, albeit with rescued materials. There is no break with the continuous nature of construction, and no challenge to the rationalities that underpin and support it. It offers a better way of building and, in the Triodos case, a method of disassembling a building without recourse to mechanical demolition that usually destroys its individual elements. However, in and of itself, it does not steer a direction away from a 'building-first' mentality, and for this, a rehabilitative culture requires a commitment to the preservation, adaptation and reuse of what *exists*, to build only on what is already built. By using technologies of demountability and disassembly, a rehabilitative building culture can be

Figure 6.10: Triodos Bank, Utrecht, the Netherlands

Source: Erik Mulder

the basis for the diminution of demolition and ending construction as we know it.

Conclusion

The decay and demolition of buildings are significant features of the (re)construction of places. They are an ever-present part of our environment and broadly accepted as a natural and necessary process in the development and evolution of the built environment. While it would be wrong to characterise all demolition as unnecessary, most occurs with little acknowledgement of, or sensitivity to, its disruptive impacts on people, ecology and the environment. Demolition is, primarily, a destructive process, which may involve the loss and/or degradation of local ecologies and habitats, particularly by the absence or poorly developed nature of appropriate means of waste disposal. As deployed as a tool of mass clearances, such as in US cities, demolition is implicated in social cleansing and engineering. It is the antithesis of what a caring approach to construction ought to be. There is a failure to engage in, or develop, the appropriate means to manage and maintain buildings and places, and the communities that reside within them.

The problem is the centrality of the demolition paradigm in shaping the rationality of building and construction. This paradigm propagates a crude, linear conception of the building process, in which demolition is a necessary, first stage in the project of modernisation, and construction is conceived as part of the ongoing, and continuous, process of human self-betterment and progress. Demolition, literally, clears the ground for the renewal of society and holds up the promise of the possibilities for new beginnings. This is a persuasive, and disarming, ideology that does not engage with the deleterious effects of demolition, but, rather, serves to emphasise its role in facilitating new market opportunities for the building industry. The paradigm is self-serving, and its deployment is intertwined with highly political, and controversial, building projects, ranging from the teardown of historic structures, to the clearance of land for the purposes of upscale, gentrified, urban renewal.

There is a need to rethink the centrality of demolition in the building process, and for a different approach to building. This has to be led by asking who will benefit from a building project because renovation and the reuse of materials, or any combination of techniques that serves to preserve a building, does not, in and of itself, guarantee a socially responsible, and responsive, architecture. Many refurbishments of high-rise blocks in places like London and Paris, while ostensibly improving the building and the place, do little more than upscale a neighbourhood and set in motion gentrification. The building technique itself cannot guarantee any particular social outcome, and, as Herstad (2017: 111) notes, the uncritical adoption of a reuse and renovation model may do no more than reproduce 'the same goals and ideologies behind the drive for demolition and landscape clearance'. This, then, represents a major challenge, not only to transform the techniques of construction, but also to realign them with political objectives relating to the social purposes of building.

Why Building More Housing Will Not Work

Introduction

On a recent train journey through the English West Country, my views of the beautiful countryside were interrupted by the sight of newly constructed housing estates at the edge of villages and towns. What were once green fields and open countryside were being converted into building sites and rows of uniform housing as part of the intensification of suburban and ex-urban development that has its roots in the early 20th century. This latest round of building is part of a new offensive encouraged by successive British governments in the belief that the best way to provide housing for all is to increase the rates of private house building and construction. The views of many politicians and social commentators are that Britain's housing crisis is the product of a deficit in the supply of properties, and that this is resulting in house price inflation that is pricing out many people from gaining access to decent, affordable dwellings. The remedy is to build more, primarily private market housing so that supply will overtake demand and, so it is alleged, depress the price of dwellings and make them more affordable.

In the chapter, I take issue with this market logic and the 'building more' argument, and critique its simplistic model of housing that does not convey how markets are manipulated and controlled in ways whereby prices are not simply responses to movements in supply and demand. I note that encouraging the speculative construction of dwellings is not a panacea for the housing crisis. Rather, speculative house building does no more than (re)produce housing that will sell at prices well beyond what many people can afford, and that is often located in places where it is not needed. People's housing needs run deeper than can be solved solely by building more, and it is wrong to think that private house builders, looking to extract as much profit as possible from house sales, ought to be in the vanguard of seeking to solve the diverse problems people face in gaining access to good-quality, affordable dwellings.

In developing these views, I divide the chapter into three parts. First, I set out the key arguments of house-building advocates for why constructing more housing is a solution to the problems people face in gaining access to good-quality, affordable dwellings. The crux of the argument is that there is a deficient supply of appropriate housing relative to demand, including spatial mismatches, with the oversupply of housing in some areas and an undersupply in others. For building advocates, the deficit in housing supply is caused by a range of factors, including, among others: builders being unable to respond to market demands, often because they lack the capacities to do so; restrictions on the supply of land for building; and the lassitude of the planning and regulatory environment that, as the authors of a government briefing paper have judged, 'is widely seen as slow, costly and complex' (Barton and Wilson, 2020: 1). I develop these points by highlighting what building advocates conceive as solutions to overcoming impediments to increasing the rates of house building.

Second, I evaluate the pro-house-building arguments, and suggest that they are misleading and fail to identity, or address, the manifold complexities relating to housing consumption. One of the observations of building advocates, as outlined by Myers (2019: 1), is that 'every home that gets built, especially if it is near good job opportunities, helps to reduce the shortage, compared to not building it'. In the world of neoclassical economics, this may be so – in the sense that any additional dwelling is one more added to the total stock – but this reveals little about how such stock is made available, if it is affordable or how far it might alleviate, or address, the manifold nature of housing problems (Been et al, 2019). These views are those of 'supply sceptics', who argue that housing supply, in and of itself, will not determine a person's capacity to gain access to a dwelling, and that to build more is unlikely to alleviate housing shortages and problems of affordability.

Third, I note that the problems facing people relating to access to housing are less to do with the alleged impediments inhibiting its supply, and more about the dominant, market model of design and construction. It follows that a different approach to 'building more' is required, with much more emphasis on the quality of what is built, and transforming the means and mechanisms by which housing is allocated or made available to people. Instead of building more, there is a case for building less or not at all, and, instead, focusing on the pre-existing stocks and creating the means to make much more of it affordable and easier for people to gain access to. This means a focus on the institutional and financial mechanisms that influence how housing is made available, and ensuring that people, whatever their financial and labour market circumstances, are provided with options, and support, to gain access to a dwelling that can meet their needs.

The case for building more houses

It has become commonplace for politicians, builders and an array of commentators to assert that the contemporary housing problem, usually defined as the lack of affordable properties, relates to a deficit of supply of new dwellings (Swinney, 2018). The argument goes that the high cost of housing can be reduced if builders are permitted to build more dwellings. By increasing supply, house prices will be depressed, property values will fall and more people will be able to gain access to housing. There is a persuasive logic to this formulation, and for policymakers and others in the political firing line to come up with solutions to the housing shortfall, the prognosis is easily identifiable. This prognosis is no more than extending the reach of the housing market by providing private builders the freedoms to build dwellings for sale, while liberalising private renting and encouraging a new genre of 'building for rent'.[1]

These arguments are to the fore in areas of high house prices, such as California. Ho (2020: 1) argues that California will need 'between 1.8 million and 3.5 million new housing units by 2025' to cater for increasing demand. The logic of building more stock to alleviate housing shortages is ingrained into the psyche of local politicians, with Chiu, Chair of the California Assembly's Housing and Community Development Committee, suggesting that 'we're not building enough homes, pure and simple' (quoted in Collins and Johnson, 2019). Such statements are commonplace, and are made routinely as 'a matter of fact'. A report by California's Legislative Analyst's Office (Taylor, 2015: 34) notes that the 'constraints on housing supply [are] the primary factor driving the state's high housing costs'. Media reports tend to reproduce such statements in caricatured ways, with the deficit of housing supply being attributed to restrictive state practices. Buhayer and Cannon (2019: 1) are exemplars of this by claiming that 'bad government ... has created a severe shortage of houses'.

This is one of the dominant strands of the pro-building argument, and it is evident across a range of countries. In Germany, Jackson (2019: 1) describes how rents have risen by more than 50 per cent in nine cities since 2005, with 16 per cent of households spending 'more than 40% of their income on housing'. The prognosis by property analysts is to construct more housing because 'the key feature of the German housing market remains a lack of supply' (Nienaber, 2019: 1). Similar views are expressed in relation to escalating housing costs in Canada, which increased by nearly 28 per cent between 2016 and 2019 (Delmendo, 2020). A widely held view about Canada's house price inflation is expressed by Taylor (2020: 1), who notes that 'there's only one way to solve a housing affordability crisis: by building more houses. A lot more houses.' For some commentators, this is unlikely unless restrictions to supply are curtailed, with Green et al (2016: 20) arguing that it is 'costly and challenging land-use regulations' that are primary factors in limiting the construction of housing.

These sentiments are evident in the UK, where there is a long-standing antipathy by real estate actors towards the state regulation of house building. This is exemplified by the Home Builders Federation (HBF, 2014a: 1), the representative body of the industry in England and Wales, which condemns land-use planning as 'too slow, overly complex and costly', a view shared by some academic commentators, such as Hilber and Vermeulen (2016: 1), who note that the planning system in the UK is 'extraordinarily rigid by world standards'. Such views are propagated at the highest levels of government, with the UK House of Commons Public Accounts Committee (2019: 2) suggesting that the government's target of delivering 300,000 new homes per year by the mid-2020s is likely to be jeopardised by 'inherent problems at the heart of the housing planning system'. Echoing the HBF (2014b), the committee note that the problem of planning relates, in part, to the slowness of the system's decision-making.

By the early 2010s, the efficacy of dismantling regulation to facilitate house building was to the fore of government policy in England, and from 2010 to 2016, English governments introduced a raft of supply-side measures. These were guided by the *National Planning Policy Framework* (DCLG, 2012), which required local planning authorities to presume in favour of construction when adjudicating planning applications for house building. There were waivers for planning permission on home extensions, and the encouragement of higher-density development around key commuter hubs. The rationale for these, and other, measures was outlined in the Housing and Planning Act as to 'remove any unnecessary obstacles in the planning system to the delivery of new homes' (DCLG, 2016: 9). In other words, politicians were seeking to create an unfettered environment to facilitate an expansion in newbuild construction.

These changes are illustrative of a long-standing mantra emanating from, primarily, pro-market interests intent on discrediting state intervention in land and property markets (Pennington, 2002; Barker, 2008; Hilber and Vermeulen, 2016). Foremost among them are academic economists, with Cheshire (2014: 1) claiming that 'we have not been building enough houses for more than 30 years – and those we have been building have too often been in the wrong place or of the wrong type to meet demand'. Others, such as Monk et al (1996: 495), note that 'the planning system imposes significant costs, which include the exacerbation of price increases'. Pennington (2002: 62) concurs and suggests that planning has led to 'the inexorable rise in the price of housing land and hence house prices' and 'the increased scarcity of supply'. Monk et al (1996: 495) also blame planning for fostering 'a narrower range of house types' that 'restrict the choices available to consumers'.

While there is recognition that other factors may influence builders' propensity to build, such as their proclivity and capacities to do so, as well as local and environmentalist opposition to construction, it is the operations of the public regulatory systems that garner most attention by building advocates. Cheshire (2018: 9) argues that the 'housing problem' in the UK is caused, primarily, by the actions of public regulators, which leads to the 'systematic undersupply of land and space' that, in turn, stymies the construction of new dwellings. For Cheshire (2018), land-use regulation operates in a political way that compounds developer risks and costs, which can dissuade builders from proceeding with a planning application for housing. Cheshire (2018: 10) cites examples of the bureaucratic inertia of local government as adding to builders' costs, characterised by planning committee members, responsible for making decisions on applications, often prevaricating and being 'subject to lobbying and political expediency'.

This can translate into the actions of local political systems thwarting development, with planning officers and politicians often siding with local protectionist interests. For pro-building groups, local opposition to construction is a significant factor in preventing building, and is construed as 'against the national interest' and contributing to the shortfall in housing provision. The understanding here is that anti-development groups obstruct housing development because they benefit from its scarcity, with the consequential deficit of supply pushing up the value of their own properties. Monkkonen and Livesley-O'Neill (2017: 3), writing about the Californian context, 'estimate that local residents have approximately 20 formal avenues to oppose housing'. For Monkkonen and Livesley-O'Neill (2017), this makes the application process for building permits for new housing a potentially time-consuming, costly and often frustrating and fruitless exercise for builders, and is likely to put them off from trying.

For building advocates, community opposition to building is 'anti-progressive', or irrational and reactionary behaviour by self-interested groups. Advocates note that it is encouraged and facilitated by planning laws and procedures that prioritise local interests over broader, societal needs. In the US, for instance, there is widespread opposition to the supply of high-density, affordable housing, and this is held up as an exemplar of how local groups stymie the supply of dwellings. Scally and Tighe (2015: 757) outline a familiar scenario; their research with a sample of 74 housing developers operating in New York State found that 70 per cent had 'experienced local community opposition to their affordable housing development projects', with the consequence of delays to construction and leasing or selling units. For Scally and Tighe (2015: 749), community opposition prevents the supply of dwellings and is 'a considerable barrier to the efficient siting of affordable housing'.

Levin and Christopher (2017: 1) also note that attempts by builders to get building permits can be prevented or slowed down by a panoply of state measures, including 'zoning restrictions, lengthy project design reviews … parking and other amenity requirements, and multi-hurdled approval processes'. Quigley and Raphael (2005: 327) concur, with their assessment of regulatory control across 407 California jurisdictions between 1990 and 2000 concluding that 'new housing construction is lower in more regulated cities relative to less regulated cities'. This research corroborates the work of Mayer and Somerville (2000), who found that heavily regulated US cities have lower levels of new housing construction. The forms of regulation vary from growth-control measures, such as growth moratoria, which, as Quigley and Raphael (2005: 327) state, reduce 'the quantity of developable land', to minimum quality standards, such as building codes requiring fire sprinklers in residential buildings, which can add over US$100,000 to the cost of a dwelling (Herriges, 2018).

This combination of regulatory controls lies behind what building advocates regard as the high rates of refusals of planning applications for house building. Hilber and Vermeulen (2016) investigated refusals of major residential projects by English local planning authorities between 1979 and 2008. They concluded that the high house prices in the South-east, relative to other parts of England, were related to the large number of planning applications turned down for residential construction, leading to a shortfall of construction of new properties. This reflects, Hilber and Vermeulen (2016) surmise, the whole gamut of regulatory controls, including the politics of housing, in which neighbourhoods in affluent areas, such as the south-east of England, are likely to resist development and have leverage in local political and planning systems. Indeed, for Cheshire (2018: 10), the problem is that planning has few rules and is open to capture by anti-development groups, with decision-making being arbitrary and 'subject to the uncertain and gameable mechanism of development control'.

Building advocates also highlight the role of planning in constraining land supply and, consequentially, limiting the propensity for builders to provide dwellings. In the English context, Cheshire and Buyuklieva (2019: 3) blame urban land-containment policies for restricting construction, and note that, as a consequence, 'the real price of land for houses has risen more than 15-fold since Green Belts were first imposed' in 1955. This statement assumes that there is a one-to-one, cause-and-effect relationship between the green belt and house prices, when, in fact, it is more complex than this (see also Dawkins and Nelson, 1992). Cheshire and Buyuklieva's (2019) study of green belt is characterised by a lack of analysis of other factors, such as changes in household incomes and builders restricting supplies of dwellings, which may also be important in shaping the price of dwellings. It is more or less impossible to generate data that can separate out 'green-belt effects' from a host of other, interlocking factors that interact with builders' behaviour in relation to the supply of, and construction upon, land.

Cheshire (2018: 12) also suggests that planning policies can restrict construction by seeking to conserve and protect sites containing buildings of historic character, further reducing the available land to build on and adding costs 'in the form of higher prices for housing and office space'. Cheshire (2018: 11) quotes the example of the London borough of Islington where the construction of 'all building of more than 7 floors' is forbidden, partly to ensure that the character of historic streetscapes is maintained. Likewise, Washington (2012: 1) asserts that 'by limiting a city's available square footage, preservation restricts supply' and 'sends prices up'. To claim that regulations to protect amenity and aesthetic values will, in and of themselves, inflate land and/or housing costs requires much more evaluation and evidence than either Washington or Cheshire provide. These authors also ignore the monetary and non-monetary costs that additional square footage of building might impose on the aesthetic and historic character of places.

The debate about housing supply and cost is particularly pointed in the US, where in certain locales, such as neighbourhoods like The East Cut in San Francisco and Brentwood in Los Angeles, the growth of population is outstripping the supply of available properties, and the highest house prices in the world are to be found. Advocates of relaxing supply-side constraints on building note that a major factor in the unaffordability of dwellings is restrictive residential zoning. In many US cities, there are stringent restrictions on the density of development, and in most cities, there is a premise in favour of the construction of low-density, single-family homes. Badger and Bui (2019: 1) note that 'it is illegal on 75 percent of the residential land in many American cities to build anything other than a detached single-family home'. In Seattle, 80 per cent of residentially zoned land is set aside for such house types, and the figure is 75 per cent in Los Angeles (Badger and Bui, 2019).

Such zoning restricts the quantity of what can be built, and for Glaeser and Gyourko (2002: 21), 'measures of zoning strictness are highly correlated with high prices'. Other researchers concur, with Kendall and Tulip's (2018: 1) study of the effects of zoning on house prices in Australian cities concluding that 'zoning can have a huge effect on land values'. They estimate that zoning has 'raised the average price of detached houses, relative to supply costs, by 69 percent in Melbourne, 42 percent in Brisbane, and 54 percent in Perth' (Kendall and Tulip, 2018: 1). The effects of zoning on the supply of land, as well as its cost, means that builders are likely to construct high-value dwellings to offset the high prices of land purchase. Conversely, for providers of social housing, there is likely to be an inability to purchase increasingly expensive land for development, with consequent shortfalls occurring in the provision of affordable dwellings.

Supply-side arguments are making major headway in government circles, and are likely to influence future policy trajectories, including a significant increase in house building. This is not surprising because there is an ideological rapport between the market-led prognosis of building advocates and the major political parties in power. In the English context, Housing Secretary Robert Jenrick announced in August 2020 sweeping planning reforms to provide 'permission in principle' to developments on land designated 'for renewal' as part of a process to speed up the building process (see Grimwood, 2020). The reforms will also permit households to add two storeys to their homes without the need for full planning permission, so encouraging, potentially, a building spree. In California, a suite of bills is being deliberated on zoning reforms to permit higher-density construction, and land zoned for office parks or retail outlets may become eligible for housing development (Levin, 2020).

This reflects what Gallent et al (2017: 2207) describe as the 'supply-side fetish', in which governments in countries ranging from the UK to the US and Australia are encouraging unprecedented house building by, primarily, seeking to deregulate planning and other 'impediments' to building. The question is, by deregulation and opening up land for construction, how far will a supply of appropriate properties ensue, and for whom? There is the issue of how far the diagnosis of the housing crisis, that is, affordability related to the shortfall of newly constructed dwellings, is accurate or a mischaracterisation of the problems people face by failing to consider questions of entry and access to housing, or how demand is expressed and manifest. It may be that revealing the complexities of how people interact with housing shows that the supply of new property per se may be trivial, even an irrelevance, or at least not as central to policy as building advocates suggest.

There is, therefore, a need to widen the scope of the critique of the interplay between housing affordability and construction through a consideration of how factors other than restrictions on the supply of dwellings may contribute to the difficulties of access to, and consumption of, dwellings. This task is important because there is much equivocation about the interrelationships between housing supply, house prices and affordability.

In one study, Fingleton et al's (2019: 25) data suggest that 'increasing housing supply in the most critical areas has little impact on (both local and regional) affordability'. Monkkonen (2019) takes the contrary view: 'constraining the supply of housing increases rents', so, by implication, increasing the supply of housing will decrease rents. Depending on which viewpoint holds sway, one points towards building more housing, the other to less, or none at all.

Building more housing is not the panacea

The debate about housing costs and the supply of dwellings is beset by polarised, often politically motivated and partisan, views that are more ideological than balanced, and rarely critically evaluative. The building lobby tends to present a case that accepts, prima facie, that there is a deficit of housing and a need to expand, significantly, the supply of newly built dwellings. Attempts to investigate the complexities of the other side of the equation, that is, housing demand, are limited. The ways in which builders and others involved in real estate seek to manipulate land and house prices by their control over when to build and release dwellings into the marketplace are not considered. In the rest of this section, I evaluate the logic of arguments propounded by building advocates, and highlight why the construction of new dwellings, in and of itself, is not a panacea in relation to the problems faced by many in gaining access to housing.

Before addressing arguments for whether there is a need to build more housing, the issue of what might cause the alleged deficit of supply of dwellings, beyond the operations of the planning system, should be considered. Cheshire (2018) suggests that his prognosis of the need to build more dwellings, based on analysis of the determinants of deficits in housing supply, is limited by the difficulties of generating data that can corroborate the claims made by building advocates. He notes that the planning system 'has an inbuilt restrictive effect' but that 'no one has been able to quantify the impact this has', and 'devising a methodology to estimate its effects is extremely challenging' (Cheshire (2018: 11). This data deficiency and methodological challenge have not stopped building advocates from drawing conclusions, and there is counter-evidence that opens up the debate to a different set of interpretations and understandings (see Gallent et al, 2017).

To blame planning for shortfalls in housing supply, or problems facing people in gaining access to dwellings, is to reduce a complex issue to a single point of causation. Planning is only one of many variables that interrelate in shaping the supply of, and demand for, housing, and there is evidence that the operations of the planning system are not necessarily as presented by building advocates. Data show that in England, the planning system is responsive to developer needs, with nine out of ten planning applications approved and administered well within the time limit for their adjudication (LGA, 2019). The quantity of planning consents held by builders to construct dwellings is evidence of a system that is both enabling and responsive to applicants. In 2020, builders held planning consents to build over 1 million dwellings in England, and in 2019, 370,000 planning permissions were granted for the construction of new housing, more than enough to meet the types of building targets that building advocates suggest are necessary (Walker, 2020).

There is, therefore, the issue of what might be preventing the take-up of planning permissions, or builders taking the next step and constructing dwellings. How far is the alleged lack of housing supply a matter of the operations of the building industry, and its disposition towards the management of supply, including 'land banking', or the hoarding of permissioned land? Jeffreys (2016: 1) notes that the ten top-listed house builders in England held more than 400,000 plots in land banks in 2016, or 'more than six years' worth of housebuilding at their current build rate'. Little had changed by the end of the decade; as Howell (2019: 1) outlines, in 2019, the top ten house builders held over 350,000 building 'plots with planning permission, and nearly as many again in "strategic" holdings'.[2] An interpretation of these figures is that builders have little interest in building quickly, or responding to government exhortations about meeting house supply figures, and look to drip-feed stock onto the market to restrict supply and keep prices high (New Economics Foundation, 2018).

This behaviour is redolent of profit maximisation, and Lai and Wang (1999) show that in the Hong Kong context, builders regard the control of land through their land banks as a means to modulate housing supply. Their research found evidence of the precision timing of the release of new housing 'by raising the housing supply at the peak season and delaying it otherwise to maximize the selling price' (Lai and Wang, 1999: 149). Huang et al (2015) also note that in the Hong Kong property market, even if governments were to facilitate an increase of land supply to developers, this may not, in and of itself, prompt a corresponding release of new housing onto the market if such releases were likely to erode profit margins. For Lee and Tang (2017), this is indicative of the hegemony of the real estate sector in Hong Kong, in which the state and property companies closely interact in (re)producing highly profitable land deals that maintain high rents and do little to facilitate the supply of affordable property.

Land markets also operate in ways whereby there is no guarantee that land allocated for housing development will lead to a supply of dwellings. There is evidence that land with planning permission for residential development attracts private equity companies not interested in house building per se, but motivated by acquiring, and holding onto, land to gain from its appreciation in value. A study by Molior (quoted in Jeffreys, 2016: 1) found that 45 per cent of sites in London 'with planning permission for new homes were owned by a company which did not build homes'. Land, as an asset class, is a speculative investment, and in contrast to the prognosis of pro-building advocates, the planning system is a sideshow in comparison to the casino-capitalist behaviour of major landowners. Bradley (2021) describes how in London, outline planning permission for housing has become a tradeable asset that is sold on, time and again, as part of a speculative, and highly profitable, market in land, and usually with no output or end product, such as the construction of dwellings.

What the trade in land and property as financial assets points towards is the social-structural relations underpinning the supply of land. It reflects the power of builders and corporate landlords to regulate flows of land and property onto, and out of, the market, and, in doing so, to influence the demand for, and price of, housing. Given the motivation of builders to construct dwellings that realise the highest possible prices, it seems problematical to expect, as building advocates do, that the private sector building industry is able, and willing, to supply the market with the numbers of dwellings that governments estimate are required to meet housing shortfalls. For builders, this would be tantamount to flooding the housing market and undermining, even dismantling, their business model. As May (2016: 1) suggests, builders 'only build in a rising market' and are unlikely to support a building strategy that could, potentially, lead to a precipitous decline in house prices.

Even if the private sector building industry were disposed to increasing the supply of housing, the issue is how far this would redress the alleged shortfall of dwellings and, in particular, provide them at prices that reach out to those in most need. One of the features of contemporary housing supply is its concentration in high-value, investor properties. The rise of housing as part of investment portfolios is characterised by major corporate investors investing in, and stimulating, the construction of high-end housing, such as in Nine Elms in London, and the lucrative returns from owning and renting property has led to the proliferation of corporate landlords buying up, and able to control, large quantities of rental property. The (re) production of housing as a pure commodity, and the syphoning of its supply into institutional control, has implications for costs and conditions of access to dwellings.

These observations are pertinent in relation to the rental market for housing, and, as Glantz (2019: 1) notes, much housing in the US is being bought up 'by anonymous shell companies using piles of cash'. Over 3 million US homes and 13 million apartment units are owned by shell companies, or organisations formed to protect a company's assets and avoid scrutiny. These companies have been joined by stock-market-listed organisations, such as Invitation Homes and American Homes 4 Rent. American Homes is a real estate investment trust that owns, operates and finances income-producing properties. It has 53,000 properties and Invitation Homes has a portfolio of 80,000 properties, primarily in Florida and the western US. These companies are the tip of the corporatised rental housing market, and indicative of the decline of individual, single-person or family landlords. As Badger (2018) outlines, in the US, the proportion of residential rental properties owned by individuals and families fell from 92 per cent to 74 per cent between 1991 and 2015 (see US Census Bureau 1996, 2015).

This financialisaton of rental housing has implications for people's access to, and consumption of, dwellings that the construction of new properties cannot easily overcome. Research into the rise of investor ownership of dwellings describes the emergence of a new tranche of 'absentee landlord at best … casually issuing rapid eviction notices at worst' (Call et al, 2014: 1). For tenants, the new landlordism proffers the possibility of a diminution of control of their housing circumstances. Preston's (2015) research, which investigated 11,000 renters living in properties in California, owned by what they call 'Wall Street Investors', shows that tenants pay more than other residents in their communities. Many have to bear the costs of repair and maintenance that landlords are ordinarily responsible for. As Preston (2015: 2) concludes, tenants are taking on the responsibilities of ownership but do not have the benefits, while being subject to escalating costs that have the potential to displace them from their homes.

While the rise of the corporate, investor landlord may facilitate an increase in the numbers of properties available for rent, the reality may well be that the supply becomes restricted to a specific, niche demand. This is the case in Berlin, where rents and house prices have increased significantly over the last 15 years, with rental levels having risen by more than 30 per cent since 2015 (Morris and Beck, 2020). The city is unaffordable for many, and this is due not to any lack of supply of housing, but to the emergence of mega-landlords owning a disproportionate amount of the stock and exercising monopoly pricing powers. Schultheis (2019) notes that Berlin's largest landlord, Deutsche Wohnen, which owns over 160,000 apartments in the city, has been increasing rents with impunity, with its actions having led to calls for them, and other corporate landlords, to be expelled from the city. Berlin, unlike other cities, is introducing rent-cap rules that may require landlords to lower rents by up to 40 per cent (Winter and Blackman, 2020).

The Berlin example indicates that an apparent deficit of supply is related, in part, to the increasing concentration of housing wealth in the hands of select groups of wealthy investors, ranging from second-homeowners to buy-to-let landlords and super-rich elites. This observation casts doubt that a supply-side strategy, which involves the construction of new housing, will provide for many people in need because much of any constructed stock is likely to be absorbed by investor interests. This is particularly the case in relation to the 'hotelisation' of housing by companies such as Airbnb. The company is described as part of the 'networked hospitality' industry in seeking to match up local homeowners, and their properties, with visitors seeking a short-term let (Bernardi, 2018a). The rise of Airbnb has been phenomenal, and from its start-up in 2007, the company's growth has been rapid. By 2018, it was worth an estimated US$38 billion, controlled over 3 million properties in 200 countries worldwide and had a presence in most cities (Bernardi, 2018b).

The quantity of properties that comprise Airbnb listings is considerable, and the company had 75,700 active properties in London and 52,000 in Paris in 2018 (Statista, 2021). The lucrative nature of short-term lets means that Airbnb is attractive to large-scale letting companies, who use the platform to advertise properties. One of the major effects has been to reduce the supply of long-term rentals, or dwellings that would otherwise be part of the mainstream housing stock. Shabrina et al (2019: 1) note that in London, Airbnb takes up to 2 per cent of the housing stock out of long-term and into short-term rentals, and, as they suggest, this figure can be as high as '20% in some neighbourhoods' and exacerbates gentrification. This process is indicative of the inflationary effects of Airbnb, with Ayouba et al's (2020) research of French cities showing that the company's operations 'puts upward pressure on rents in Lyon, Montpellier, and Paris', and Segú (2018: 1) reporting that Airbnb is responsible for a 4 per cent increase in rents in Barcelona.

The Airbnb effect is not confined to the hotelisation trade, but also evident in the construction of properties for rent. One significant initiative in England is 'build-for-rent', in which the government set up a £1 billion fund in 2012 to encourage builders to construct dwellings for rent. The rationale is that the increase in rental supply will diminish escalating rents and associated housing costs, and contribute to new tranches of affordable dwellings. However, 'build-for-rent' has attracted finance and investment companies keen to cash in on schemes that deliver a stream of stable and long-term income. T. White (2018) describes a study of build-to-rent properties constructed in London, which were 11 per cent more expensive than older, pre-existing, non-build-to-rent properties located nearby. He outlines a development in the Elephant and Castle in South London, with the rent priced at nearly £1,900 per month, and notes that the conditions of entry require a salary of '£60,000 a year to qualify as a tenant' (White, T., 2018: 1).

The irony of build-for-rent is that far from achieving a stated objective to widen the rental market by increasing the supply of property, the presence of major real estate investors, looking for high returns, has shaped the scheme towards the provision of, primarily, high-spec, high-value dwellings. Given that the metropolitan government of London defined an affordable rent for a two-bedroomed dwelling in 2020 as no more than £164.24 per week, build-for-rent is not for people on low incomes (Webb and Murphy, 2020). While it might absorb a particular tranche of demand and, arguably, free up other properties for those on lower incomes, build-for-rent highlights that supply, in and of itself, is no guarantee that the requisite, relevant forms of, housing will be provided that can redress problems of access to, and affordability of, dwellings. Build-for-rent can be thought of as a supply-side approach that, by supplying a particular type of property within specific price brackets, is simultaneously contributing to a broader housing crisis, related to inflated rents and people being priced out of places where such schemes are constructed.

The same can be said for the buy-to-let initiative in the UK, in which governments encourage homeowners to purchase second homes to rent as part of an initiative to increase the supply of private rental property. The policy has existed since 1996, and it is illustrative of the financialisaton of housing, or the propagation of speculative investment and securing capital gains by property transactions. Evaluations of the scheme suggest that the newbuild buy-to-let market is dominated by wealthy, overseas investors purchasing property in bulk (Leyshon and French, 2009: 456). Buy-to-let properties tend to be overvalued and rental prices high, and Paccoud (2017: 839) notes that 'buy-to-let has become a prominent tenure trajectory in gentrifying neighbourhoods'. For Paccoud (2017: 839), buy-to-let enables a rapid route for investors to benefit from asset appreciation but it does not provide for people on low incomes and shows evidence of 'long term trajectories of displacement in surrounding areas'.

This brings to the fore the different ways in which housing is supplied, and how it is segmented and channelled into specific markets, and often off-limits to many people. This is evident with the second-homeownership market, which is an illustration of how the supply of housing stock becomes concentrated in the hands of a few. Hilber (2018) notes that the number of second homes in the UK doubled between 1995 and 2013, and numerous reports document second homes left empty for long periods of time, catering for wealthy outsiders and restricting the supply of dwellings to local people. In the picturesque town of Southwold in Suffolk, it is estimated that second-homeowners own 900 out of 1,500 homes, and many are part of property portfolios, or vehicles for investment, and not necessarily for habitation (Iqbal, 2018). Evidence on newbuild in many of the second-home 'hotspots' is that such supply is unlikely to be affordable to local people, thus questioning the efficacy of new construction in such places without requisite checks and controls on who has the means to buy and/or gain access to them.[3]

Whether second homes, investor-led rental properties or hotel-style, short-term lets, the nature of housing supply and conditions relating to its availability, particularly pricing, are all important in influencing how far a supply-side approach can redress the major, seemingly intractable, problems relating to the consumption of dwellings. It may be that new construction is not needed, but that the ways in which existing stock is made available is the issue. This is the view of many academic and policy commentators, with Chance et al (2016) suggesting that there is not a deficit or shortage of housing in the UK, insofar that the construction of new houses outpaced the increase in population and household formation in the period between 2001 and 2011, a trend that has since continued. Coupled with loft conversions and extensions to existing homes, they suggest that 'there are more rooms per person than ever before, with more than enough to allow everyone to have a spare bedroom' (Chance et al, 2016: 55).

In this respect, the problem is not necessarily a lack of supply per se, but the distribution and use of space, and, as Chance et al (2016: 56) suggest, some people have 'far more space than they need, while others struggle to find a home that they can afford'. Murphy (2018) outlines the English Housing Survey for 2014 to 2015, which indicates that 51 per cent of owner-occupied homes in England, or 7.3 million households, were underoccupied, in which at least two bedrooms were not used on a regular basis. By comparison, the equivalent figure was 39 per cent, or 5.3 million, households for 1995 to 1996, indicative of a worsening situation (see Murphy, 2018). Similar sentiments are outlined by Mayhew (2020), who in looking at the paucity of accommodation for elderly people, notes that they tend to stay put in their larger dwellings due to lack of appropriate supply. Mayhew's (2020: 1) research indicates that there will be 20 million surplus bedrooms by 2040, suggesting that 'if people lived in homes more suited to their needs, 50,000 fewer homes would need to be built each year'.

There is also the issue of empty homes, and in purely quantitative terms, it appears that there are more than enough empty properties to meet all existing housing needs in the UK and other countries. By the mid-2010s, there were more than 11 million empty homes in Europe, with 3.4 million homes vacant in Spain, 2 million vacant homes in each of France and Italy, and more than 700,000 or 3 per cent of the housing stock in the UK that is empty (Neate, 2014). In the US, there are more than 17 million homes that are vacant but no system to overturn such vacancies (US Census Bureau, 2018; McIntyre, 2019). Building advocates suggest that vacancies emerge when people look to change their housing circumstances, often to acquire more space or downsize, and that local planning restrictions on adapting existing dwellings will force people to move. For pro-building advocates, a solution is to relax restrictions, but this sidesteps the issue that there are many different types of vacancies related to a complexity of different processes.[4]

This critique of empty properties says nothing about the swathes of new, never-occupied, speculative housing constructed across countries such as China and Spain. Nor does it say anything about the major displacements of people from homes in US cities, in which thousands of abandoned and empty homes are testament to the failures of market provision. The question remains: why build and supply more homes when there is a major surfeit of existing properties? The presence of an empty property, in and of itself, does not mean that it can simply be filled, or be part of the solution to the shortfall of housing.[5] It may be that some empty places can address a shortfall, but the issue at stake, as discussed in Chapter 3, is how does such a situation transpire in the first instance in which construction is permitted without a realistic evaluation of who will live in the properties. Part of the problem is speculation and permissive systems of planning that fail to address what may be needed.

May (2016: 1) notes that the supply-side argument is flawed because 'demand is almost unbounded ... so supply can never "meet" demand'. If demand is 'unbounded', the supply-side logic implies that there would be a never-ending building programme and the sanctioning of 'building without limits'. The question is how demand is estimated, by whom and using what methods, and how this might be translated into making dwelling space available in ways whereby the costs of speculative building, including the provision of buildings that remain empty and unused, can be mitigated or even avoided. The complexities of how people interact with the domestic environment do not permit any easy way of estimating what a level or quantity of supply should be, or, indeed, the types or forms of dwellings, including costs or prices to a consumer. To leave such complexities to speculative provision carries dangers of perpetuating a building culture in which to build becomes an end in itself.

For building advocates, their understanding about allocative mechanisms points to the market, in the form of individual builders and consumers, making the key decisions about what to provide and consume, based on market research and intelligence. While this system works to a degree, it fails more often than not by its inability to intervene in, and ameliorate problems relating to, the social provisioning of dwellings, in which the power of the wealthy, the elites and corporate investors to co-opt and control the market is paramount. Builders can manipulate supply and price, institutional investors can corral property, and large-scale, corporate landlords can set rental levels that perpetuate gentrification and contribute to displacement and homelessness. The broader cultural context of building is important here too, and this propagates the idea of housing not as a home, but as an investment and commodity, or part of a wealth portfolio. Under this maxim, the underlying dynamic of seeking to construct more dwellings is unlikely to change.

Conclusion

The debate about the housing crisis, both in the UK and elsewhere, is narrowly construed around the need to build more dwellings. The understanding is that the crisis relates to a deficit of supply that drives up housing costs and makes properties unaffordable. Deploying a market logic, building advocates note that by increasing the supply of dwellings, house prices will be lowered and people will be able to afford access to housing. What is required is to remove barriers to building more dwellings and to let the market operate without interference by government, particularly from local politicians and planning officials. It is assumed that this will facilitate an appropriate level of supply that will be sufficient to meet demand, as though synchronisation between the two will occur. There are factors that make this unlikely, if not impossible, and there are examples of where a surfeit of goods and services fail to meet, or respond to, demand, including Sen's (1977) account of the Bengal famine, in which people were dying while shops were full of grain and foodstuffs.

While pro-building arguments have a persuasive logic, the 'building more' mentality cannot be sustained, or supported, given the evidence showing that construction per se is not the solution to the housing crisis. The increase in housing supply by building does not necessarily lower prices because much of what is built is constructed, purposely, for high-value investment, beyond what many people can afford. Builders have the capacity to restrict the supply of what they build, and to manage the construction process in ways whereby they can maintain high prices for properties. The rise of portfolio landlords, purchasing swathes of properties en masse, creates oligopolistic systems of housing supply and control that also enable prices to be kept high, irrespective of how much additional stock is built. Even if the construction of new housing is sanctioned, much stock will be absorbed as second homes and 'safe deposit box' investments for wealthy investors, highlighting that the market supply of newly built housing is no guarantee that people in need will be able to access it.

So, what ought to be done? Foremost is to recognise the complexities of people's interrelationships with housing, in which there is no singular housing problem, but many problems relating to the allocation and consumption of dwellings. The so-called 'housing crisis' has many dimensions and causes, the solutions to which require much more than the building of new dwellings. It is necessary to pull back from the one-track mentalities of building advocates, who appear to be part of a powerful grouping who do not engage with, or convey, the intricacies of people's relationships with housing and the consumption of domestic space. There is little recognition, or value, of the environmental impacts of new building projects, nor acknowledgement of evidence which suggests that for every single dwelling that is constructed, local soils and ecologies are disturbed and upwards of 80 tons of carbon dioxide is released (Berners-Lee, 2010). Such considerations ought to be factored in to any decision about whether to build or not.

It is also fallacious, and disingenuous, to expect the private sector house-building industry to address, let alone solve, the multiplicity of people's needs, though this is implied by building advocates in seeking to liberalise the flows of supply of dwellings. The building industry is, not surprisingly, self-interested in pushing the supply of new construction, or at least ensuring a favourable, deregulated, political environment that enables freedom to design and build without restraint. The dangers of this are manifest in builders not only managing the flow of supply, and hence able to set the price, but also pursuing profit maximisation by regulating the quality of the product. Enabling private house builders to build more is often the equivalent of building less in relation to the size of dwellings. The aphorism 'more is less' seems apt in relation to house builders, as 'the size of the average house in Britain has shrunk by 20% since the 1970's' (Hemingway, 2018: 1). This points towards the need to control for not only quantity of supply, but also its quality.

Instead of encouraging the ongoing financialisaton of housing, and conceiving of the dwelling as an investment vehicle and a means of capital gain, it should be reconceived much more as a home, or place of habitation. This would make a break with a build-for-profit mentality, or a rationale that is hard-wired in to the continuous production of the product, that is, the dwelling, as part of the process of realising value. The last 20 years have seen the marketisation of housing provision, and the co-option, even capture, of its supply by a host of wealthy and corporate investors, compounding access difficulties for people on low incomes. To supply more dwellings in a context where there is already an abundance of properties, albeit unevenly owned, controlled and distributed, seems to fly in the face of what ought to be done. There needs to be more focus on distributional issues, and to ask awkward, pertinent questions regarding who has access to and control of, particularly, the existing housing stock and its supply.

Given that the major problem relating to housing is affordability, the model for supplying low-cost dwellings in places like the UK is neither low in cost nor sufficient in quantity to address the problems of those in housing need. Local authorities barely build anymore and social housing providers have been forced to adopt a model in which they charge rents that are not far off the full market price. Housing associations and a new genre of social housing providers are implicated in exacerbating the housing crisis by selling land and property that could otherwise be used to supply low-cost, affordable dwellings. They have become market-oriented in seeking to maximise profits from land and property transactions. Batty (2018: 1) describes how housing associations in London have made over £82 million from selling homes in five boroughs between 2013 and 2018. It is part of a trend that has seen 150,000 homes for social rent being lost to the sector since 2012.

The decrease of the housing stock that ordinarily would provide for people on low incomes is part of a broader process that points to issues relating to people's incomes and relative wealth as the main factors in how far they can access decent, affordable properties. Over the last 20 years, average housing prices have far outpaced incomes, having 'risen by over 160% in real terms since their low point in the middle of 1996' (Mulheirn, 2019: 1). This reflects, in large part, corporate investor involvement in purchasing property and inflating its value. For many people in the UK and elsewhere, their incomes have also collapsed in a context of austerity in public policy and welfare cutbacks, particularly in relation to housing benefit. Here, I concur with Mulheirn's (2019: 1) observation that 'tackling these problems directly would be a far more potent (and less economically costly) way to improve affordability than boosting market supply'.

Building That Matters to People

Introduction

In previous chapters, I have set out some of the broader socio-political and economic dynamics and processes that shape the construction of the built environment. In this chapter, I explore the substance of how building and construction can affect people's quality of habitation and everyday lives, and how what we build is significant in shaping human welfare and physical and mental well-being. It is a truism to say that the primary objective of a building is, or ought to be, the facilitation and support of people's functioning and activities. These activities are many and varied, and constantly evolving and changing; yet, buildings and spaces are often constructed in ways that render them static, or impervious to the ways in which people seek to interact with(in) them. From major road systems that do not permit ease of pedestrian access from one part of a city to another, to the construction of buildings with poor acoustics and sound insulation, the design of the built environment is not always attuned to, or understanding of, the sensory nature of the human body.

This point was brought home to me when spending time with Ann, who depends on using her wheelchair to move around the built environment.[1] Ann struggles to get to her local shops because the environment does not enable her to propel her wheelchair with any ease. The pavement outside her house is broken and uneven, and there are no kerb cuts at the main road she has to cross to get to the parade of shops. Ann has to 'bump down' the kerb and hope that she does not topple over out of the wheelchair. This is one of many instances in which the design and construction of buildings and space is insensitive to Ann's bodily scale and needs, and has the potential for harm and hurt. Similar experiences were described to me by Reiko, who, as a vison-impaired person guiding me around Tokyo in July 2014, highlighted physical obstacles, including poorly sited street furniture, and said, "I walk every day in places not designed for people like me, everything is cluttered and I am always walking into things."

Ann's and Reiko's experiences are common and illustrate the prevalence and potency of a building culture with the potential to undermine and debilitate the body. There is often an absence of human scale, and sensibility, in the design and construction of the built environment, and incongruity between the form and functioning of a place and the values and habits of those who live there. For some observers, modernist building cultures encourage the construction of formulaic or template-type places that are neither flexible nor malleable, but impose pre-fixed spaces that may limit human capabilities and performance (Lynch, 1981; Imrie, 2003). This reflects the scale economies of construction, with the propensity towards the standardisation of building parts and materials that are fitted together as a series of fixtures that often lack the means of adaptability (see Lynch, 1981).

I divide the chapter into two substantive parts. First, I develop the argument that the culture of building and construction does not sensitise its practitioners to the bodily interactions between people and the built environment. Designers and builders are not taught about how different bodies interact with(in) the constructed environment, or about the significance of different social and cultural identities in shaping how people interact with, and embody, buildings and space. Design and construction discourses are antithetical to the crafting of embodied and socially sensitised spaces, and the expectation of building professionals is that people will adapt or change their behaviour to whatever built environments they encounter. If people are unable to do so, as is often the case, construction is implicated, potentially, in the (re)production of debilitating spaces, in which specific bodies may be subject to violations, subtle forms of violence and social exclusion.

It need not be like this, and in a second section, I consider examples of the design and construction of places in ways whereby there is an attempt to sensitise them to the manifold needs of people. I evaluate the potential and possibilities of what I term 'inclusive construction' to challenge, and transform, the values and conventions embedded in much building practice in ways whereby the process may be opened up to a multitude of outcomes, or ways of ordering space and objects that disrupt the discourses of modernist building cultures. For Lynch (1960: 111), such disruption requires a body-sensitised design that enables the construction of buildings and spaces that have 'a certain plasticity, a richness of structures and clues' to enable individuals to navigate, and use, environments with ease. It also requires an understanding not only of how constructed space shapes people's physical interactions with buildings, but also how cognitive and emotional well-being is intertwined with the form and performance of the built environment.

157

In developing these themes, I focus on three illustrations in which the building process is people-centred and sensitive, based on the construction of spaces that support and enhance people's capacities to interact with places in ways whereby their physical and emotional well-being is paramount. The examples are: a landscape garden located in hospital grounds, providing a place of calmness and respite for people recovering from serious illness; dwellings designed by the American architect FLW, characterised by simple and intuitively crafted interiors; and school buildings and grounds designed and constructed to respond to the learning needs of autistic children. In each case, the different design and constructed elements provide people with the potential to shape how they choose to occupy, and inhabit, the places, and they defy any attempt to caricature users, or mould them to any specific form or patterning of behaviour.

Disembodied by design and construction

Construction is integral to shaping people's health and well-being, as well as their sensory and physical experiences of the built environment. From the size and siting of doors and corridors to facilitate the flows of people and materials through buildings, to the provision of toilets and bathrooms that enables basic bodily functioning to occur, the constructed environment has profound and far-reaching effects on the human body. These effects are evident at all phases of construction, and not just the end, built product. The mining of building materials from quarries and the demolition and dispersal of waste products contribute to a range of sensory, bodily outcomes, ranging from air, noise and water pollution, to exposure of people to toxic building materials.[2] Likewise, the construction of pavements without tactile paving, or non-visual cues or means of orientation, is commonplace and redolent of a culture that cares little for people whose bodily functions do not conform to a norm, or what the medical, and other, professions define as 'the average body'.

Most building and construction practice is shaped by a conception of the body as an average or a norm to which few people approximate. The norm tends to characterise, or caricature, people and their behaviour as conforming to a 'type' (see Figure 8.1). This is defined by the normal body, which is conceived as a biological entity that functions and performs according to medical criteria. Such criteria are mobilised to describe the functioning of the body, and the norm, or that which is usual, typical or standard, is defined as the measure for the design and construction of buildings and spaces. This norm tends to revolve around an identikit human being, defined as fully functioning with respect to physical biology but

Figure 8.1: The modular man

Note: This figure of the modular man was located in the Pavilion Le Corbusier in Zurich in 2004. It is a measure of the body as a proportional system to enable architects to conceive of a building's structure, and form, in relation to the body's dimensional configurations, as represented by the modular man (see Le Corbusier, 2004).

Source: Rob Imrie

rarely conceived of in relation to sex, ethnicity, gender or any other social identity, or emotional, sensual and mental capacities and capabilities. The outcome is that builders construct buildings that do not engage with, or respond to, the complexity of what people are, or their different bodily needs and capacities.

This is evident in the design and construction of dwellings that rarely depart from a template, as well as the standardised series of measures that are replicated across time and space. The basic design of dwellings has barely changed since the early 20th century, and it represents an example of a building type that is not sensitised to local social and cultural variations, or to different demands relating to the use of domestic space. Schrader (2013) documents the construction of European-style volume dwellings to house Maori people in New Zealand, noting that in the period of the 1930s, they 'did not suit the inter-generational living arrangements of Māori communities'. The pattern was repeated in the 1960s and 1970s when migrant Samoan people in New Zealand were rehoused in newly constructed dwellings. MacPherson (1997: 152) observes that the design briefs for them 'made assumptions about the lifestyle and requirements of the typical family which required builders to design dwellings around the lifestyles of the European nuclear family'.

This was a problem because, as Bautista (2011: 69) suggests, 'Micronesian households tend to be large and complex', requiring a different type of dwelling environment to those designed and constructed for a small, nuclear family. Cheer et al's (2002) study of the experiences of Samoan and Cook Island families rehoused in Auckland shows that the dwellings were overcrowded, with large numbers of people forced to sleep in bedrooms and overspill into common living areas. Privacy was compromised and the lack of space meant that close contact heightened the risk of spread of disease. As one of the respondents in Cheer et al's (2002: 506) research said: 'There's not enough breathing space for everyone. If one person gets a cold then everyone does.' Pene et al (2009: 79) also recount similar experiences of Tokelauan people living in New Zealand, where there were 'serious difficulties created by inappropriately sized and configured housing'.

These illustrations reflect Parker's (2020: 1, original emphasis) observation that designed environments are 'an idealisation of how people *should* inhabit a space', echoing Lynch's (1981: 159) understanding of the design template as 'a way of seeing the world and then a moral', or a diktat about how people ought to live. In the New Zealand examples, the spaces were a cultural imposition, or an understanding of the world that was not sensitive to the needs of would-be inhabitants. Young (1990) refers to this as 'cultural imperialism', in which conceptions of the body are filtered by a dominant value system that fails to recognise, or respond to, sociobiological variations. When translated into the construction of buildings and the design of space, outcomes are often at odds with what is needed to make a building accessible and usable. In Figure 8.2, a dwelling features a stepped entrance that ought not to be there and, as I recorded in my research diary, 'builders have been required to construct no stepped entrances for years, but they can't seem to stop (re)producing places that won't work for people with mobility impairments'.

This is not untypical, being part of a building rationality premised on the reduction of complexity to archetypes and identikit construction that 'regards variation and difference as a nuisance' (Sayer, 2011: 85). Such mentalities serve to discipline bodies into specific templates and standards shaped by a rationality of scientism in which the design and construction of places is based on 'a science of codes, plot ratios, setbacks, percentages of open space, standardized road patterns' (Newman and Kenworthy, 1999: 287). Lefebvre (1991: 361) has described the production of designed environments as the normalisation of 'a coding of space', or 'a moral discourse on straight lines' in which the complexities of how bodies interact with objects are often reduced 'to blueprints, to mere images'. There is little recognition of complexity and contingency, or the indeterminacy of how people may interact, potentially, with designed objects in ways whereby design is never a fixity, but something that is always in the making.

Figure 8.2: A stepped entrance to a dwelling, preventing ease of access

Source: Rob Imrie

The culture of the design and building professions does not inculcate understanding of the built environment in these terms. Construction is not future-sensitive, and its practitioners rarely think about, or respond to, the future-directive nature of built environments. Rather, there is a preoccupation with the end product as a fixity, or object that, once designed, is fit for, and fitted to, those who will use it. The derivation of 'the fit', or the bodies that interact with the designed environment, is prefigured in relation to the cultural materials of anthropometry, or the application of 'scientific methods to human subjects for the development of design standards' (Roebuck et al, 1975: 6). Figure 8.3 shows a typical, linear itemisation of what designers and building professionals are taught to regard as the methodological ingredients of anthropometry that, in combination, will enable, so it is alleged, the construction of buildings sensitised to the needs of people.

While the criteria are not without value, as an approach to the construction of buildings, there are a number of problems. Foremost is that the method characterises the user based on biological data that cannot reveal anything about a person's social and cultural characteristics. This is a physical, biological reductionism, as though all encounters between people and buildings are comprehensible by, and filtered through, the interactions between biology and design. There is no account of how a person's values and social identity,

Figure 8.3: Anthropometric criteria for design and construction

---

1. Determine the user population
2. Determine the relevant body measurements
3. Determine the percentage of the population to be accommodated
4. Determine the percentile value of the selected anthropometric dimension
5. Make necessary design modifications to the data from the anthropometric data
6. Use mock-ups or simulators to test the design

Source: Adapted from Roebuck et al (1975)

such as sex, gender, class or disability, might shape such interactions, and with what effects. The method also ignores, or, at least, fails to articulate, the importance of cognitive and behavioural stimuli, including the role of emotions, in shaping a person's experiences of, and interactions with, buildings. The approach is also static in its prior determination of who the user is, when it can never be clear what type of user will transpire to interact with the built environment.

Anthropometric methodologies and methods dominate the limited design education that building professionals are given in relation to bodies and buildings. They encourage the construction of buildings and spaces that, designed around criteria that conform to an 'average fit', create misfitting spaces, or buildings and places that fail to fit or respond to a host of different users and/or forms of interactions with the built environment (Lynch, 1981). For particular people with bodies that misfit, the experience of interacting with buildings and the environment can be profound, even sometimes life-threatening. One example is the imposition of 'normalised time' in the construction and operation of highways, in which crossing points for pedestrians operate according to a conception of how long it takes for the anthropometrically measured body to cross a road. Similar temporal rhythms are evident in relation to a host of other urban infrastructure, such as the opening and closing of automatic doors on train carriages.

In both instances, people's abilities to cross a road, or access a train, are shaped, in part, by a remote process in which someone, somewhere, inputs data to regulate the temporal rhythms of infrastructure in ways that impose a standard and regularise time. Such temporality may be indifferent to the contrasting bodily capabilities of people, and for those with particular neurological conditions, such as obsessional slowness, the rhythms of a place can create anxiety and stress (Lam et al, 2008). For others, such as one of my research subjects, Reiko, getting on and off the metro trains requires her to be well organised by ensuring that she is standing in the right location on the platform prior to the train turning up. As she said: "I need to navigate myself to the point near where the doors will open, as if I'm standing any distance from them, there's not enough time for me to get into the carriage, the doors open and close too quickly."

Reiko's experiences reflect the application of a rationality primarily concerned with the speed and efficiency of motorised movement, which, in doing so, places particular kinds of bodies in danger. Bradbury and Cumber (2014) note that the time to cross controlled pedestrian crossing points in London was reduced to six seconds at 568 locations between 2010 and 2014. Research shows that such timings are impossible for many people to attain, and that this puts them into dangerous situations, and this is particularly so for children and people with visual and mobility impairments (Asher et al, 2012). The technology can induce people to try and 'beat' the time, or otherwise to use other, non-controlled parts of the road (Lupton et al, 2002). In using a local crossing point where I live, I recorded in my research diary the gauntlet of traversing it as a 'stressful and difficult process that gives priority to cars and leaves the most vulnerable, the pedestrian, at risk' (see Figure 8.4).

Such situations reflect the design and construction of spaces around a mobile, agile body, assumed by building practitioners to be the embodiment of normality and the benchmark for the construction of space. While infrastructure that accommodates the normal, mobile body may work well for those with the requisite sensory capacities, for others, from autistic

Figure 8.4: A crossing point in Esher, without pedestrian controls

Source: Rob Imrie

to vision-impaired and deaf people, it can be destructive of any 'sense of meaning' and undermine or reduce a person's capacity to make sense of their surroundings. For Mensch (2008: 4), the undoing of 'the role of the bodily "I can" in making sense of our surrounding world' is akin to a violation of, and against, the body. One of my research subjects, Elaine, described the emotional turmoil after her employer refused to adapt the workplace to accommodate her increasing reliance on a wheelchair: "The place wasn't built for wheelchairs, the able-bodied people there couldn't be arsed with the likes of me, I was a hindrance … my illness was getting worse and I was getting to do less and less things."

For Elaine, with a progressive, deteriorating motor disease, the design of her work environment was the embodiment of "people who don't have any sense of what it's like to lose the ability to walk". She felt the place was "built without much thought" and "badly organised and managed", and for her, the environment was a series of spaces that were hostile and not amenable to ease of use. The spaces were not only redolent of a physicality that resisted her attempts to use the place, but also illustrative of a sociocultural value set akin to what Bourdieu (1998) refers to as symbolic violence. Such violence is never physical, but subtle, coded signifiers of the order of things, or the imposition of the norms of a dominant group over those who have less social power. Elaine, while critical of the work environment, felt that it was nothing out of the ordinary to be confronted with physical barriers, saying: "I face restrictions on my movement everywhere; it's just the way things are."

Elaine's attitude revealed a weariness in trying to challenge and change a building culture that appears indifferent to the multiplicities of ways that people may choose to interact with(in) the built environment. Such indifference reflects, in part, the broader educational, pedagogical environments that builders and others are exposed to, in which teaching about (dis)abled embodiment, design and construction is rare and restricted to conveying dimensional standards relating to the size and structure of buildings. Little is taught about the interrelationships between mental health, emotions and the nature of building, or the interdependencies between space, senses and bodily comfort. Much of the constructed environment is conceived by using one- and two-dimensional drawing and computer graphics, in which interactions between users and artefacts are desensitised to the body. The body is otherwise rendered subservient to abstract, computer models that degrade, even eliminate, the sensory complexities of bodily–environmental interactions.

This translates into building projects that pose challenges to the ever-changing nature of bodies. One example is the emergence of the interior 'fitted environment', or the creation of a fixity in how places are crafted and built. Interior spaces are usually designed to conceal the working elements of a building by hiding stuff out of sight in order to create a sense of ordered and uncluttered space. From water pipes to gas boilers and electric wires, the infrastructure necessary for the functioning of buildings is often embedded under concrete, or encased in plasterboard, and only accessible if building parts are dismantled and/or destroyed. This is a 'tight-fit functionalism' that predefines and presets the uses of space, and it ossifies the spaces of a building (Rabeneck et al, 1973). Such functionalism has the potential to inhibit how people can live, while creating layers of complexity in servicing the built environment.

Interior design often has a fixity that may force people to adapt their bodies to enable the ease of use of facilities. An example is a cafe I visited in Copenhagen in June 2014, in which the seats and tables were bolted to the floor and could not be moved. The seats were a fixed distance from the tabletops and the floor, and from my observations, I felt they would be a tight squeeze for people whose bodies are larger than average; for people of short stature, they would be impossible to sit on. I noted in my research diary that 'they do not permit people to face each other and conversations have to be conducted sideways on, and groups of more than three people are not able to sit and converse with any ease'. There was no evidence of demountable or interchangeable elements, and no flexibility in relation to changing the use of the space. In my diary, I observed that 'the seats are poorly arranged and they won't let people be spontaneous, you can't move them about, and they are uncomfortable to sit on and they control every aspect of my body'.

The fixity of the cafe's seats, and the forcing of my body to fit them, is illustrative of a broader debilitating culture in which building and construction has the capacity to render bodies 'less than able' by impacting on the body's physiological performance and well-being. This is particularly to the fore in relation to the rise of passive bodies relating to the obesity epidemic, in which the design and construction of spaces is implicated in minimising bodily effort, or the usage of body parts, in engaging with the environment (Booth et al, 2005). From the installation of lifts, escalators and walkways in buildings to encourage people to minimise their walking, to the construction of roads to enable ease of access to places by motor vehicles, the built environment is, increasingly, using technology in design and construction to create inactive spaces, or environs that reduce bodily exertion and effort (see Figure 8.5). The implication is the (re)production of inert bodies, or bodily interactions that render the body less than active and static.

This technologisation of building reflects, in part, the modernist ethos of seeking to control nature, or, in this instance, bodily movement and physical exertion. Moore (2012: 19) refers to the disembodied experiences inbuilt into

Figure 8.5: The moving pavement, Chicago

Note: The first electric moving pavement, or sidewalk, was built for, and exhibited at, the 1893 Columbian Exposition in Chicago. It could carry up to 6,000 people, with a maximum speed of 6 mph.

Source: https://upload.wikimedia.org/wikipedia/commons/thumb/e/ef/The_Moving_ Sidewalk_On_Pier_—_Official_Views_Of_The_World%27s_Columbian_Exposition_—_83_ %28cropped%29.jpg/1280px-The_Moving_Sidewalk_On_Pier_—_Official_Views_Of_The_ World%27s_Columbian_Exposition_—_83_%28cropped%29.jpg

modernist Dubai, where he regards the built environment as engaging the eye 'but not the body'. People's sensual interactions with the environment are mediated by a range of denaturalised artifices, in which, as Moore (2012: 19) suggests, 'you are not invited to move through' the buildings 'unless by lift or escalator'. The body is controlled by the direction of moving walkways that do not encourage spontaneous engagement with the environment. The sensations of the natural environment are suppressed, and by entering Dubai's buildings, one encounters 'mechanical clamminess', in which 'climate is an awkwardness, to be banished by air conditioning' (Moore, 2012: 19).

These observations draw attention to the broader, sensory impacts of building, in which the construction of environments, both the process and the end product, is poorly understood in relation to its bodily effects, particularly in relation to mental health and well-being. There is a plethora of literature about sick building syndrome, and an understanding that construction noise and the materials used in a building, such as particular colour schemes, can influence people's feelings about, and engagement with, specific spaces (see, for example, Lahtinen et al, 1998). For people with autism and other neurological conditions, the physical form of buildings and spaces is integral to feelings and emotions; yet, much of the constructed environment is chaotic and jumbled, lacking legibility or any sense of clarity and calmness. For many people, the construction process is disruptive and a sensory overload, and for autistic people, there is little thought about how to build a place that enhances acoustic qualities, while minimising noise and using natural, earthly light.

Instead, the construction process pays lip service to guidance and advice about how to craft places that respond to human sensibilities and scale, and there is continuous output of unattractive and ill-fitting buildings and spaces that fail to engage with the socio-psychological needs of people. The economics of building, with the emphasis on quantity and throughput of output, undermines attention to design detail and the micro-relations between bodies and buildings. Building culture is characterised by social hierarchies that tend to impose form, with limited user input or scope to enable self-build. This is not a democratic or open process, and it is compounded by the reproduction of building types that are directive of how to inhabit and embody a place, which, as the New Zealand examples illustrate, ignore sociocultural variations and changes in lifestyle. Building types are inimical to a progressive, bodily-centred approach to building and construction, with the question outstanding: how might it be possible for it to be otherwise?

Constructing otherwise for inclusion: three examples

A genre of writers and commentators lament the poor quality of buildings and the construction of spaces that fail to respond to the diverse needs of people (Turner, 1976; Habraken, 2005). This has led to numerous sketches of what ought to be different and how changes in the social relations of design and construction, and the values of building professionals, can proffer alternative, more progressive, ways of designing and building (Lynch, 1981; Papanek, 1984). A common observation is by Papanek (1984: ix–x), who suggests that there is a 'need for high social and moral responsibility' on the part of building professionals to 'stop defiling the earth itself with poorly designed objects and structures'. Others have argued for an open, people-focused process, ranging from FLW (Lloyd Wright, 1932: 300), who commented on the importance of engaging in 'democratic building [that] belongs to the people', to John Turner (1976), who campaigned to promote self-build housing and localised, vernacular design and building.

In their different ways, both Turner and FLW were set against a building culture that, through the economies of standardisation and the formulaic use of materials, was impervious to the multiple ways in which people experience, and interact with, the built environment. FLW (Lloyd Wright, 1908) felt that such experience was specific to individuals, and that this ought to be the basis for achieving a quality of building but was usually ignored by builders imposing a formal architectural order. This, for FLW (Lloyd Wright, 1908), was akin to building without integrity and unlikely to provide an environment that would work well for people. Instead, writers have pointed to the importance of flexible and open building, and the use of materials and processes that enable multiple uses of spaces, as well as the scope for ease of adaptability and change. Since the late 1950s, debates about supportive architecture, social design and, latterly, inclusive building and construction have come to the fore, and each, in different ways, point to the observations of people like FLW in seeking to create inclusive spaces that work well for everyone.

In the rest of the chapter, I consider three examples of 'inclusive construction' that, in their contrasting styles, seek to respond to the multiplicity of ways in which people interact with the built environment. Inclusive construction can be understood as a process that is customised and human-focused, being shaped by a political critique of conventional building. The process has an ethical and political commitment to body-centred design and the construction of buildings and infrastructure that are legible, meaningful and usable to people, irrespective of their bodily capacities and capabilities. Unlike much contemporary construction, which rarely future-proofs buildings or thinks beyond their immediate uses, inclusive construction is premised on adaptable, flexible and demountable fixtures and fittings, permitting future interventions to enable the redesign and ease of adaptation and reuse of a space.

In discussing these ideas, I draw on data derived from a European Research Council project that I directed between 2013 and 2016.[3] The project's aim was to explore practitioners' involvement in the construction of the built environment, evaluating how far their design and building practices were attuned to, and responsive towards, the complexities of the body. I draw on the ideas and work of three designers involved in the building process in, respectively, the UK, the US and Australia. I demonstrate the contrasting ways in which their ethical and political commitment to creating inclusive places was foregrounded and significant to the outcomes. In each instance, there is evidence of sensitivity towards the creation of caring spaces by identifying, and acting on, the fragile interdependencies between people and objects. This shows attentiveness to, and responsibility for, how the different elements of design and construction ought to come together as practical, body-sensitive projects.

Creating spaces of play and interaction with nature

The coming of modernity and the industrial age is associated with the emergence of a highly mobile and active society, with people forever on the move, restless and jumbled together in what often appear to be chaotic circumstances. Berman (1982: 16) refers to the maelstrom of modernity to describe the 'moving chaos' of the streets and the 'perpetual disintegration and renewal' of places, including the speeding up of 'the whole tempo of life'. For Berman (1982), there is a constant upheaval and a sensory overload, characterised by the sounds, sights and smells of the environment, or what Mansell (2016: back cover) refers to as 'the sonic maelstrom of mechanized society'. A significant part of this is the continuous construction of buildings and infrastructure, and the never-ending sounds of loud and intrusive mechanical devices, from piling rigs and digging machines, to machinery for garden maintenance, such as leaf blowers and lawnmowers.

This is compounded by the dominance of the environment by roads, in which no one is far from the noises and smells of motorised transport, or the dangers they pose to pedestrians and other users. The first element of building projects is to (re)construct roads and to insinuate the motor vehicle into the environment, a process particularly evident in newly built housing estates, or domestic spaces constructed, purportedly, for retreat and rest. By the early 20th century, commentators were characterising the coming of motor vehicles as heralding the 'age of noise' (Whyte, 1932). For Huxley (1930), the new mechanical age was a tipping point in society that was leading to a diminution in human happiness, a narrative that has since become important in thinking about the interrelationships between buildings, mental health and well-being. Evans (2003), like others, notes that much of the constructed environment is inimical to mental health, and that the key challenge is to create spaces of calmness and repose.

This observation is to the fore in the work of the landscape architect Mike Westley (MW), who specialises in inclusive design and building relating to care and learning environments, including hospitals, gardens, play spaces and schools.[4] MW is knowledgeable about the interrelationships between disability, sensory perception and mental and emotional health, and his work with the UK's Sensory Trust, coupled with his landscape architectural background, provides the basis for his commitment to designing environments that accentuate the positive well-being effects of access to good-quality landscapes (Landscape Institute, 2013). This is particularly

Figure 8.6: The Inclusive Design Play Space

Source: Rob Imrie

evident in his design of the Royal Cornwall Hospital Inclusive Design Play Space, known as 'Play 4 Life', a project based in Truro in the UK (see Figure 8.6). The play space was commissioned in 2007 and completed in 2012, and is described by MW as a "diverse landscape [to] entertain, inspire and absorb the users, taking them out of the hospital environment and into the world of their own imagination".

The rationale of the play space was to create a series of outdoor 'interlocking rooms', or environs, in which, for MW, "children, their families and carers could find a place of respite", and where clinicians can interact with them by engaging in "therapeutic horticulture, or therapeutic activity in a green space". In distinction to mainstream construction, it was important to ensure the space was accessible to all, or, as MW said, to facilitate "equal alternatives, not necessarily designing down to a common level of ability to enjoy, but to try and build, wherever possible, alternative approaches to enjoying the same basic elements". Prior to its construction, the play space was a car park, a hostile space defined by concrete and continuous vehicle movements. Now, the space has easy access for wheelchair users, play facilities that people with mobility impairments can use, soft, rubberised paving, a wide range of rest areas and seating options, and an abundance of planting, including what MW described as a sensory "plant trail that people can follow while in the space".

For MW, it was important to design tactility into the play spaces to provide a "strong sensory experience which takes the user into an inspiring space, the world of the garden". The pathways use recycled rubber called tiger mulch, which, as MW said, is "a fantastically interesting thing to walk on … and the path changes to gravel and means that there is a story of texture through the feet going on". The space uses a multitude of plants to provide a range of textures and smells that, for MW, give "people a chance to reach out in a tactile way, to navigate themselves around the space". The gardens have an intuitive route through them, characterised by what MW described as the "repetition of its curves and of the verticals". This was part of the design intent to provide a flow but also a sense of legibility, and to take people on a journey through the site. As a place of repose and recovery, the therapeutic nature of the space was crucial, as MW said, "to provide people who come here from the stroke recovery unit and who work on reacquainting themselves with their senses and with their balance … and take time out away from it".

The project is a reaction and challenge to the denaturalisation of environments, and an attempt to provide a restorative and playful environment with a combination of areas, some for seclusion, and others to be part of the public, collective presence that the spaces encourage. Figure 8.7 shows one of two 'willow domes' or 'small rooms' that, for MW, enable people "to find a sense of release or seclusion at any one time". The 'willow rooms', when in full summer greenery, are concealed from general view, and, as MW said, "It is a favourite space for teenage children in the summer months, where hammocks are hung within the willow domes, there will be covers over the top of them to guard against summer showers and there is an element of den building, and just hanging out and chilling out." MW described the multifunctionality of the rooms, in that "Musicians, entertainers, people will be here at different times, food is eaten here, celebrations made here."

The garden is inspired by a literature about how the thoughtful design of play spaces can encourage both children's and adults' engagement in play, and help with recovery. Thought has gone into the provision of both natural and sculptural elements that, for MW, create a "playable landscape which isn't overtly a playground" (Nestor and Moser, 2018). Figure 8.8 shows sculptural objects that MW described as having multidimensional qualities, as they "are themselves seating elements, climbing elements, visual stimulation elements, there is a glass set within them, people knock sticks against them and play them like musical instruments, giant glockenspiels". The idea was to create objects that would encourage interaction with the landscape, and "To have

Figure 8.7: One of the interlocking rooms

Source: Rob Imrie

Figure 8.8: The sculptural garden

Source: Rob Imrie

things which weren't totally expressly about play elements, but which had a playful nature to them." For MW, the objective is to take "people out of their world of illness", to reduce negative feelings and emotions, and to provide a place in which anxiety is managed, even dispelled.

The play space garden is an exemplar of principles that design and construction practices ought to imbibe. The space was conceived from an in-depth collaborative engagement between MW, hospital managers, nursing staff and, crucially, patients, including children; it was not an imposed space. The space challenges conventional building wisdom about stasis and permanence, or that an environment has a fixity or finality, and it does this, primarily, by the seasonality constructed into the gardens and a continual reworking of the planting, including changes to the layout and the introduction of new plants. There is incompleteness to the space that provides scope for user interventions to change it. The space comprises visual and sound barriers that enable a masking of the environment beyond it, and it contains elements that stimulate the emotions. It is far from the deadened space of much contemporary building and construction.

Breaking the box and the significance of organic building

The dwelling is the most significant building that people occupy, yet the design and construction of domestic space leaves a lot to be desired. Most older housing stock is unable to cater for people ageing in place, and newer, volume-build dwellings, while providing statutory elements such as downstairs toilets, are often part of charmless, edge-of-town environments disconnected from services, and places that encourage the use of motor vehicles as the main means of mobility. Volume house builders tend to construct dwellings for an idealised, nuclear family that, if it ever did exist, does not reflect the make-up or fluidity of contemporary households, or the varied and changing ways that people seek to use domestic spaces. Place Alliance (2020: 8), in a national audit of UK-based house builders, notes that most new dwellings are poorly designed, of mediocre quality and usually constructed amid 'unattractive and unfriendly environments dominated by large areas of hard surfaces'.

These observations are not new, but part of a long-standing critique of the volume house-building industry. In the early 20th century, the American architect FLW (Lloyd Wright, 1932), described the modern house as formulaically designed and an affront to human dignity, noting that the form and structure of most buildings was to make the human being feel insignificant. For FLW (Lloyd Wright, 1954: 14), the modern dwelling was 'readymade architecture' that was 'stuck up in thoughtless fashion', creating buildings in which 'houses are more boxes than homes'. The box was a building that was enclosed, confined the user and failed to relate to, or be part of, the outside, or interlinked with nature. Edward Tafel (1979: 44), who worked closely with FLW, echoes his reference to the mass construction of housing as large boxes 'broken up into small rooms, not very comfortable … and laid out with almost no regard for actual human needs and patterns of living'.

These views were the basis of FLW's approach to design and building. He espoused the importance of craftwork and customisation, including the rejection of building by code. The modern house was the antithesis of craftwork, an incongruous object and impervious to its setting. It had 'no sense of space … the thing was more a hive than a home' (Lloyd Wright, 1954: 14). For FLW (Lloyd Wright, 1932: 177–8), the 'typical dwelling' was ill fitting for people because it had no 'appropriate sense of proportion whatever … all materials looked alike to it or to anything or anybody in it'. What was required was an organic architecture, or an approach to construction in which 'the size of the human figure should fix every proportion of a dwelling, or of anything in it. Human scale was true building scale' (Lloyd Wright, 1954: 16). This was a guiding idea for FLW (Lloyd Wright, 1932: 145): 'human use and comfort should have intimate possession of every interior … [and] should be felt in every exterior'.

One of his most interesting works reflecting such views is Jacobs 1, a single-family home located in Madison, Wisconsin, in the US (see Figure 8.9). The dwelling was commissioned by Herbert and Katherine Jacobs in 1935 and completed in 1937, and is based on FLW's understanding that 'the reality of the building consisted not in the four walls and roof, but inhered in the spaces within, the space to be lived in' (Lloyd Wright, 1939: 2–3). The dwelling was crafted as a series of flowing, interlocking spaces, and it was the antithesis of the house 'as a box', or what FLW (Lloyd Wright, 1932: 141) otherwise described as 'cellular sequestration'. Jacobs 1 was the first Usonian house designed by FLW, being an affordable dwelling that, by the measure of other houses he designed, was small, one-storey and constructed on concrete slabs with piping for radiant underfloor heating.[5] Blake (1960: 100) describes the Usonian concept as a 'space-in-continuous-motion', in which, as FLW said, 'let walls, ceilings, floors, now become party to each other but part of each other' (quoted in Silzer, 2019: 1).

This was FLW's (Lloyd Wright, 1932: 162) expression of the principle of plasticity, or, as he said, the 'freedom of floor space and elimination of useless heights … a sense of appropriate freedom'. In the Jacobs 1 house, such plasticity was characterised by the absence of wasted spaces, such as attic voids, or the use of fixed walls and partitions that could otherwise interrupt rhythm and flow. Fixity of structure was anathema to FLW and he never spoke about walls, but rather 'wall screens', to denote the possibilities of ease

Figure 8.9: The exterior of the Herbert and Katherine Jacobs First House, Madison, Wisconsin

Note: The house is called 'Jacobs 1' as it was the first of two dwellings that FLW designed for the Jacobs family.

Source: https://upload.wikimedia.org/wikipedia/commons/8/86/Jacobs_First_House_-_back_02.jpg

of adaptation of a structure to be part of a flexibility of space (Lloyd Wright, 1932). For FLW (Lloyd Wright, 1932), the layout of Jacobs 1, with flows between rooms and the interconnections between its constituent spaces, was integral to its integration, in which there was no value in anything as a singular object, but only as a part of the whole building. FLW (Lloyd Wright, 1932) contrasted the integrative nature of 'good architecture' with the volume housing that he conceived as a collection of disintegrative parts, the garage, the separate living room and the attic void, all constructed without unity, hence no point or purpose.

FLW was the purveyor of bringing the outside into the inside of the dwelling, and creating buildings that were more or less indistinguishable from their surroundings. He explained this as the dissolution of walls, or 'space not walled in now but more or less free to appear ... the interior space opening to the outside and see the outside coming in' (Lloyd Wright, 1954: 75). The flat roofs and horizontal lines of some of his dwellings were an attempt to design them as extensions of the earth and indissoluble from the ground. Facilitating natural artifices, such as air and sunlight, was important in embedding the building into its environment, and for FLW

Figure 8.10: Graycliff, Buffalo, USA

Note: Graycliff was designed by FLW and constructed between 1926 and 1931. The main building pictured here enables people to see through the house from one side to the other, and for those living in the dwelling, to feel as though they are enveloped by outside space.

Source: Rob Imrie

(Lloyd Wright, 1954: 112), this was important as people 'derive countenance and sustenance from the "atmosphere" of the things they live in and with'. This reflected FLW's (Lloyd Wright, 1931) belief that 'light is the beautifier of the building', an idea that he translated into the use of large windows, often floor to ceiling, to bring people 'face to face with nature's play of shade and depth of shadow' (see Figure 8.10).

In contrast to the imposition of a style or house type that, for FLW (Lloyd Wright, 1954: 167), stifled living, his dwellings were designed to be lived in throughout the life course, and, as FLW (Lloyd Wright, 1932) noted, the house 'can, without deformity, be expanded, later, for the needs of a growing family'. There was a bodily sensitivity to FLW's conception of the spaces in insisting that 'windows and doors [be] lowered to convenient human heights' (Lloyd Wright, 1932: 143), and for floors to be kept free of carpets and steps that would otherwise impede ease of mobility and movement (see Figure 8.11). This is illustrative of an ethical sensibility towards people's interrelationships with the environment, and reflective of FLW's understanding that the objective of building is to 'give dignity to daily life' (Lloyd Wright, 1932: 333). Such dignity, for FLW (Lloyd Wright, 1932), was unlikely to be provided by the building industry, but instead required flexible forms of standardisation that, as Boyd and Pfeiffer (2007) note, rejected 'average' form in favour of materials with flexibility in use to enable people to adjust them to suit their needs.

Figure 8.11: The living room of Jacobs 1

Note: The Jacobs 1 living room is spacious and enables ease of flow and movement.
Source: https://upload.wikimedia.org/wikipedia/commons/e/ec/Jacobs_First_House_-_living_room_02.jpg

FLW's architecture contrasts with contemporary design and construction by working closely with the building's context to ensure that there is a symbiosis between the environmental setting, particularly the landscape, and the constructed artefact. For FLW (Lloyd Wright, 1932: 490), house types were anathema to the crafting of a vernacular, quality building; as he observed, 'style is important. A style is not.' He rejected waste and the use of superfluous materials in a building, and derided an excess of consumption, as a house 'should be simple, containing as few rooms as will meet the conditions under which you live' (Lloyd Wright, 1932: 21). FLW (Lloyd Wright, 1932: 474) conceived of his dwellings as a sensuous, sensory experience, receptive to the body and crafted as 'a democratic building', not imposed or handed down, but responding to 'the inner vision' of inhabitants. The speculative dwelling was anything but this, and for FLW (Lloyd Wright, 1932: 313), it was the 'death of the soul' and the killing of 'any imaginative spirit'.

Constructing spaces to enhance mental health and well-being

Beyond responding to basic human requirements for sufficient lighting, heating and toilet and washing facilities, buildings are rarely constructed with people's diverse bodily needs in mind. This is particularly so in relation to mental health and well-being. Building practitioners have limited knowledge of, or training about, the interrelationships between a building's form and materiality, and people's sensory and cognitive functioning. There is a literature that draws attention to the sensual nature of a building, in which its smells, sounds and textures, and the immediate environment, are implicated in bodily reactions and feelings, including people's emotional and mental well-being. For instance, Hoisington et al (2019) note that while building occupants' mental health is enhanced by access to nature and natural light and air, many buildings are synthetic and denaturalised, sealed from outdoor elements, and dependent for their functioning on artificial sources of light and atmosphere.

Noise is also a major source of mental health issues, with buildings constructed close to sources of vehicular movement and comprising materials that do not prevent sound transmission, with consequences for sleep disturbance (Dzhambov and Lercher, 2019). Sensory stimuli of this type are relevant to a growing cohort of the population, that is, people with autism, who are sensitive to sounds, touch, tastes, smells, light, colours and temperatures. Autism is described by the National Autistic Society (2020) as a 'developmental disability', or a neurological condition that can affect how people communicate, interact, behave and learn. Humphreys (2008) notes that the qualities of space that work well for autistic people include calmness, order and simplicity, minimal materials and detail, the use of natural light, and good acoustics. These qualities are missing from much of the built environment, and evidence suggests that design and related professionals have little or no understanding of how to craft and construct buildings with reference to the needs of autistic people, or anyone with neurological or cognitive impairments (see Humphreys, 2008).

Rather, the design and construction of spaces is inimical to easing sensory overloads, and may exacerbate sensual stimuli, destabilising people with a range of cognitive impairments. This understanding informs the work of the Australian architect Paul Hede (PH), who is well known for his pioneering design in relation to autism and the built environment.[6] He has a significant portfolio and was directly involved in the design and construction of schools in the state of Victoria, Australia, that cater for autistic children, including the Northern School for Autism, the Western Autistic School and the Eastern Ranges School. Each school exemplifies how learning and teaching spaces can be designed to respond to the needs of children with autism, while highlighting key principles of good design in relation to the construction of spaces that work well not only for autistic people, but for everyone.

The starting point for PH is an attentiveness to the multi-sensory nature of the body, and the significance of embodiment in how people make sense of the world. In a wide-ranging interview I conducted with PH, he outlined some of his thinking and noted the complexity of the subject matter, in that

"Some people with autism are hypersensitive to sensory inputs, such as sound and light, while others are hyposensitive, and need plenty of stimulation to be comfortable." He amplified by highlighting the challenges of designing for autistic schoolchildren, noting that they are not a singular grouping, or, as he said, "It's not a homogeneous set of kids we're designing for, it's a range." This encompasses a broad base of behaviour and, as PH observed, autistic people "like order, they like things in place, they can overreact to sound, light, flickering, they can be prone to self-stimulation, running off patterns and things like that, air-conditioning sounds can drive them mad, they can get frustrated and lash out on someone".

Much of the modern world is designed and constructed in ways likely to accentuate the problems that autistic people experience in interacting with the environment, and for PH, the challenge in designing the schools was to ensure that they were flexibly designed to respond to the range of autistic children and their needs. As PH said, "It's important for them to be able to adjust the space in order to cope with it, or to enjoy it, or expand it or whatever, and adjustability is the thing, is key." This overarching idea was an integral part of the design of the Northern School for Autism located in the suburbs of Melbourne (see Figure 8.12). The classrooms have a series of spaces to cater for how autistic children choose to interact with teachers and the learning process, including a high- and low-ceilinged space, accentuated corners in some classrooms, a quiet work room, a discreet outdoor courtyard, and a kitchenette. As PH said, "You're giving them choices about the amount of connection that they have, so although they're in an included environment, they can leave it, they can go outside, into other places ... the school scales down from larger general spaces to small learning nooks."

This freedom for children to move and wander, and to manage their bodily feelings, is enhanced by the subdivision of the school into separate sub-schools that, as PH (quoted in Bozikovic, 2015: 1) describes, provides them with 'access to controlled separated play areas via courtyards attached to their learning areas ... and little spaces that children feel happy in and can control'. The provision of these diverse spaces ensures that the children have a degree of choice over how, and in what ways, they wish to be part of the school environment. Part of the design rationale is that, as PH observed, "A space has got to offer the opportunities for a student to be included on the basis that they feel comfortable." This requires a flexibility of design, and the understanding of staff, to facilitate how an individual student is able to engage with the learning environment. As PH said, for students, it means " 'I can go over here', and 'I can sit here', and 'I don't have to have anybody looking at me that way' and 'I don't want to look at them'."

The school embodies the idea that a 'sense of place' should not only be perceptible with the eyes, but also perceived by all of the senses. For

Figure 8.12: Northern School for Autism – an aerial view (top) and the learning area (bottom)

Source: PH

PH, designing a school environment to work well with the multi-sensory nature of the body is paramount to good design, particularly in relation to colour, sunlight and air. The Northern School for Autism features a central courtyard, and natural sunlight is able to penetrate all parts of the building, providing warmth and a connection with nature (see Figure 8.13).

Figure 8.13: Northern School for Autism – internal junior courtyard

Source: PH

The architecture makes students aware of the natural environment, as PH noted, "We wanted to get the direct sun, that north sun, so it didn't have to be an air-conditioned building. It had to be a highly natural environment that children can feel comfortable in." Colour has also been used, carefully employing subdued colours as a calming mechanism because, as PH said, "We want them to learn and feel that the school is a relaxing place, we want them to feel calm." In contrast, the Western Autistic School has strong colour to prepare students to move to mainstream schools, whereas students at the Northern School for Autism are likely to remain there for their entire career.

There is an inclusivity here that responds to the diverse needs of schoolchildren with autism. For PH, the schools provide safe, secure, flexible and sensory-attuned spaces, and environments designed around autistic people's perceptions of the world. This is a sensory, bodily architecture that propagates the understanding that for a building to work well, designed space needs to intercede with, and respond to, what Norberg-Schultz (1988: 29) terms 'psychological nature', or the existential, bodily needs of people. This intercession between the environment and people's socio-psychological perceptions and behaviour is palpably missing in contemporary building projects. PH's approach to design and environment provides cues and impetus for a different approach to building. By placing sensory experiences at the fulcrum of his work, PH imparts not only a critique of disembodiment by design, but also a positive redirection for practitioners to attend to the interrelationships between body, cognition and environment as the basis for the design and construction of the built environment.

Conclusion

The buildings and the spaces that people inhabit are integral to their functioning and well-being, yet there is evidence that much of the built environment fails to provide the support and the care that is required to live well. There is often a dissonance between constructed environments and basic biological functioning, characterised by the design of places that are not well attuned to natural bodily rhythms, such as 'sleeping and waking, alertness and inattention' (Lynch, 1981: 122). The layout of new housing estates is an example in which the failure to separate motor vehicles from where people rest and retreat from the world can create noise and disruption to patterns of sleep. The design of environments includes steps and gradients that prevent people with mobility impairments from accessing places, and many public buildings are designed without good acoustics and means for ease of use by vision-impaired people. The design of the built environment also encourages physical inactivity, and so is implicated in the emergent obesity epidemic.

The predominant approach to construction is the design of functional spaces that respond to predefined uses, and users, shaped by tried-and-tested design templates relating to building form and performance. These templates rarely refer to the human body or acknowledge the complexities relating to how people interact with(in) the manifold elements of the designed environment. Where the body is referred to, it is usually a reductive description of bodily form, or an opaque, caricatured conception that conceives of the human being as a uniform type, and a passive, one-dimensional figure, bereft of sensory complexity. These conceptions shape practices that perpetrate social inequalities and unfairness by design because they do not respond to, or respect, the feelings of people whose bodily capacities and capabilities do not conform with or fit into the bodily type. By failing to acknowledge, and respond to, bodily diversity, building practitioners are implicated in the perpetuation of immoral spaces, or environs that constrain life opportunities and choices.

In contrast, the potential for the design and construction of environments to liberate and be life affirming is the message of the three cases outlined in the chapter. Each highlights the problems of reductive conceptions of the body, and the importance of re-establishing a body-centric approach to the design and construction of the built environment. FLW conceives of building as reacting against a synthetic architecture, and sees the importance of creating an organic symbiosis between nature and the built environment. Here, the body is in, and of, or integral to, whatever is designed. MW relates such ideas to the spiritual and emotional dimensions of life in relation to the caring potential of play space, or environs that provide respite and calmness, and a distancing from the sensory overload of much of the constructed environment. PH highlights the normality of cognitive and mental issues, and the need for building practitioners to develop some understanding of the neurological and socio-psychological implications of design.

The cases point towards the importance of building and construction starting with the body as the key point of reference, and asking questions about the interrelationships between the bodily senses, emotions and the design and performance of the built environment. This reflects Merleau Ponty's (1962: 206) understanding about the body that 'we are in the world through our body', and, as such, it is through the body that our experiences of buildings and spaces are manifest. The case studies reflect this understanding, and also that bodies are not static objects, but dynamic and self-conscious, and interact with designed objects in unpredictable ways. A difficult but necessary challenge for design and building practitioners is to incorporate biodynamic functioning into the design and construction of the built environment by engaging with the complexity of ways in which bodies interact with(in) space. To do so is an important part of practitioners acknowledging their ethical and moral responsibilities towards crafting a caring and responsible environment.

9

Constructing for Species Survival

Introduction

There is much awareness of the harm caused by construction to the environment but little that is being done to prevent or mitigate it. While politicians and the executives of leading corporate organisations deliberate and debate about the effects of building, their inaction is evident by the acceleration in global construction activity, including significant increases in the rates of material extraction, use of energy and deterioration of the earth's ecological and environmental systems. From Amazonia to Indonesia, vast tracts of land are being laid to waste to provide raw materials for construction and the trappings of Western lifestyles. The destruction of tropical forests is generating one of the largest mass extinctions to beset the earth, with, as Weisse and Goldman (2020: 1) note, the tropics having lost 11.9 million hectares of tree cover in 2019. Much of this was used in building projects, ranging from the construction of walls, floors and ceilings, to the reconstruction of boardwalks in US beach resorts (Rainforest Relief, 2013).

The loss of habitat and biodiversity is referred to by some observers as 'ecocide', or a process of widespread, global devastation and destruction of ecological systems (Higgins, 2010). Construction is at the forefront of ecocide and asset raiding the natural world, and in places like Amazonia, the demand by the building industry for its products is interlinked with land grabs, illegal logging and mining, and threats to the lives and habitation of indigenous people (Funes, 2019). Viana (1998, quoted in Taccioni et al, 2003: 8) estimates that in the 1990s, over 80 per cent of logging in Amazonia was illegal, with large quantities of timber sent to reputable building contractors, particularly relating to hardwood flooring. The US company LL Floorings, formerly Lumber Liquidators Flooring, is one of many that have flouted laws relating to the illegal importation of hardwoods, and in 2015, it was fined US$13.15 million by the US federal government for using timber that had not been sourced by legal means (US Department of Justice, 2016).

The actions of LL Floorings and countless other building contractors are implicated in a global supply chain that is depleting resources and despoiling the environment. Oil is one of the major, non-renewable resources consumed by the building industry, and, as Trubiano et al (2019: 1) suggest, 'nearly everything in our built environment is permeated by chemicals derived from fossil fuels'. This ranges from the use of unplasticised polyvinyl chloride (UPVC) in windows and doors, to the fuel used in machinery to excavate sites and construct buildings. Plastics are a particular problem because they are high in embodied energy, that is, the total sum of energy necessary for an entire product lifecycle. They do not waste or decay and cannot be absorbed back into nature. The extraction of oil, the main ingredient in plastics, also leads to thousands of spillages and marine contamination every day, an outcome from which the building industry, and those that consume its products, cannot be absolved.

The reliance of construction on fossil fuels and materials that, in their extraction and use, are a threat to the environment, combined with the effects of building on climate and local micro-ecologies, poses the question of what ought to be done to mitigate the environmental effects of the building industry. In its current form, the operations of the building industry are, potentially, an existential threat to species by the continuous use of non-renewable resources and activities that transmit high levels of carbon dioxide, or gases that contribute to global warming. In the next part of the chapter, I consider how building and construction practices are implicated in environmental change, where the problem is about not only too much construction, but also the forms and types of building activities. These include the processes underpinning the production of the materials used in constructing the built environment, as well as the materials themselves, many of which are chemically treated and processed, and of doubtful ecological value.

I then turn to discuss and evaluate the responses by actors in the building industry to the alleged environmental effects of construction. In recent years, there has been a shift in the attitudes and practices of industry actors, with commentators noting the emergence of green building and construction (Snook, 2018). Many in the building industry have adopted plans to change practices, and there is awareness of the need to reduce carbon footprints by reusing and recycling materials, using water-conserving features, reducing dependence on fossil fuels and harnessing renewable energy sources. I outline and discuss the adaptation of parts of the building industry towards a green agenda, and note that while there are many different initiatives, these are not confronting the crux of the problem of building too much, too badly. Its spokespeople are engaging in 'greenwashing' by making inaccurate and/ or inflated claims about what is possible *within* the current paradigm of building and construction.

I conclude the chapter by asking the question: what can be done to transform the continuous construction of buildings and infrastructure? The environmental impacts of construction cannot be overcome by the judicious management of resources and the development of technology, as claimed by industry spokespeople. This leaves intact the underlying structural dynamic of the construction industry, which is the production of buildings and infrastructure for profit. Unless that dynamic is broken, there is little likelihood of a slowdown, or redirection, of the operations of the industry, and of a reduction in the degradation of nature. What is required is a break with the 'building more' paradigm in favour of an eco-sensitive approach that asks fundamental questions about what a building is for, and for whom. I refer to the ideas of biophilia, or the 'love of nature', as the basis for a new way of building in which nature, and its needs, are placed at the fulcrum of the relationships between people and their inhabitation of the planet.

The unsustainable nature of building

The biggest challenge facing humankind is the survival of the species in a context of the rapid degradation and despoliation of landscapes and environments, including the widespread loss, and extinction, of flora and fauna, and the depletion of the earth's natural resources. Climate change, coupled with the spread of urban settlement, is heightening risks to life and property, and people are increasingly exposed to major, precipitous events, such as floods and fires (Bubeck et al, 2019). Other manifestations of human-induced, environmental crises include: deforestation, in which more than 50 per cent of the planet's mature forests have been cut down; air pollution, which the World Health Organisation (2020) estimates kills 7 million people per year; and the loss and degradation of fresh water supplies (Morris, 2010). These outcomes reflect people's appropriation and reworking of land and its resources, where, as Watts (2019: 1) notes, 'the human footprint is so large it leaves little space for anything else'.

The construction of the built environment is at the forefront of people's deleterious impacts on the planet, and as previous chapters have outlined, it is one of the most destructive human activities and at the heart of the collapse of the world's ecological systems. A variety of data relating to the impact of construction on the environment are alarming, with sources noting that the construction sector is responsible for a quarter of the earth's air pollution, pollutes 40 per cent of its fresh water resources and contributes to over 50 per cent of the content of landfill sites (GoContractor, 2017). The sector's contribution to global warming is significant by the production of buildings that consume large quantities of energy, both in their construction and operation. These operations are typified by large quantities of vehicular movements, the sourcing of products from all over the globe and the liberal use of materials, such as concrete, that have few environmental credentials.[1] These all contribute to an energy-intensive sector, and as the United Nations Environment Programme (2019) estimate, nearly 40 per cent of energy-related greenhouse gas emissions stem from the activities of construction.[2]

These data show that there is no building or construction activity that is not, simultaneously, part of the destruction of specific ecologies and environments. All building, irrespective of where or what it is, intrudes on the character of nature and natural resources, and it changes, often irrevocably, the ecological and environmental qualities of places. It would be misplaced, though, to characterise the relationships between people and nature as though they are divisible and separate. People are part of nature, and in intervening in, and changing, the nature of natural materials, people are acting upon themselves and the habitats and species that they depend on for their survival and well-being. Such actions do not destroy nature per se, but change its form and dynamics in ways that can challenge, even threaten, the survival of species, including the human race. This understanding is helpful for drawing attention to the significance of human actions, and their potential socio-environmental effects, though these are rarely highlighted or featured by the building industry.

The culture of building does little to problematise or question its interrelationships with nature, and building practitioners have, until recently, rarely acknowledged people's dependence on the natural environment or the effects of construction in changing the quality of ecology and environment. Rather, nature has been regarded, primarily, as an infinite resource of raw materials to be exploited and monetised, and used to satisfy human wants and desires. For Milani (2000), the construction industry engages in profligate behaviour by extracting far more from the earth than is used. Over 90 per cent of extracted materials for use in construction are rendered as waste and discarded. The harm done to nature by construction, ranging from the disfigurement of landscapes to the pollution of air and water, is rarely costed or paid for by the building industry, and, as Milani (2000: 18) observes, construction benefits by virtue of the 'use of drastically undervalued nature' (see Figure 9.1).

This undervaluation of nature permeates every aspect of the design and construction of the built environment. From the bulldozers that excavate sites and destroy fragile, biodiverse environments, to the common usage of materials, such as cement, with high levels of embodied energy, the ecological costs of building tend to be regarded as an externality, or necessary by-product, of construction. The disregard and devaluation of nature is evident with unrelenting road building and damage to wild areas. Construction of

Figure 9.1: An abandoned aggregate quarry near Adelaide, Australia

Note: This disused stone quarry lies within the boundaries of Anstey Hill Recreation Park, and it originates from the late 19th century. After its abandonment, it has left scars and the landscape has not been restored to its original state.

Source: https://upload.wikimedia.org/wikipedia/commons/e/e1/Stone_quarry_adelaide.JPG

roads is a catalyst and conduit for further incursions into, and development of, fragile habitats, and research by Ibisch et al (2016) notes that while 80 per cent of the earth's terrestrial surface remains roadless, it is fragmented by roads into 600,000 fragments that are too small to support significant wildlife (see Figure 9.2). For Ibisch et al (2016), places without road networks are quickly disappearing, and with a projected increase of 25 million km of new roads by 2050, there is urgent need, they suggest, to protect and conserve roadless areas.

This pattern of significant threats to, and destruction of, wildlife and flora and fauna is a trademark of major mega-projects, in which there is often disregard by developers of a locale's heritage and the intrinsic ecological qualities of a place. This is evident with the plans for a high-speed rail route in England, the HS2 network (Barkham, 2020). As intimated in Chapter 2, the proposed route will damage or destroy 693 local wildlife sites and up to 108 ancient woodlands that have existed since the early 17th century (Woodland Trust, 2020). These woodlands have 'unique and complex communities of plants, fungi, insects and other microorganisms' that are

Figure 9.2: BR-319 highway, Brazil

Note: The BR-319 highway is 540 miles in length and connects Manaus, Amazonas, to Porto Velho, Rondônia in Brazil. It was completed in 1973, opening up pristine forest to economic exploitation.

Source: https://upload.wikimedia.org/wikipedia/commons/7/79/BR-319_The_road_ahead.jpg

irreplaceable (Woodland Trust, 2020: 1). The Wildlife Trust also note that wetlands, wildflower meadows and historic wood pasture will be lost, and, as a spokesperson for the organisation said, 'HS2 will destroy precious carbon-capturing habitats.... It will damage the very ecosystems that provide a natural solution to the climate emergency' (quoted in Drury, 2020: 1).

The protection and enhancement of ecosystems seems anathema to a culture of building characterised by its propensity to intervene in, and radically transform, nature to create new, modified, naturalised environments that contain the seeds of ecological destruction. The emergence of the air-conditioned building in the mid-20th century illustrates how a technology, the electrically powered air-conditioning unit, transformed the design and construction of the built environment (Cox, 2010). As the epitome of modernity and the quest for the calculability and control of nature, this technology enabled a new type of high-rise environment to emerge in which ambient conditions, relating to air temperature, humidity and quality, were amenable to regulation and control (Graham, 2015). Buildings no longer had to let the outside in, or subject people to poor air quality or fluctuations in temperatures, and people's levels of comfort were not dependent on the whims of nature, or the natural rhythms of the climate.

The air-conditioned and controlled building has come to dominate major cities, and, as Sisson (2017: 1) suggests, 'the great commercial buildings of the modern era owe their existence to air conditioning'. By cooling the air inside a building, air conditioning is, simultaneously, warming the air outside the building, and by the beginning of the 21st century, air-conditioned environments were a major source of carbon emissions and global warming (Buranyi, 2019). Sisson (2017: 1) notes that by 2014, 87 per cent of US homes 'had some form of air conditioning', which was contributing 500 million metric tons of carbon emissions annually. There are more than 1.6 billion air-conditioning units in use globally, a figure projected to increase to 5.6 billion by 2050, partly to offset and combat the rise in temperatures due to global warming (Dean et al, 2018). This illustrates the paradoxical nature of designing a built environment that by rendering buildings impermeable to the outside environment, creates a dependence for its functioning on an ecologically destructive technology.

This paradox is at the heart of the culture of building that in distancing itself from the construction of environments that depend on the use of materials with little or no embodied energy, has created places that function primarily by technological means and the use of high levels of energy expenditure. The history of urbanisation is the production of the energy-intensive city, from road networks that encourage the consumption of fossil fuels and the transmission of toxic gases, to the rapid growth in the construction of tall buildings that require large quantities of energy to function. These buildings, such as Chicago's Willis Tower, increasingly dominate cityscapes, and, as Saroglou et al (2017) suggest, they consume more energy than low-rise buildings due to the reliance on lifts and use of energy to pump water to high elevations (see Figure 9.3). Godoy-Shimizu et al's (2018: 845) study of 611 office buildings in England and Wales illustrates this, noting that 'when rising from five storeys and below to 21 storeys and above', the mean intensity of electricity and fossil fuel dramatically increases, with a doubling of carbon emissions.

The construction of such buildings and related infrastructure is proceeding apace, despite the evidence of its failings. This reflects the contradictions of a culture that is wedded to a belief in the power of technology to overcome the limits to building by providing a constant supply of new techniques to control nature and to rework it into new, often synthetic, products. The use of plastics is an apt example, in which much of the built environment is overwhelmingly synthetically constructed and comprised of laboratory-engineered materials that have the capacity to extend the lifespan of a range

Figure 9.3: Willis Tower, Chicago

Source: Rob Imrie

of products. Plastics are used in every part of a building, from its insulation to piping, window frames, doors, interior design, paints, floors and wall linings; the list is endless. The durability of plastic is the problem, insofar that once insinuated into the built environment, it cannot be eradicated or easily recycled or reused. As Cousins (2018: 1) suggests, its extensive use by builders is likely 'to leave a toxic plastic legacy for future generations'.

That this legacy is in the making is related, in part, to the methodological nature of construction, or its approach to the environment with little or no knowledge of it, and little intent to understand it beyond the technicalities of site planning, excavation, preparation and building. The culture of building rarely encourages its practitioners to think about a building site as a vital, living organism, or part of a broader, holistic environment that has intrinsic value, or a value in itself, for itself. Rather, landscapes and ecologies tend to be regarded as just another resource to be costed, or factored into a cost calculus as part of the broadcloth of a construction project. In evaluating an ecology or environment, project managers, or those in the vanguard of conducting environmental assessments prior to construction, will usually overlook or disregard intrinsic values in favour of instrumentalist values. These conceive the worth, or the value, of an ecology in terms of what it can contribute, or provide, to satisfy human wants and/or desires.

Here, ecology is a means to an end rather than an end in itself, and the value ascribed to it in building projects is shaped by an econometric rationality in which monetary and market valuations are paramount. This approach to valuing ecology has the danger of ignoring the deleterious impacts on nature that accrue from the pursuit of transforming it for economic benefit. This instrumentalist rationality underpins most construction projects, in which assessment of their environmental impacts, where they are carried out, are, as Laurance and Salt (2018: 1) note, 'full of holes' and 'designed to fail', and do not take into account the complexity of ecological systems, or the fullest possible range of a project's impacts on the environment. More often than not, construction projects proceed with little or no evaluation of their 'ecological impact'. There is often a broader, strategic interest at stake, or political and economic interests that outweigh attempts to provide appropriate, non-monetary valuations of nature and the socio-ecological costs of its transformation.

There are numerous examples, from road building in Amazonia to dam projects, such as the Chalillo dam, in Belize. This project went ahead despite local opposition and a legal challenge relating to the likelihood of biodiversity loss, deforestation, loss of landscape and aesthetic degradation. By 2005, the dam was in full operation, as protests had been ignored, and by the end of the 2010s, research data were showing that food and water security had been degraded, with local communities drinking from expensive bottled water where previously they sourced clean water from the riverine environment (Crocker, 2019). The environmental assessment for the site, a requirement by the Belizean government, was carried out on behalf of the developer, Fortis, by Amec, a global engineering company that, as Barcott (2008: 200) recounts, was 'hired to persuade the Belizean government to greenlight the project'. For Barcott (2008), the process did not consider any sense of value, or valuation, of nature beyond goals relating to measures of economic development and output.

This sums up the disposition of the building and development industry in relation to ecology and the environment, and the question is: how, then, should nature be valued? Can a different methodological basis to the valuation of the natural environment, beyond an instrumentalist approach, be insinuated into the logics of the building industry? Kenner (2014) notes a shift by development interests towards valuing nature as 'natural capital', defined by the Natural Capital Coalition (2020: 1) as 'a stock, and from it flows ecosystem services or benefits'. This conception of nature as stock is meant to identify, and account for, the totality of renewable and non-renewable resources in the natural world. This is a basis for informed judgements about how human actions affect the quality and quantity of nature's resources. While the approach is an attempt to instil responsible and respectful behaviour towards nature, by regarding biodiversity as intrinsic to planetary well-being, it does not escape instrumental values, or the understanding that the assets of natural capital, the air, soil, plants and animals, combine 'to yield a flow of benefits to people' (Natural Capital Coalition, 2020: 1).

For some observers, the potential of the natural capital approach to provide insights into, and checks on, the diminution of nature is not being realised because major organisations, including corporate business, are incorporating it into an econometric methodology that regards nature as a series of assets that can be costed and given a price.[3] An instance is the World Forum on Natural Capital (2020: 1), which suggests that 'nature is priceless', but then makes the case for pricing nature and evaluating it in economic terms. The World Forum on Natural Capital (2020: 1) describes 'street trees in California as worth '\$1 billion per year in ecosystem services, through atmospheric regulation and flood prevention', and notes that 'Mexico's mangrove forests provide an annual \$70 billion to the economy through storm protection, fisheries support, and ecotourism.' These illustrations value nature not as 'priceless', but as a commodity for exchange, and, as Sullivan (2016: 1) suggests, prioritise 'economic, as opposed to ecological language and models ... that [otherwise] elicit care for the natural world'.

Such care for the natural world ought not to be reduced to quantifiable measures, or embedded within an instrumentalist logic. For Kenner (2014: iv), there needs to be a new way of valuing nature that shifts the focus 'from mainly expert bodies including consultancies, specialist companies, academia and conservation NGOs'. Kenner (2014: v) asks the important question: 'who should do the valuing and whose values ... [ought to be] taken into account?'. There is no single answer to this, but the problem of the culture of building is its relative distancing from, and indifference to, what Sukhdev (2014: 1) describes as 'those who are closest and most dependent on ecosystems', who often espouse non-economic valuations of nature. Kenner (2014: vi) refers to the Dongria Kondh indigenous community, who live in the Niyamgiri hills in India and defend their environment for its spiritual value, in which the hills that they live in are 'their God and soul'. How might this particular sense of value, and similar, non-econometric values of nature, challenge and transform the prevailing orthodoxy?

Construction and the fallacy of the green agenda

The prevailing orthodoxy of instrumentalising nature, treating it as a commodity and doing little to prevent its ongoing exploitation is fast translating into stark and alarming data about the loss of biodiversity and habitat, and the onward acceleration of climate change. At the present rates of human exploitation of nature, there is the likelihood of the mass extinction of species, and, as Ceballos et al (2015: 5) suggest, there is evidence 'that current species extinction rates are higher than the pre-human background rate'. Similar scenarios of ecological destruction are highlighted by climate scientists, who said in October 2018 that the world has until 2030 to keep global warming to a maximum of 1.5 degrees centigrade, beyond which there is likely to be a catastrophic failure of environmental systems (IPCC, 2018). The Intergovernmental Panel on Climate Change (IPCC, 2018: 489) suggests that nothing short of unprecedented changes in lifestyles will suffice, including 'accelerating energy efficiency' in the built environment and the adoption of 'zero-energy buildings' and 'green building technology'.

The IPCC report is one of many published since the late 20th century that have been instrumental in galvanising governments to adopt 'green policies'. The objective has been less to stop people's exploitation of nature and more to manage it, or develop the means to mitigate and reduce the worst impacts of human activities on the environment. The notion of green growth, or ecological modernisation, has taken centre stage, and state strategies range from market environmentalism, or encouraging private sector companies to take responsibility for conserving nature, to the obfuscation of the risks of economic activity on the environment, seeking to depoliticise or deflect critique that might otherwise challenge the centrality of growth (Lee, 2015). As a political, state-centred stratagem, green growth appears to be crisis management, or what While et al (2004: 551) refer to as a 'sustainability fix', to 'safeguard growth trajectories in the wake of ... the global "ecological crisis"'.

A whole industry has sprung up to respond to, and engage with, the degradation of ecology, and green growth has fast become a major focus for activity in the building industry. Builders are encouraged by their trades organisations to think much more about all stages of the building process in relation to adopting methods to eliminate waste and reduce dependence on materials with high levels of embodied energy. For instance, in 2005, the HBF (2005: 1), with partners, set up the Sustainability in Housebuilding initiative 'to help the spread of good and sustainable practice throughout the ... housebuilding industries'. Likewise, the Portland Cement Association (2020: 1), based in the US, notes that it and its members, who propagate the use of one of the most ecologically destructive materials used by builders, are 'committed to sustainably producing the highest quality product'.[4]

There are thousands of similar statements stemming from all corners of the building industry, shaped by steers from government. These tend to be guidance without legal status, and provide accreditation if particular standards of sustainable building have been attained. In the UK, this is exemplified by the Building Research Establishment Environmental Assessment Method (BREEAM), which certifies buildings with low environmental impact. The scheme seeks to encourage 'value in higher performing assets and aims to inspire and empower change by rewarding and motivating sustainability' (BREEAM, 2018: 6). In the US, the equivalent is the Leadership in Energy and Environmental Design (LEED), a certification programme devised in 1994 by the US Green Building Council, and since adopted in over 40 countries (Cidell, 2009). Like BREEAM, it recommends courses of action but does not mandate them, and, as Cidell (2009: 632, original emphasis) concludes, 'economic motivations are still at the fore', with the emphasis on 'business as usual, but not *too* much'.

This reflects the status of the development of sustainable or green building products and processes, in which 'green growth' has been mobilised as a clarion call in seeking to show builders how they can profit from going green, while responding to, and overcoming, environmental problems relating to their operations. Green growth is presented by supranational agencies and governments as an 'opportunity and reward, rather than costly restraint' (Bowen and Fankhauser, 2011: 1157). The OECD (2011: 4) typify this by describing green growth as a panacea or means to foster 'economic growth and development, while ensuring that natural assets continue to provide the resources and environmental services on which our well-being relies'. Here, green growth is not a challenge to the growthist rationalities of society, but tapping into them and extending the tentacles of economic growth by encouraging firms to seek out market opportunities by developing new green products, technologies and services.

For builders, these opportunities revolve around the development of a host of new building techniques and technologies, relating to energy, recycling, refurbishment, air quality, heating, humidity, materials and waste management. There has been a rapid increase in green consultancies and commercial outlets selling a plethora of products marketed as 'green', and it is estimated that by 2022, the global green materials market will be worth US$365 billion (Grand View Research, 2018). One of the major growth areas is smart or intelligent technologies to modulate user behaviour in buildings. Many buildings feature a host of smart features, ranging from building automation to enable remote operations of lighting, heating and energy systems, to heat-recovery systems to control air humidity and quality. These systems reflect the technology-led nature of the green growth movement, in which faith is placed in the power of technical innovation to overcome the profligate use of energy and natural resources.

While smart technologies, such as remotely controlled heating systems, may enable efficiencies in energy use, they are not sufficient, in and of themselves, to offset the continuous growth in energy consumption in the construction industry. In some senses, they are a diversion from the main issue, that is, that too many buildings are being constructed, with many pre-existing buildings badly built and requiring much more than technology to overcome poor energy retention and performance. Smart technologies, and other techniques, are enabling the construction sector to make reductions in energy usage, and a report by the United Nations Environment and International Energy Agency (UNEIEA, 2017: 7) notes that the 'buildings sector energy intensity (in terms of energy use per m2) continues to improve at an annual average rate of around 1.5%'. However, the report observes that the 'global floor area continues to grow by about 2.3% per annum, offsetting those energy intensity improvements' (UNEIEA, 2017: 7). These data question the relevance and impact of smart technology and building.

Waste is also to the fore in green growth thinking, including the idea of the circular economy. The Building Services Research and Information Association (2020: 1) define the circular economy as maximising 'the utility of the existing infrastructure across the product value chain, where the waste from one system can be utilised as the input in another system'. This emphasises the recycling of buildings and their materials, and the construction of durable, flexible and demountable structures that can be used time and again, albeit in modified forms (van de Rijdt, 2020). This is a rejection of building as a linear process, being seen rather as part of an iterative cycle. An example of circularity is the notion of 'urban mining', which describes the wealth of mineral assets vested in buildings and infrastructure, and encourages builders to think much more about the recovery of precious and non-renewable materials, such as lead in batteries (Koutamanis et al, 2018). For Koutamanis et al (2018: 33), urban mining is the recognition that the excavation of the anthroposphere, or the people-made environment, 'is an attractive alternative to depleting natural ones'.

These ideas seem persuasive, but the notion of circularity is premised on a constant reworking of growth, that is, using recycled and/or reusable building products to feed back into the (re)production of the built environment, or the basis for renewed rounds of economic growth. As Valenzuela and Bohm (2017: 27) put it, the 'ideals of growth have assumed the command of the discourse of sustainability', and in the building context, circularity is not so much an approach to the curtailment of building projects, but an encouragement to (re)create the means for the expansion of construction and its products. So too with urban mining, which, while laudable, and with value in a world where anthropogenic effects cannot be eradicated, does have limits. Graedel (2011: 49) notes that urban mining 'is successful when the economic incentives are high', such as extracting rhenium from gas-turbine blades. Otherwise, 'without economic incentives or other imperatives, our society seems likely to persist in mining and processing virgin metals, using them once or twice, and letting them dissipate back into the environment' (Graedel, 2011: 49).

The green growth agenda also advocates carbon offsetting projects to mitigate the deleterious effects of building and other human activities. The logic of this is that investments in unsustainable building activities, such as major road-building and infrastructure projects, can be compensated by equal investments in sustainable or green activities. In doing so, carbon emissions associated with a building project can be offset by buying carbon credits in emissions reduction projects, such as investing in, for example, reforestation or renewable energy technologies. This 'pay to pollute' approach does not challenge the rationality of 'building without limits', and its logic permits construction to proceed without checks or limits on the scale or form and performance of buildings, as long as offsets are made. The continuation of building, and its deleterious effects on climate and ecology, is justified and legitimised by a process that is 'sleight of hand', or 'buying off' objections and dissenting voices. The problem is that whatever is done to 'offset' can never be the equivalent of, or replacement for, that which is lost by a building project.

The net effect is the continuing deterioration of the planet's resources. An example is the construction of infrastructure for major sports events. The International Olympic Committee (2020: 1) has stated the intent to contribute to the planting of an Olympic Forest from 2021 onwards in order 'to support communities in Africa's Sahel region working towards the sustainable use of forests, rangelands and other natural resources. It will help to mitigate and adapt to climate change.' While major building programmes will be occurring for the Olympics in Paris in 2024 and Los Angeles in 2028, the International Olympic Committee will assuage their conscience by purchasing reforestation offsets far removed from the original sources of carbon emissions, as though emissions are the only issue. Offsetting in remote countries does not address the non-carbon environmental effects of building in and around the Olympic sites, relating to local water use, changes to micro-ecologies, air pollution and the social disruption to communities affected by major construction projects.

The International Olympic Committee's belief that reforestation can achieve the offsetting claims that they make is also questionable, and Greenpeace (2020: 1) notes that 'a newly-planted tree can take as many as 20 years to capture the amount of CO_2 that a carbon-offset scheme promises'. Greenpeace (2020: 1) suggest that such schemes are unlikely to provide the requisite offset because forests are at risk from being 'wiped out by droughts, wildfires, tree diseases and deforestation' (see also Kill, 2013). The problem, though, is that offsetting does not require builders to change what they do, or think through the ethical import of their actions. As Greenpeace (2020: 1) state: 'offsetting schemes provide a good story that allows companies to swerve away from taking meaningful action on their carbon emissions'. Meaningful action ought to overturn whatever is causing carbon emissions, but offsetting does not require this, and, as Knapton and Horton (2019) suggest, by failing to discourage or prevent consumption, offsetting projects may just as easily lead to an increase as to a reduction in carbon emissions.

Despite these critiques and reservations concerning the green growth movement, it has rapidly translated into a series of fast-growing, lucrative markets. It has potential to change perceptions of what makes a good or bad building, and to provide suggestions, and means, to redress some of the human impacts on ecology and the environment. However, awareness of the green agenda and the impacts of construction on ecology has not permeated far into the building industry or challenged, or changed, its proclivity to build and construct continuously. There is slow uptake of green technologies and techniques, with builders being risk averse and reluctant to change practices. Ahn et al's (2013) study of the US building industry found evidence of builders' reluctance to 'go green' due to the perception of the sector as entailing high costs and long payback periods. Heffernan et al's (2015: 34) research of the UK house-building industry shows that builders are 'failing to respond to the non-mandatory stimuli for the delivery of zero carbon homes'. This is due to a range of reasons, including perceived risk and costs, and reluctance to do more than is specified by statute or law.

The issue is even more pronounced in the fastest-growing parts of the globe, and in China, the building industry is a long way from adopting or responding to the green growth movement. Given that China is constructing more buildings than anywhere else in the world, it is necessary that builders, and politicians, there take stock and reflect on the ecological and environmental effects of construction. However, research indicates that this is far from the case, and Shen et al's (2017) study of real estate activity in Chongqing, China, indicates a lassitude by builders in relation to the interrelationships between building and ecology. In a survey of local builders, the research shows that they do not have knowledge or understanding of 'green building materials', nor do they have experience in using green procurement. Others note that the problem of slow uptake of green ideas is that there is a lack of fiscal and other governmental incentives to encourage developers to adopt green building techniques (Li et al, 2014).

This reflects the voluntary nature of the green growth agenda, both in China and elsewhere, being based less on legislating for change, and more on industry awareness and knowledge translating into practice. For critics of the green growth agenda, this is unlikely to lead to the radical, far-reaching changes required to thwart a global ecological crisis, and the term 'greenwashing' has been popularised to characterise companies who proclaim their green credentials without the substance to back it up. Watson (2016) describes an advertising campaign in 1994 by the US real estate investment trust company Weyerhaeuser. The adverts stated that in relation to its forestry activities, the company was 'working with scientists and environmental groups to study problems faced by fish in their natural state. As you can see, we're taking it very seriously' (Letto, 1995: 1). As Watson (2016) suggests, by destabilising salmon habitats, the effects of Weyerhaeuser's operations were the reverse of their claims.

The claim by Weyerhaeuser to be operating in an environmentally sensitive way is a widespread practice in the construction sector, as well as others. A typical example is the global infrastructure company Balfour Beatty (2019: 2), which notes that they 'position sustainability at the heart of what we do'. To substantiate this, Balfour Beatty claim to have reduced carbon emissions associated with their projects by 51 per cent since 2010, with less than 3 per cent of waste sent to landfill sites (Balfour Beatty, 2020: 1). These are laudable figures that sit uneasily alongside, and in contradiction to, most Balfour Beatty building projects. These include road building and maintenance, such as the contract to manage and maintain the M25 motorway around London. The contract is implicated in supporting, and encouraging, motor vehicle usage, and the operation of the road consistently breaks regulations relating to air quality, with high levels of nitrogen dioxide and carbon dioxide emitted close to residential areas (MacKerron and Mourato, 2009).

It is not surprising that despite the claims of companies like Balfour Beatty, the plethora of green initiatives globally seem to have made little difference to mitigating the harmful, and escalating, ecological effects of building and construction. As the Balfour Beatty example indicates, what is often labelled 'green' or 'sustainable' by the building industry may be no more than a smokescreen, or a partial representation of reality. This reality is usually no more than the attempt to mitigate some of the effects of building activity by adhering to legal technical standards and increasing efficiencies relating to energy and material use, including the disposal and management of waste. For Balfour Beatty and similar organisations, green growth does not encourage a questioning and critique of the *raison d'être* of building. Rather, it assumes that building, in and of itself, is unproblematic and 'a good thing', and to question otherwise would be tantamount to undermining the prevailing business model.

This translates into more building activity, in which, as Lee (2015: 353) suggests, 'narratives about green growth become intertwined with conventional development preoccupations in public policy'. Lee (2015), referring to the South Korean context, notes that green growth policy promotes construction, and cites the example of the Four Major Rivers Restoration Project. The project, started in 2009, was an attempt under South Korea's

Green New Deal policy to restore the ecology of its river systems. It was a huge engineering and construction project, involving the building of dams, reconstruction of riverbanks by lining them in concrete, construction of 16 weirs and dredging of waterways. Over US$20 billion was spent, and the outcome was significant profits for the construction companies that were awarded contracts and little or no impact in terms of ecological enhancement. Data suggest the reverse: that water quality has diminished and disruption to the flow of rivers has led to worsening algae blooms (Jeong-su, 2013). For Lee (2015: 353), the case is illustrative of how green growth may facilitate the output of a construction-oriented neo-developmentalist state, while compromising ecological quality.

The problem for the future of planetary integrity is how to redirect a movement that, for Dale (2015: 1), has no ecological credentials, but is 'a collection of tradable ecosystem services' that are made 'circulatable and accumulable'. These services extend the reach of the market into ecology and the environment, with the promise of what Dale (2015: 1) describes as 'eco-balanced affluence engineered through ethical enterprise and smart markets'. Here, green growth is reinforcing the instrumentalist values inherent in the natural capital conception of the environment, and it is propagating continuing human exploitation of the natural world. For Monbiot (2014: 1), the contradiction is perverse because what is killing the planet is held up as its saviour, or, as he observes, the deployment of 'the pricing, valuation, monetisation, financialisation of nature in the name of saving it'. How, then, might this contradiction be challenged or changed to avert ecological degradation?

Towards a construction that cares for the environment

The operation of the construction sector, in contributing to the ongoing despoliation of places and the eradication of nature, cannot be sustained in a context whereby planetary survival is at stake. There is a need to politicise the impacts of building on the environment, and to critique proffered solutions, such as those emanating from the green growth agenda, as part of the problem and not the means to avert ecological destruction. The environmental agenda has been depoliticised by politicians who, in wielding the promises of modernism, note that the appropriate management of resources, coupled with technical innovation, can solve any crisis and ensure the longevity of the species. The record shows this to be a chimera: while we live in a world characterised by technical skills and know-how, the earth's life support systems are becoming ever-more compromised and impoverished.

Counter-views to the technocratic, build-without-limits rationality have emerged, including a politics of degrowth, post-growth, indigenous political ecology, permaculture and radical ecological democracy, to name but a few (Merchant, 1992). What they have in common is a concern with the integrity of nature and to care for the environment in recognition that species survival is dependent on ecological well-being. They question how far anthropocentrism should be defended, and how people ought to rethink their relationships with(in) nature. Should a biocentric outlook be the basis of a new 'natural' approach to building in which all living things are ascribed inherent value? Instead of a builder approaching the environment, or a site on which a building will be erected, as an object and exterior phenomenon, a biocentric view reveres the land and, in Escobar's (2001: 146) terms, 'the landscape is endowed with agency and personhood'. It is not a thing to be owned as property and exploited, but rather to be respected and nurtured.

This perspective informs practices that go beyond green growth, including biophilia, which is the 'love of life', or the understanding that for people to function and live well depends upon the nurturing of, and care for, nature and the environment. Biophilia expresses the importance of the interconnected and related nature of organisms, in which to insert a building into a place without any connectivity to the setting, or sensitivity to the ecological fabric, undermines one of people's primary needs for 'ongoing connections with the natural world' (Heerwagen, 2009: 39). The quality of these connections depends on deconstructing building structures that keep nature at bay by reducing the use of artificial, or adapted, natures, as exemplified by air conditioning.[5] They also depend on people nurturing nature and working within its rhythms to harness its powers in order to provide for the sustenance and reproduction of the natural world.

Such views are reflected, in part, in the propagation of natural or eco-buildings based on rejecting industrial-scaled built environments which use products that expend high levels of embodied energy, both in their manufacturing and transportation (Pullen, 2020: 1).[6] The natural building is bespoke and customised and seeks to use locally sourced materials that are abundant and renewable, contain few chemical components or treatment, and have minimal need for technology to manufacture and assembly them. They are, so it is claimed, attuned to their local environment and climate, and do not depend on sources of fossil fuels for heating or air conditioning (Pullen, 2020). The building materials that are used range in diversity, including mud, cork, straw, sheep's wool, reclaimed wood and plant-based polyurethane rigid foam. One of the more intriguing materials is cob, which comprises a mixture of subsoil, straw and clay, and sometimes with added lime (see Figure 9.4; see also Evans et al, 2002).

Figure 9.4: A Pacific Northwest cob home

Note: Credit is due to Gerry Thomasen.
Source: https://upload.wikimedia.org/wikipedia/commons/3/33/Home_at_Hollyhock.jpg

The notion of natural building is part of the International Living Future Institute's (ILFI's) living building movement (LBM). The LBM follows biophilia ideas by asking existential questions about people's entanglement with(in) complex ecologies and, as McLennan (2012, 2019: 1) notes, raises ethical considerations about how people ought to interact with other species, or how 'we do good in the world while meeting our needs for shelter'. For McLennan (2019: 1), it is not sufficient to pursue the half measures that typify green growth, such as 'to build buildings that are a little less bad than conventional', 'to pollute more slowly' or to 'warm the planet just a little less'. This will change little and only slow rates of ecological degradation and destruction. In contrast, a living building has a regenerative, enhancing effect on ecology and, as McLennan (2019: 1) notes, 'a net positive impact on an ecosystem, with no harmful emissions ... [and adapted] to place and climate just like trees and plants surrounding them'.

Te Kura Whare in Taneatua, New Zealand, is an example of a living building (see Figure 9.5). It was constructed in 2014 for the Tūhoe, a Maori indigenous group, as a meeting place. The building is based on the understanding that people need to live within the means of nature and the environment, and never diminish or denude the spaces that surround them.

Figure 9.5: Te Kura Whare building, Taneatua, New Zealand

Note: Credit is due to Phillippa Flannery
Source: Phillippa Flannery

Like many indigenous groups, the Tūhoe regard the land as sacred and to be revered, having cosmological beliefs in which all living matter is conceived as 'coming from – and returning to – the same source, sharing the same substance and, crucially, the same identity' (Strang, 2005: 51). The building reflects such values by generating its own energy from solar-powered panels, and collecting and purifying water for public use. Te Kura Whare was constructed from locally sourced materials left untreated by toxic chemicals, and it has natural ventilation. Its waste is treated by using locally constructed septic tanks and a botanical wetland (Warnock, 2017).

Te Kura Whare differs from most conventional buildings, yet it is embedded in a technocentric construction culture. Much of the building is dependent on technology and technical know-how, and in the course of its construction, some waste was sent to landfill sites (ILFI, 2020). The building is a product-based artefact comprising a paraphernalia of gadgets, including lighting, solar panels, a fire sprinkler and fire storage tank. Its construction has impacted on the earth by the excavation of local clay to make 6,000 earth bricks, and its production of carbon emissions has been assuaged by 'offset' payments into local environmental projects (ILFI, 2020). In the construction of Te Kura Whare, concrete was used for underground water tanks and the building's foundations. The inescapable observation is the difficulty for any building project to overcome these contradictions of anthropogenic behaviour, in which whatever is built will compromise, in some form, ecological integrity.

This is evident with the LBM, which, while pushing standards beyond what is required from the green growth movement, is a variation on a theme, as it does not question the need to build or push back against the growthist rationality of the building culture. The ILFI mimics the green industry's approach to accrediting and certifying living buildings, and, in doing so, is fuelling a new range of products and services, and contributing to an expansion in both the production and consumption of building materials. This is related, in part, to the ILFI creating the Living Building Challenge, which Roberts (2018: 1) describes as 'the world's most rigorous green building standard and certification process'. The ILFI describes one of its goals as encouraging builders to attain a 'level of performance' in their buildings by adhering to 16 standards that, in combination, represent the 'living building'. Attaining such standards requires a high level of material consumption, and the question is: how does this mitigate the effects of building per se on ecology and the environment?

The observation from the case of Te Kura Whare is that it does mitigate some effects, but not all, and, in some senses, may well be causing others. This is a matter for close evaluation of buildings with living building certification, but, to date, there are few, if any, such studies. However, scrutiny of some of the claims relating to buildings with ILFI certification is revealing. In relation to one building, the Phipps Center for Sustainable Landscapes located in Pittsburgh, the claim is made that because the building adheres to ILFI standards, it exists in 'harmonious co-existence with nature' (see Figure 9.6). There is no definition of what harmony means, nor any data deployed to show what the harmonious coexistence is or entails. As an aesthetic object, the building conjures up the observation made by Bookchin (1979: 26) about urbanisation, that is, the 'encroachment of the synthetic on the natural, of the inorganic (concrete, metals, and glass) on the organic, or crude, elemental stimuli on variegated wide ranging ones'.

For the LBM and advocates of natural building, there is a need to scale down some of the claims, and to acknowledge that the notions of 'the natural' and 'the living' are misnomers, as they convey the sense that to build 'naturally' is to escape the confines of the anthropogenic. This can never occur, and so the challenge is how to approach building and construction in ways whereby anthropogenic effects are redirected to create a built environment that is not reliant on growth, or the (re)production of more buildings and infrastructure. In reducing dependence on fossil fuels, creating natural ventilation and using materials with low levels of embodied energy, the LBM is part of the solution. However, it requires more, and there is a need to decouple the LBM from the commodification of living building products, or any sense that it is part of 'business as usual'.

Figure 9.6: The Phipps Center for Sustainable Landscapes, Pittsburgh, USA

Note: Credit is due to Dllu

Source: https://upload.wikimedia.org/wikipedia/commons/9/9f/Phipps_Conservatory_23.jpg

This decoupling would enable a break with the mindset that there is always 'more to build', and challenge what Minkjan (2019: 1) describes as the 'constant reconfiguration' of the built environment and its 'extension into new territory'. Building and construction need to be decoupled from the growth paradigm and the dynamic to produce and consume more of the material world. This is at every level of building activity, including the constant, consumerist push to encourage people to purchase the latest household fads and gadgets, or to extend into lofts and basements to increase their consumption of constructed space. The growthist rationality is particularly evident with the continuing expansion of cities, and the proliferation of infrastructure mega-projects. Given this scale of building, the question is the relevance of the LBM, in its present form, to attend to, and transform, not only the socio-ecological effects of the operations of the global construction industry, but also the politics that underpin and provide it with the supportive political infrastructure.

What, then, can be done to transform building and construction in ways whereby the needs of people's habitation are met, while ensuring the reproduction and nurturing of fragile ecologies and environments? There is no easy or singular answer that is not part of systemic social, cultural and political change, including a reorientation of the economy. While the

LBM demonstrates what is technically feasible in constructing buildings that minimise their impacts on the environment, there is a need to scale up in ways whereby all buildings and infrastructure, including the pre-existing built environment, can adhere to, and develop, ecological principles. Fry (2009) notes that to build is always a political and ethical action, and this is a useful maxim to begin a line of questioning relating to what building is for, for whom and in what ways we build. From the construction of major road systems, to the large, volume-constructed, housing estates, there needs to be a thoroughgoing, existential exposé of the point and purpose of building.

Much building activity is occurring without asking these fundamental questions, interrogating political and public policy, or challenging the motivations and actions of actors in the construction industry. Building needs to be politicised around a degrowth agenda, or the development of a politics that will challenge the prevailing growth-oriented orthodoxy. This is a message highlighted by a range of environmental and ecological groups in exhorting construction companies to change their behaviour, or to pull back from the scale and nature of building projects. The problem is the deeply embedded nature of building within a political economy of construction. How might a degrowth agenda be put in place with a premise against new building and construction, and the onus placed on the management and maintenance, including adaptation, of existing stocks of buildings and infrastructure, without adding to the ecological footprint?

This is only one of many possible routes that begin, in Fournier's (2008: 528) terms, to 'escape from the economy', and to offer the possibilities of a future of producing and consuming less. To 'degrow' is not to stymie the possibilities of growth per se, but to change what is grown, or what is conceived as growth, which is usually a monetary return or a measure such as GDP. In contrast, to degrow is to shift from the econometric, quantitative meanings of growth, and to change what we do, such as building, into a practical politics that enables people to become good ecological citizens, and for ecology itself to grow and flourish. Thus, instead of the construction of roads that lead to the growth in numbers of motor vehicles, carcinogenic pollutants and carbon emissions, why not craft places to cater for a growth in cycling, walking and a mixture of gardens and open spaces?

These are alternative possibilities and scenarios that relate to a sense of caring for the environment as part of a process of caring for humans. To care relates to a sense of obligation, and responsibility, or what is just in relation to the inequities that occur by virtue of unfettered building and construction. These are many and varied, and range from rapid deforestation and loss of habitat in places like Amazonia, to the siting of social housing beside major road systems that pump out toxic gases. In both instances, the growth impulses of construction are implicated in the denudation of a natural resource and the perpetuation of social inequalities by, in the first instance, species losing their habitats and, in the second instance, having to consume dirty air. To step back from, and critique, the growth impulses shaping such outcomes is to harness a sense of ecological citizenship that, as argued in Chapter 10, should be the basis for a different way of thinking about, and acting towards, building and construction.

Conclusion

The impact of construction on ecology and the environment is far-reaching, with most building activity inattentive to nature and the rhythms of the natural world. Construction is thoroughly anthropogenic in propagating a 'human-first' perspective that conceives of nature as subservient to the needs of people, and in the service of shaping the world for human gratification. Insofar that construction has the capacity to transform nature in deleterious ways, it is assumed that these can be mitigated by recourse to technical solutions and the management of building processes. This is the position adopted by the green growth agenda, which is based on a weak version of sustainable development that does not question the *raison d'être* of building and construction, or why we need to build. It does not challenge the economic growth rationality that shapes most building activity, and there is no evidence that the policies it advocates can do more than slow the rates of ecological degradation.

Part of the problem is the tendency for nature to be regarded as an exterior object awaiting human intervention. For FLW (Lloyd Wright, 1932), the issue with the building industry is its inability to grasp the organic nature of the building process, or the relationships between human interventions in the production of space, the spaces themselves and the consequent reshaping of people's modes of habitation and their environments. The building process and the building itself, in whatever shape or form, disturbs and disrupts ecological systems and transforms the nature of natural environments, and is implicated in the (re)production of new natures or natural formations. In seeking to understand the interrelationships between building and ecological change, the ongoing task is to acknowledge these because they highlight that whatever is built has consequence for people's lives, and for the places that they and the other of the earth's species inhabit.

Such understanding ought to place the entanglements between building and ecology at the apex of construction, or at least require building practitioners to think through, and articulate, how nature will be nurtured and placed at the fulcrum of the process in any building context. The LBM (2014), with other eco-building approaches, provides insights into what is possible, and these steer practitioners towards how a building can be crafted to reduce its impact on hydrological, biotic and atmospheric matter and materials. The LBM (2014) gives advice on creating healthier buildings made of natural materials that can breathe and are free of chemicals, while directing practitioners to reducing environmental impacts by using locally sourced, vernacular materials that are low in embodied energy. All of this is educative and useful for practitioners. The LBM (2014: 40, 8) also exhorts building professionals 'to nurture the innate human/nature connection', and notes that 'nothing less than a sea change in building, infrastructure and community design is required'.

These observations stop short of a political programme for change, as though change will somehow transpire. In a manifesto document by the LBM (2014), two statements highlight the scale of the problem. The first notes that new building ought to lead to: 'greater biodiversity; increased soil health; additional outlets for beauty and personal expression; a deeper understanding of climate, culture and place' (LBM, 2014: 7). However, why build anew in the first place given that any constructed object will compromise the environment? The second statement aligns LBM to the market as the means to deliver sustainable building, or, as they say, 'to realign incentives and market signals that truly protect the health, safety and welfare of people and all beings' (LBM, 2014: 3). The question is: how do we realign these, and with what political agenda, since the market commodifies, and in doing so, leaves intact the growthist impulses of the construction sector?

This is not to single out the LBM, as much of their work is positive, but to highlight the apolitical nature of such organisations operating in a field that is avowedly political and requires the articulation, and deployment, of political ideals, ideas and strategies. Without these, how will it be possible to confront, and turn around, the vested interests in the building industry, or the power of construction states and major corporate construction companies? These interests are unlikely to easily relinquish their hold on, and domination of, building contracts given the projected figures for construction into the middle of the 21st century and beyond. In a world where we are already awash with buildings, many of which are underused and unused, it seems incumbent on organisations like the LBM to demonstrate that another way forward, beyond building, is possible because, without this, there seems little likelihood that ecologies and environments will be able to support the reproduction of the species.

10

Building and Construction
That Cares

Introduction

> [T]he most fundamental problem that architecture has within itself, which is also a problem that is inherent within our society, [is] we have too much stuff, we have too many buildings. (Betsky, 2017: 1)

The built environment is the most potent representation and material manifestation of people's presence on the planet, and in the course of its construction, ongoing management and maintenance, and the daily rhythms of use, it has profound effects on people's lives and the qualities of ecology and the environment. Our lives are shaped by the design and emplacement of buildings and infrastructure, and there is a directionality embedded into them that influences much of what we do, how we do it and how we experience places. From the pavements and roads that provide the connections directing people from one place to another, to the juxtaposition of buildings and their interior design that shape how people move within and between spaces, the designed and constructed environment is formative in influencing social encounters and interactions. It is also closely intertwined with the functioning of the world's biosphere, and is significant in the ongoing degradation and deterioration of local and global ecosystems.

Such is the importance of the built environment that there is a need to build in ways whereby it works well for all species, but the reality is that this is very far from being so. Too much of the built environment is based on speculation in land and property, or the propagation of a casino capitalism characterised by investments in risk-taking ventures that prioritise the construction of high-value-added buildings and infrastructure. This reflects the construction of buildings as a commercial asset, or part of an exchange economy in which their use, and usefulness, appear to be less important than the maximisation of returns from investment. This translates into a political economy of building and construction that is implicated in the production of buildings as a series of commodities, or tradable assets, in which spatial development is characterised, disproportionately, by a built environment that reflects the pursuit of value enhancement in the (re)production of space.

This logic translates into too many buildings consumed by too few people, and too many people not having access to adequate spaces, or inhabiting badly designed and functioning dwellings. These socio-spatial inequalities are also manifest in many people being forced to live in areas exposed to toxic water and air pollution, and often located in places at risk of human-induced environmental events, such as floods and landslides. For some indigenous people inhabiting areas of rapid deforestation, in which extracted timber is made into flooring, furniture and a range of building products, a process of ecocide is evident that, in undermining the ecological fabric, is potentially a process of genocide. This is the loss of habitat that sustains local populations that, due to its exploitation, can no longer provide the sustenance for living, or means to reproduce local biospheres.

A potent example is the rise of sea levels related to the melting of the icecaps due to global warming, and the threat to habitat and lives in low-lying areas. Lindsey (2020) notes that the global mean sea level has risen by 24 cm since 1880, with 30 per cent of this rise since 1995. One outcome is the flooding, and possible submergence, of islands, such as Tuvalu in the Pacific Ocean and the Maldives in the Indian Ocean. Storlazzi et al (2018) suggest that the impact of sea-level rise and wave-driven flooding on island infrastructure will lead to them becoming uninhabitable. Many islands in the tropics are less than 4 m in height. Their ecosystems are vulnerable to seawater infiltration and the contamination of fresh water sources. Tuvalu is most under threat, with beaches sinking due to wave erosion, and soil salination preventing the growth of crops. The government has plans for the evacuation of its 11,000 citizens, with estimates that the island will be unoccupied by the middle to end of the 21st century (Briney, 2019).

The case of Tuvalu is a human and ecological disaster in the making, but it is evident almost everywhere, albeit in different forms. At root is the exploitation of the planet's resources, and their recombination into people-made products and environments that constitute the anthropogenic biosphere. Here, new recombinant natures are constantly in the making in response to human activities, or the (re)production of synthetic environs that affect, often in deleterious ways, the reproductive systems of both biotic and abiotic matter. In Tuvalu's case, recombinant natures are part of the (re)production of carbon emissions and the warming of the planet, and highlight the potential dangers of the continuation of human practices such as building that, in its present form, is a key repository of embodied energy and a source of potential climate destabilisation.

In this concluding chapter, I reflect on the main messages of the book and develop the proposition that we need to rethink the point and purpose of building. I discuss Betsky's (2017) observation that there is a need to slow down, even to stop, constructing new buildings and infrastructure, and to adapt what already exists. This includes rethinking how space should be reused, and to transform built environments into flexible, multifunctioning places connected to nature in ways whereby a building seeks to nurture, not destroy, the natural environment. This does not preclude the possibility of the replacement of buildings and/or infrastructure by new structures, particularly for people living in places where there is an insufficient supply of good-quality, habitable environments. It does mean that new construction is not a priority where adaptative techniques and interventions can be made, and this includes avoiding demolition and its disruptive social and environmental costs.

These observations are brought into sharp focus by the COVID-19 pandemic, in which the pre-existing built environment seems increasingly unsuited to coping with a world trying to deal with a major socio-ecological crisis. From the stay-at-home employees no longer wanting to inhabit air-conditioned office environments, to the millions of people looking for access to open, green spaces as a means of both socially distancing and escaping the confines of dwellings without gardens, there is a momentum towards a much more socially responsive, and responsible, architecture and building that eschews its commodification, or the production of spaces for profit. COVID-19 draws to our attention the idea that buildings and spaces ought to be attentive to the physical and mental well-being of people, and also, simultaneously, responsive to ecology and the needs of the planet's species.

In developing these ideas, I divide the rest of the chapter into three themes. The first considers the importance of a challenge to the political economy of building, and the significance of post-growth. It will be difficult to sustain a world that provides for all people, including the reproduction of the biosphere, if current trajectories of building continue, shaped by a political-economic logic that knows no bounds, or limits to growth. A second theme considers the significance of the COVID-19 pandemic in changing people's interrelationship with space and the built environment, and how far it is a basis for overturning the dominant, consumerist model of construction. Despite negative impacts on society, the pandemic provides a prompt for reappraising and challenging the prevailing building culture and forms of spatial development. There is a need to rethink what we build, why we build and how to construct in ways whereby the health and well-being of living species is paramount.

The final theme outlines alternative ways of thinking about, and practising, building, in which what is required is a sea change in the culture of construction, underpinned by a democratic, participative approach to the design and production of places. I discuss the importance of the building process being understood, and practised, as holistic and relational, and to recognise the intricate interrelationships between people, ecology and building, in which the objective or outcome of any construction project ought to be a symbiosis. This requires a different value and knowledge set and different skills to those ordinarily imparted to building professionals, including a change in the social relations of construction. Here, I discuss the importance of politicising the actions of building professionals, and underpinning their work by changes to the pedagogic and learning environments that, in their present form, do little to encourage critique of, or critical reflection on, the ethical and practical implications of building and construction practices.

Crafting a built environment for use, not exchange

Much of the book has documented the proliferation of building and construction, and its ubiquitous presence, around the globe. The irony is that while there is much awareness of the socio-ecological impacts of building, there is more construction occurring than at any time of human history, and projections suggest that the rates and scales of this will increase markedly over the course of the 21st century (World Green Building Council, 2016). One response is to leave the status quo untouched and to permit the continuation of unfettered construction, and rely on people's technical know-how and the use of technology to mitigate its deleterious effects. A whole industry has emerged around mitigation strategies, from smart cities to the use of green growth products. Yet, as intimated in Chapter 9, they are focused on addressing the symptoms or effects of deleterious building activity, while sidestepping, and not confronting, the underlying causes.

This raises the question of what is the point and purpose of mitigating the symptoms of building activity when this will do little to change the deleterious effects of construction on people and ecology? Where is the political challenge to, or the means to overturn, the underlying dynamics of the economy of construction, characterised by the production of buildings for profit and the reproduction of spaces that facilitate wealth acquisition for corporate, state and individual interests? The dynamic of the capitalist land market is key in shaping the proclivity to build, and, as outlined in Chapter 4, speculative real estate development, motivated by investors seeking to capture upwards movements in land values, is responsible for large swathes of construction. For investors in construction, the objective is the growth of assets, and enhancing the exchange value of a building is part of a quantitative paradigm that values materialism and the acquisition of material goods as, seemingly, part of a rich and virtuous life.

For Adam Smith (1776), this was a fallacious understanding of materialism and its impacts on morality but nonetheless a powerful part of a broader ideology legitimising the worth and value to people of acquisitiveness and consumption. The rise of capitalism after the 18th century revolved around such ideological substrata, in which behaviour that propagated economic growth was conceived as virtuous and the basis of the good life that a person of virtue was duty-bound to pursue. The rationality of these powerful, and disarming, ideas of the interrelations between self-worth, virtue and consumption is at the fulcrum of contemporary society, and it shapes behaviour in the construction sector. It is part of a self-serving rationale by actors in the building industry in which to engage in the development of land and property is to pursue growth without limits by extracting the highest-possible exchange values from transactions in real estate.

This exchange-value character of land and property shapes the form and substance of the built environment, and it serves to (re)produce commodified spaces, implicated in transforming the socio-ecological quality of places. As recounted in Chapter 4, contemporary urban change is characterised by hyper-speculative development and the construction of spaces that encourage expansion of the oil economy, while denuding the planet's precious resources. The proliferation of the areal size of cities is interlinked with the development of a built environment constructed, increasingly, around suburban sprawl and tall buildings, and generating exorbitant demands for both water and energy consumption in central city areas. This is compounded by a built environment that extends into areas of environmental risk, often disregarding the risks posed to people by living in flood plains or close to sources of potential wildfires. The impulse to build, and to extract value from the process, often outweighs environmental, and other, considerations.

The speculative nature of building has spawned places that are increasingly unequal and unaffordable, or constructed as investment spaces to provide assets for private equity and real estate organisations. Property-led development is creating gentrified spaces, and transforming places into quasi-private entities, or environments that, in their exclusivity, command high exchange valuations. Richter et al (2017) refer to such places as the epitome of the anti-social architecture of contemporary urbanism, in which much design and construction is antithetical to sociability and a collective presence in space. Here, the construction of buildings and objects increasingly serves and services private places, and is part of a widespread privatisation of the built environment. Much of this environment is foreclosed to the public and only accessible under specific conditions of entry, and construction activity is increasingly associated with the production of vanity projects, or places that pander to wealthy, elite groups.

Vanity projects, such as the Shard in London, are integral to a speculative urbanism that, as documented in Chapter 4, is part of the wasteful culture of building by providing buildings that do not respond to, or provide for, social need. Speculative behaviour is the epitome of a building system in thrall to exchange values, flooding places with an abundance of building types, or variegated investment products, in anticipation of generating high monetary returns. The outcome is properties priced well beyond what many people can afford, often being bought by wealthy investors as 'buy-to-leave' investments rather than places to be available for occupation and use. Here, the speculative city is often one of empty or barely used buildings, awaiting upturns in land values and property prices so that they can be traded on. Meanwhile, homeless people wander the streets among the empty buildings, testament to an exchange-value, transactional system that is bereft of any moral standpoint or compass.

The growthist impulses of construction are also part of geopolitical behaviour, and in the book, I have conveyed the significance of state-building programmes involving the acquisition and development of territory. The history of humanity revolves around colonial and postcolonial state, territorial development, in which building and construction are integral to the opening up, and settlement, of territories. Such settlement is simultaneously the disruption and unsettlement of pre-existing social and ecological relations, and the rupture and displacement of people and species from places. Here, construction is deployed in a variety of ways, from its potency as a 'weapon or war', or means to contain and control populations, to a developmental role in the provision of access to, and extraction of, resources, ranging from aggregates to forestry and hydroelectricity. In turn, such resources are part of the broader industrial growth trajectories of states, and are the necessary ingredients in supporting the expansion of building and construction.

This ongoing commodification of construction extends its reach into every aspect of building, and is at the apex of the capitalist economy in fuelling the consumption of non-renewal resources, and stimulating the demand for thousands of building, and related, products. There is no corner of the globe, or any aspect of human activity, that is not implicated and involved in the production and consumption of goods and services related to building, and much of what is produced is 'lifestyle' oriented and part of a consumer capitalism, or the production of stuff that perpetuates waste. This is typified by the rapid growth of the home market, or the wholesale commodification of domestic lifestyles, with builders, and assorted manufacturers of everything from doors to bathrooms, radiators, ventilators, artificial grass, flooring and loft extensions, seeking to sell stuff to adorn and add to the value of a dwelling.

To scale back on building, and to change its character and *raison d'être*, will require far-reaching changes not only to the political actions of states, but also to the rationality of an exchange-value economy that perpetuates the virtues of unfettered production and consumption. How might this be addressed and achieved in ways whereby there is not only a break with the powerful, and deeply embedded, rationality of economic growth, but also a practical, political means to achieve a different way of reconceiving space and the built environment? There is a need to challenge, intellectually and politically, the technocratic and instrumentalist character of exchange-value relations that smokescreen the construction process as a neutral act, or a straightforward, non-partisan, monetary transaction. These relations do not raise, or question, the how and why of building and its socio-ecological effects; rather, they render the process as apolitical, as though any social and environmental effect or outcome of construction is a by-product, or an externality.

The notion of 'externality' is a misnomer because externalities are never benign or neutral, but part of the logic of an economy that seeks to minimise the costs of construction by offshoring them to third or external parties. This is a frequent occurrence characterised by, for example, water degradation related to the building of hydroelectricity dams, or the construction of roads that generate noise and air pollution in their use. These illustrations are redolent of an irresponsible and careless, even uncaring, approach to people's interactions with the environment. What is required is much more care in how we build, with careful deliberation about where we build and with what materials. To construct ought to be a life-enhancing, not life-threatening, process and a positive addition to a place that nurtures ecology and environment for its intrinsic value, in which nature is 'a visible, palpable, presence in daily human experience' (Milani, 2000: 130).

In conceiving of nature and its resources as subservient to, and in the service of, the economy, the growthist rationality of building reinforces the sense that ecologies are purely products, or, as Gibson-Graham and Miller (2015: 7) note, 'passive inputs for production and consumption measured primarily by their market value'. For Gibson-Graham and Miller (2015), this conceives of the economy as a distinctive sphere of activity, as an individualised, monetised calculation, whereas ecologies exist 'out there' as objects to be exploited by people. The power of this conception is manifest in the violence wrought on nature by construction, and other human activities, and, as Gibson-Graham and Miller (2015: 8, original emphasis) suggest, to counter this, there is a need to recognise the interrelationships between the economy and ecology, or to see the 'economy *as* ecology'. This is to recognise that economic activities are indelibly part of nature, affecting, and being affected by, their interdependence.

It follows that to sustain the sustenance of people with(in) nature requires much more respect towards, and understanding of, the fragilities of our being in the world, in which the growthist rationality that conceives of people as decoupled from nature has the potential to denude, and destroy, the fabric that is the sustenance of life. For Gibson-Graham and Miller (2015: 14), to reconceive the economy as ecology is to ask the ethical question: 'how do we live together with human and non-human others' in ways whereby the objective is not unfettered economic growth, but the production for necessity and sufficiency, or the 'dignified survival of all living beings and communities'? In contrast, the construction of the built environment is the production and consumption of excess, albeit unevenly distributed, and for Gibson-Graham and Miller (2015), such excess needs to be eradicated by a post-growth society. Here, societal and species betterment is premised on a community of sharing, characterised by what Gibson-Graham and Miller (2015: 15) describe as 'ethical negotiations of multiple rationalities and ways-of-living'.

This is to create a building culture whereby what is built and consumed is for its value in use, not exchange, and responsive to the needs of people and other biotic matter. There is, however, no easy way to extricate society from unrelenting consumerism, or an economic ideology that legitimises wastefulness and ecologically unsustainable growth, and building for the sake of building. The idea of a post-growth economy, underpinning Gibson-Graham and Miller's (2015) sentiments, offers the potential for a society shaped by a qualitative paradigm, or what Blewitt and Cunningham (2014: back page) refer to as 'a better life based on having fewer material possessions, less production and less work', and an emphasis on 'well-being, community, security and conviviality'. Here, growth is defined less by econometric criteria relating to the production of quantities of materials for exchange, whether bricks, mortar or house furnishings, and more in relation to the growth of, for example, the ecological mix, the diversity of species or the adaptation of a building that reduces, even eliminates, the presence of toxic materials.

A post-growth future does not suggest that we should not build; rather, it is a matter of what we build and how we build, and the factors that motivate and shape the building process. It is a future that rejects the present economic paradigm of growth with seemingly few limits, of speculative capitalism and of a trajectory that, if it continues, will likely implode on its own contradictions, or what Crownshaw et al (2019: 117) describe as 'an involuntary and unplanned cessation of growth'. For Crownshaw et al (2019: 131), a post-growth world requires a fundamental change in how we organise society, and 'a de-emphasis of material consumption as the singular path to wellbeing'. It also requires valuing community and the common good, and instilling care of, and for, people and species into everyday life, or those habitual, human practices that are sensitised, and responsive, to the indeterminacies of socio-ecological relations.

Pandemic spaces and recrafting the built environment

To recreate a world that revolves around the needs of both people and non-human species is no easy task. It requires radical and far-reaching changes to the institutional, political and economic organisation of society, and transformations to the systems of governance and resource allocation, including the inculcation of the population into a different way of thinking about, and interacting with, each other and the biosphere. All of this may be difficult to imagine transpiring, yet the question is: what are the alternatives, or the means of living within our environments that do not lead to the inability of the biosphere to reproduce itself, and, with it, the means to sustain people and the species? Here, the ways that we live, by the ways that we build, are of paramount significance, a statement that has resonance with the emergence of the COVID-19 pandemic, which may well provide a necessary challenge to the prevailing order.

While a sustainability agenda has been around for some time, and has provided impetus into rethinking the nature of building and construction, nothing has fundamentally changed. This makes the emergence of COVID-19 potentially important for how it may change people's interrelationships with buildings and space, and while this may be of a temporary nature, it provides insights into what might be possible. This is not surprising because the history of human settlement and building revolves around health and welfare concerns, and previous pandemics and outbreaks of disease have been important in changing the form and quality of the built environment. In London in the mid-19th century, cholera outbreaks were a consequence, in part, of dense urban living and people drinking untreated water, and dumping sewage and other waste into rivers. Once water was identified as the source of the disease, new infrastructure was installed to supply clean water and safely dispose of sewage, and more liveable, less threatening, environments emerged.

Unlike cholera, which led to a specific form of urban, infrastructural change, COVID-19 prompts questions about the *raison d'être* of the design and performance of the built environment as a whole. It is, potentially, a challenge to conventional wisdom, and practices, about how buildings and spaces are constructed and used, and how far they are 'pandemic-proof' and able to safeguard health. Here, there is debate about how COVID-19 ought to be understood, with the recognition that it is not a discrete occurrence, but systemic (Murshed, 2020). It reflects the interdependence of the human and non-human world, and how people's exploitation, and misappropriation, of nature's resources has consequences for the well-being of the world's population. The source of COVID-19 is an economic system of food production characterised by human interference in, and exploitation of, specific ecosystems, enabling chains of interaction between people and non-humans, with the consequential transmission of the virus and its rapid spread.

This spread is directly interconnected with human lifestyles and the operations of a political economy that revolves around high levels of mobility and movement, and a closeness of physical interactions in confined and compressed spaces. The spread of COVID-19 highlights the limits of the major speculative building projects of the 20th and 21st centuries, of the indoor shopping centres that depend on mass footfall, and of the corporate, air-conditioned, office environments, with shared spaces that provide little protection from the spread of an infectious disease. COVID-19 also highlights how the construction of the domestic, residential environment is contributing to new forms of social inequalities and injustices, in which governments' 'stay-at-home' policies as part of a strategy to prevent the ease of spread of the virus highlight the differences between those who have access to a garden or a private open space, and those who do not, and who have no option in accessing open space but to use public space or parks, where the risks of catching the virus are heightened.

The pandemic draws attention to the intimate interconnections between people and the biosphere, in that whatever is built ought to be done with knowledge and understanding of how buildings and biotic ecologies interact. As experiences of COVID-19 suggest, if we harm nature or transgress natural rhythms and processes, then we run the risk of harming ourselves and the broader biosphere. In drawing a parallel with the built environment, there is a need to respect the place-based relationships between buildings and their settings, or the sites where they are constructed. For FLW (Lloyd Wright, 1932), the notion of organic architecture was premised on avoiding the imposition of a building on a site, as the site and the building ought to be a symbiosis or part of a dialectical relationship. This was part of a broader appreciation of sustaining ecological quality and integrity by minimising people's impact on the earth, and for FLW (Lloyd Wright, 1932: 238), a key principle for guiding construction was 'no speculation in natural resources [and] of earth, water, air, or sky'.

Such sentiments are to the fore in the post-growth movement, and proponents of eco- and living buildings conceive, in part, of the need to interact with, and transform, what we have built, and to develop a building culture that stops using the planet's resources. Instead of continuously building and rebuilding, there needs to be much more emphasis on remaking and reusing the materials of the built environment. The architect Aaron Betsky (2015) makes the case to work with what we have, to scale back on new construction and to adopt techniques of adaptive reuse as the future of building. As Betsky (2015: 1) suggests, there is a need to end vanity and speculative building, and to 'replace the notion of the genius designer creating monuments for the ages out of his (not her) head, and imposing them on the rest of us with the idea of an architecture that reimagines our world' (see Figure 10.1). For Betsky (2020), the imperative is to stop 'wasting both space and unrenewable natural resources on making new buildings'.

Figure 10.1: Hudson Yards, New York City

Note: Betsky's (2015) comments are directed at speculative mega-developments that bear testimony to the faults and failures of speculation. Referring to Hudson Yards, he suggests that 'it is almost criminal to use up so many natural resources to build such large structures for so few people, and to close it off from the city perceptually and physically' (Betsky, 2019: 1).

Source: https://upload.wikimedia.org/wikipedia/commons/5/56/Hudson_Yards_from_
Hudson_Commons_%2895131p%29.jpg

One approach is to consume fewer buildings while redistributing spaces to enable everyone to have access to a minimum quantity, and quality, of environment. For the Finnish architect Alvar Aalto, a rational space was the minimum dwelling, or the construction of small dimensions, in which he conceived of large dimensions as a problem and a potential drawback (see Frampton, 1998). For Aalto (cited in Pallasmaa, 1984: 199), while the house had to be divided to accommodate and respond to biological functioning and needs, large spaces were unnecessary and internal spaces could be created, and changed, by 'moveable and foldable furniture', or demountable design. This view chimes with broader debates about the importance of flexibility in design, including Habraken's (1972) conception of buildings as 'supports', in which people ought to be provided with a building structure that they can 'fill in' or flexibly adapt and change according to their changing needs and lifestyles.

There are variations on these views that challenge why we need to keep building when adaptation of lifestyles, and habits, can facilitate a very different type of built environment. Ellsworth-Krebs (2018: 1) questions why societal values often tend to regard 'bigger as always better', and suggests that 'we need to make do with less and learn to appreciate it'. Her thoughts are important because the trend, in many countries, is to consume more of everything and to demand much more space for living. In the US, it is estimated that in 2016, the average size of newly built homes was 2,430 square feet, over 1,000 square feet larger than 100 years ago (Property Shark, 2016). For Ellsworth-Krebs (2018), instead of building so big and consuming so much space, living in smaller spaces can be feasible by careful construction and lifestyle changes, which range from soundproofing walls to create a better sense of privacy than having more rooms, to the use of sofa beds to create temporary guest bedrooms that need not be empty for the majority of the year.

The rise of the 'tiny house' movement, described by Ford and Gomez-Lanier (2017: 394) as 'minimizing, de-cluttering, and downsizing', provides an illustration of what might be possible (see Figure 10.2). The movement has its roots in the early 1970s as a countercultural critique of the excess of consumption in society. Its objective is to encourage people to live modestly by reducing their environmental footprint and, as Alexander (2015: 8) suggests, to pursue 'sufficiency, frugality, moderation, restraint, localism, and mindfulness'. Tiny homes in the US tend to be 20 per cent of the size of the average dwelling, with low running costs and waste, and less use of raw materials. While evidence of the effects of tiny homes is lacking, some research shows that those who subscribe to it, and live in tiny dwellings, seek out a simple way of living. They try to create an autonomous life free from dependence on a building that ties one to utility and other companies, and

Figure 10.2: The Nest House, Argyll and Bute, Scotland

Note: The Nest House is a tiny house designed and built by Jonathan Avery of Tiny House Scotland. Such houses range in size from 10 to 50 m².

Source: https://upload.wikimedia.org/wikipedia/commons/4/47/JA6_4484.jpg

full of 'experiences and relationships as a means toward happiness' (Mangold and Zschau, 2019: 15).

The tiny house has potential to be part of what Fry (2011) refers to as a quality-based economy, in which the objective is to minimise the production and consumption of objects, and to engage in their maintenance and repair. Fry's (2011) view advocates for a caring approach to building, or the crafting of spaces by attending to the fragile, perilous existence of the multiple microcosms of the planet and their interdependence. For Fry (2011), instead of the continuous excavation of the earth as part of the preparation of new construction sites and sourcing of building materials, there is a need to develop what he describes as a 'metro-fitting culture'. This process does not just mend and repair or take objects back to what they were, but refashions them to adapt to the emergent world. It recognises constantly changing socio-ecological conditions, and the need to craft a built environment that is easily adaptable to these by being sensitised to, and crafted out of, the ecological fabric of places.

To metro-fit the built environment is not an easy task because it is not only a matter of the physical redesigning and rebuilding of infrastructure, but a different way of organising an economy, including all of the infrastructural systems relating to the functioning of a place. To metro-fit is to create a system-wide 'arcology' in which the point of crafting a space ought to be to enhance its functioning as a living system by pursuing a frugal resilience or doing more with less (Soleri et al, 2012).[1] Metro-fitting requires the abandonment of modernist projects that consume fossil fuels, and the dismantling, and refitting, of buildings that operate with high levels of energy use. It involves greater flood management, the re-siting of buildings away from areas of environmental risk and the prevention of construction that compromises life. It rejects the exploitation of resources sourced globally by reducing global flows of goods and services, and insinuates local ways of living, with city spaces becoming a 'catchment' for life's key elements and with the localised production of food and sourcing of water.

Towards a built environment that cares

To realise a built environment that is sensitive to the socio-ecological fabric of the planet depends on attending to the fragilities that comprise it. This is the point and purpose of care, and Amin (2006) outlines some helpful suggestions about how one might reconceive of building and caring. This is premised on a progressive politics of care and well-being that, as Amin (2006: 1012) notes, recognises 'the "being-togetherness" of life in urban space ... demanding attendance to the politics of living together'. For Amin (2006: 1012), caring is premised on recognising our commonalities and differences, or an urban solidarity in which outcomes ought to 'benefit the more rather than the few, without compromising the right to difference'. To care is not just 'to build', but also, as Amin (2006: 1014) suggests, to attend to 'continual maintenance and repair'; it is to assure the publicness of what is built by its inclusive qualities and to encourage a plurality of being and dissent, or the means for people to shape the politics and processes of the construction of urban environments.

Such sentiments begin to steer thinking towards a purposive politics of urban design and building, and for Papanek (1984: 333), a manifesto of rights is required to combat 'the worst excesses of a profit seeking system' that is implicated in creating short-lived, often obsolete, products that do not work well for the socio-ecological fabric of the earth. Papanek (1984: 339) suggests that a bill of rights should include people's rights 'to have access to a variety of products and services', and for them to be heard and represented in the design and building process. This reflects a system of construction that is far removed from those that consume the built environment, the populace of users. They are conceived by the building industry never as individuals or citizens, but as consumers of stuff, to be kept at arm's length from the process. There is a hierarchy here that maintains a social and political closure, or a non-transparency of the actions and operations of the building industry.

Papanek's (1984) observations are suggestive of the need for fundamental changes to defining what building is for, and to decouple its production from profit and asset acquisition. This is not an easy task and requires much more than procedural and technocratic 'fixes', or public sector management interventions. The likelihood is that the break between building and profit, or construction as the production of assets, will not transpire easily, but this ought not to work against measures to open up the building industry, including the state's involvement, towards accounting for its activities and actions. This should include moves towards radical transparency, or the subversion of 'dominant attitudes towards disclosure's limited and prescribed role in the political sphere' (Birchall, 2014: 85). It recognises that most calls for transparency are clichéd and revolve around disclosures that do not disclose. Instead, a new political-ethical approach will need to break entrenched hierarchies and procedures, and to destabilise systems of operating, such as procurement and contract bidding, as ways of opening them up to a resistant, critical scrutiny.

This is to regain popular, community control of an activity that affects every aspect of life, and to provide a democratic basis for shaping what is built, for whom and for what purpose. Part of the agenda ought to be a right to determine life by the redesign of buildings and spaces that do not undermine the lives of people and species. This point is pertinent in relation to the poor water quality that many people and non-human species often have to drink, the toxic air quality in cities and the production of plastic waste that will never degrade. In designing the built environment, the right to life ought to be part of an ethical disposition of the building industry in which every stage of crafting and creating the material basis of building is subject to rigorous checks and controls. One example is to separate where people sleep from where motor vehicles move about, and to ensure that there is a distancing between the two as part of a broader objective of creating calm spaces as free as possible from the toxins emitted by vehicles.

Part of a right to determine life is also to craft a building culture that is sensitive to the needs of the body by constructing in ways that attend to the mental and physical needs of people. Throughout this book, I have outlined some of the disembodied practices of construction, in which there is often a fixity of building structure, the ossification of space and the making of places lacking relational qualities or sensitivity to changes in how people and non-humans may seek to interact with their environments. An embodied approach to building, which is the antithesis of the preset, predesigned spaces that typify most contemporary, industrial-scale construction, needs to be developed. There is need to scale buildings and places that relate to the human body, and to create legible places that enable people with different cognitive functioning to interact with(in) them. This is to develop an understanding of the interrelationships between the senses and building, or, as Pallasmaa (2017: 108) suggests, to inculcate into the professions the significance of 'human embodied existence [as] the prerequisite for a dignified life'.

The question is how to develop change within the building and construction sector in ways whereby its activities are less likely to harm the planet, and better able to enhance the liveability of spaces. Across the world, there are many instances of the politicisation of building, or the uprising of dissent and opposition by local groups to construction activities, yet none of this has led to significant change in the industry. Opposition to the activities of the construction sector is localised and fragmented, and cross-cuts many different types of contexts, from local residents groups opposing building in their neighbourhoods, to campaign groups, such as Reclaim the Streets, seeking to create safe, walkable places free from motor vehicles (see Figure 10.3). Such groupings rarely intercede or communicate with one another, and often do not share similar political ideals, or conceive of their campaigns as sharing like-minded objectives. This is particularly so with single issue groups, in which opposition to a local project is temporary

Figure 10.3: Reclaim the Streets

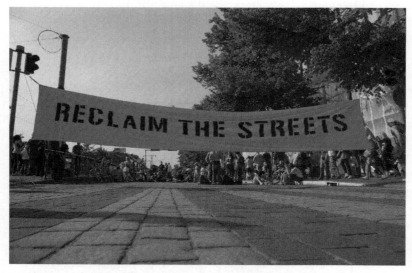

Note: Reclaim the Streets was formed in 1991 as an anti-roads campaign to transform highways into public spaces to cater for pedestrians and other, non-motor-vehicle users.

Source: https://upload.wikimedia.org/wikipedia/commons/5/51/Reclaim_the_streets.jpg

and focused and rarely thought about as symptomatic of broader, systemic, culture of building.

To transform what amounts to an apolitical stasis, and to create a basis for thinking about building beyond the immediacy of its effects, is not easy, but part of a response is to change people's perceptions, and understandings, of construction and its place-based outcomes. This is an argument for developing education, resources and political power in order to provide people with the intellectual, and practical, tools to proffer alternative spatialities to those propagated by the corporate construction sector, and with the means to control their actions. Here, building would be reconceived as politics, and the building process democratised in ways whereby there is, in Fry's (2011: 42) terms, 'a seismic shift in political, economic and cultural agendas'. For Zibechi (2012: 28), a key to progressive change is to deinstitutionalise professional practice and to challenge, and change, the 'institutional knowledge that usually lies in the hands of specialists'.

This suggests a different pedagogic culture able to change conceptions of what building is or ought to be, based on instilling an ethical scrutiny into its purpose. Construction is usually conceived of, and taught, as the building of a fixity or creation of a permanent object, usually unrelated to its context or surroundings. Building professionals are taught about construction as a technical issue, based on an engineering approach and solution, with little sense of the politics that relates to it, or the sociocultural significance of a building. A conception of time and the future-directive nature of building is weakly developed within the pedagogic experiences of professionals. As Fry (2011) suggests, construction leaves imprints on the earth that are not easy to eradicate, and whatever is built has consequences that transpire over time. There is a responsibility to think about, and act upon, the unfolding effects of building, and for temporal considerations to be at the forefront of the construction process.

A critical pedagogy for building ought to challenge the modernist discourses of construction, to reject any notion of nature as an exterior object, and to not overlook the interrelationships between people, buildings and ecologies. A critically disposed building profession ought to cultivate relational knowledges, with, for example, its practitioners developing understanding of how and why construction materials are extracted, processed, deployed and disposed of. FLW (Lloyd Wright, 1932: 249) commented on practitioners' limited knowledge of materials and processes, noting that what held them back from practising in a way that was sensitive to the organic, site-specific context of building was the organisation of the professions into specialisms. To develop an arcology, or how building is indelibly part of its socio-ecological context, requires practitioners to become knowledgeable of all aspects of the process, or, as FLW (Lloyd Wright, 1932: 249) advised trainee architects, to 'go into the field where you can see the machines and methods at work … stay in construction direct and simple until you can work naturally into building design'.

For these sentiments to translate into a caring culture of construction will require not only pedagogic changes, but also a politics of building. As conveyed in this book, to build is to act on, and through, the environment, and to transform people's lives and the biosphere. This occurs, primarily, through powerful, vested interests that are not always coterminous with a broader, common good. Our building culture encourages what Raymond Williams (1989: 22) describes as the tendency to propagate avarice in which the working of land and the construction of buildings is part of a dispossession, or objects that are often lost to common usage and environmental degradation. A politics of building requires overturning the socio-institutional relations involved in dispossession, from the air that we breathe to the earth that we live upon, and the insinuation of a common good relating to how we build and where we build in ways that attend to the health and well-being of *all* species.

Conclusion

Throughout this book, I have conveyed that there is too much building that is poorly crafted and constructed, inattentive to people and the pressing social needs of our times, and implicated in what some commentators regard as the onset of the irreversible despoliation and destruction of ecologies and environments (Soleri, 1969; Fry, 2011). From the construction of major transport networks and commercial and residential property in rapidly urbanising countries, such as China and India, to the popularisation of self-build and home improvements, we are living in a period of unprecedented building in which there are few places untouched by building and infrastructure projects. The ubiquity of building far exceeds what human beings need to survive as a species, yet there is much that is constructed that is unavailable to people, or part of an exchange-value economy that, through pricing mechanisms, is implicated in the (re) production of significant socio-spatial inequalities relating to building provision and its consumption.

This is one of many perversities relating to the economy and culture of building, and much more care in the crafting and construction of places is required to ensure that whatever is built and/or adapted is attentive to the fragilities of the socio-ecological make-up of places. This seems unlikely while construction remains a significant part of a global growth culture, or developmentalist paradigm, in which the rationality of building is premised on growth without limits. Supported and orchestrated by state power, construction is pivotal to the (re)production of capitalist economies, and reflects, and reproduces, its central tenets, that is, the propagation of commodities and exchange. To craft a building culture beyond this is an ongoing task, and here I concur with Soleri et al (2012: 15), who note that for architecture and building to become part of a 'coherent human ecology, a reformulation is necessary that puts distance between it and our present reigning materialism'.

Notes

Chapter 1

[1]   Synthetic processes are purposive human interventions in nature, and ought not to be regarded as 'non-natural' or separate from, or existing outside of, nature.

Chapter 2

[1]   This period of time is commonly referred to as 'prehistory', characterised by nature dominating social and cultural patterns and processes.

[2]   Camões and Ferreira (2010: 1573) suggest that the development of concrete by the Romans was the most important legacy that they 'left to mankind in the art and technique of building'.

[3]   The increase in construction activity is likely to continue. Robinson et al (2015) predict that the volume of construction output will grow by 85 per cent to US$15.5 trillion worldwide by 2030, with three countries (China, the US and India) accounting for 57 per cent of global growth.

[4]   Construction and demolition waste (CDW) is a major problem in the EU. The European Commission (2019: 1) states that CDW 'accounts for approximately 25% to 30% of all waste generated in the EU and consists of numerous materials, including concrete, bricks, gypsum, wood, glass, metals, plastic, solvents, asbestos and excavated soil, many of which can be recycled'.

[5]   This point is made by a number of commentators, including Sandilands (2018: 1), who notes that 'lack of media coverage' contributes 'to the limited public response to the sector's waste problem'. He refers to the construction industry as the 'silent sector' to denote its activities bypassing public perception and slipping under the radar of political scrutiny and comment.

[6]   There is little likelihood of a decline in sand dredging. Sand is an important building material and its value attracts mafia gangs. Tweedie (2018: 1) reports on criminal gangs stealing sand from pristine beaches 'and paradise islands ... being dredged and sold to the construction industry'. In India, Mahadevan (2019: 1) notes that sand mining is worth US$2 billion per year, and that 'civil administration is retreating before a mafia-like nexus of political, business and bureaucratic interests'.

Chapter 3

[1]   Soft power is a process of political ingratiation, or the use of persuasion and diplomacy, rather than coercion, to forge relationships between states. The exercise of soft power may include policies of cultural influence to forge mutual identification between states

and the creation of chains of obligation, as evidenced by major Chinese infrastructure investments in African nations (see Nye, 2008).

2   A variation on the notion of the construction state is the 'real estate state' coined by Stein (2019). For Stein (2019: 45), the real estate state is 'government by developers, for developers', in which planning commissions and review boards are composed 'of people whose futures are tied to real estate'. Stein (2019) conceives of the real estate state as shaping planners' actions towards policies and plans that promote the industry's interests by rezoning areas to facilitate ease of development, encouraging tax breaks and reducing regulations that might otherwise impact on development investment.

3   A total of 800 miles of 'bypass' roads' have been constructed by the Israeli state in the West Bank that connect Jewish settlements to each other and to Israel. They are for use by Israeli citizens and/or residents, and illustrate the significance of building in seeking to secure political control of territory.

4   Like India, China's spending on construction is phenomenal, and Bach (2016: 1) refers to China as the 'paradigmatic infrastructural state', noting that in 2015, 43 per cent of the country's total investment, or US$2.3 trillion, was spent on infrastructure. This was more than 14 per cent of China's GDP. In the wake of COVID-19, commentators note that the Chinese government is expanding infrastructure spending as part of a process to modernise the country and spend its way out of the economic downturn caused by the pandemic (see Wong, 2020). It is estimated that expenditure on infrastructure will exceed US$2 trillion per year between 2020 and 2025 (see Desai, 2020).

5   The Madeira River runs through Amazonia for 900 miles. It is one of the major, navigable waterways for the shipment of soy and corn grain by cargo barges. The Madeira River project is, primarily, two hydroelectric dams: the Santo Antonio and the Jirau. Major environmental effects have ensued, including a 'large increase in newly flooded areas significantly greater than predicted by an environmental impact assessment in 2005' (Li et al, 2020: 17). Cunningham (2018) describes how people's lives have been disrupted by the Santo Antonio dam, including loss of local fisheries, the pollution of drinking water and people forced to relocate to cities outside of the region.

6   One of the earliest writings about the mercantile system is *The Wealth of Nations* by Adam Smith (1776). For Smith (1776), the mercantile system was a private network of monopolies that dominated the economic affairs of early-modern Europe. Private companies lobbied governments for the right to operate exclusive trade routes, while closed guilds controlled the flow of products and employment within domestic markets. Smith (1776) regarded mercantilism as a 'closed system' promoting the interests of specific groups.

Chapter 4

1   The sub-prime mortgage crisis was pronounced in the US, precipitated by a mixture of housing speculation by financial institutions and the availability of cheap credit and mortgage finance (see Albanesi et al, 2017). This led to an exposure of households on low incomes to risks of defaulting on mortgage repayments, a process that ensued in the wake of the collapse of housing markets at the end of 2007. People walked away from properties they could no longer afford, and in many US cities, the legacy is swathes of abandoned and empty dwellings.

2   A notable builder was Nicholas Barbon, who acquired sites all over London at cut-price rates after the Great Fire and developed techniques to construct identikit-type dwellings. These tended to be tall, thin terraces or buildings that enabled the maximisation of lettable space, and, as Parsons (2012: 62) notes, the 'workmanship was sometimes lamentable'.

3   Roger North's autobiography was not published until after his death, and readers can access it in the edited book by Peter Millard (2000).

4   This is particularly so in relation to office and retail space, and it was estimated that in 2017, 24,400 commercial properties in London were empty (Bosetti and Colthorpe, 2018: 31). Bosetti and Colthorpe (2018: 31) note that 22,500 of these 'have been empty for at least six months', and 'the total vacant floorspace' is 27 times that of Europe's largest shopping centre, Westfield London, located in White City, West London.

5   Not much has changed since the mid-1970s, and by the end of the 2010s, Centre Point was less than half-occupied after the owner, Almacantar, halted sales as the asking prices, ranging from £1.8 million for a small one-bedroomed apartment to £55 million for a two-storey five-bedroomed penthouse, were not attracting offers. Rather than reduce the prices, the owner has kept space empty (see Neate, 2018b).

6   Weiler (2013: 394) quotes from a report published by the Royal Town Planning Institute that Centre Point was the epitome of an 'empty office syndrome ... that has become the symbol of the unacceptable face of capitalism'. The Labour MP Anthony Crosland (1972: col 1091) said in a Parliamentary debate that there was a 'mood of helpless resentment at the inability to stop these damned developments'.

7   St George Wharf Tower has been described by Booth and Bengtsson (2016: 1) as 'under occupied, astonishingly expensive, mostly foreign owned, and with dozens of apartments held through secretive offshore firms'. Atkinson (2019: 10) notes that 'The Tower has a quarter of its flats held through offshore companies'.

8   In 2014 and 2015, with my research colleague Dr Mike Dolton from Royal Holloway University of London, we interviewed 12 actors in Nine Elms, including representatives from house-building companies, local planning officials, community group representatives and residents. We mapped the area and I kept a diary to record feelings and thoughts. Some of my diary-recorded thoughts are reproduced in this and subsequent chapters.

9   Writing in the same period as Parker (1911), Ryan (1902: 347) argues that speculative behaviour is deeply embedded in questions of morality: 'socially, it is productive of great and widespread evils; and morally, it is vitiated by a very considerable amount of dishonest "deals" and practices. As an individual action, speculation, at its best, is morally questionable.'

Chapter 5

1   For some scholars, gentrification was a feature of Roman cities, and Dufton (2019: 263) documents the displacement of 'less affluent' communities, followed by 'subsequent waves of gentrifying elites' in North African Roman settlements. Dufton (2019: 263) argues that there is 'evidence for the architectural dynamics of Roman gentrification'. This contrasts with Williams and Smith (1986: 206), who suggest that gentrification is 'a feature of the advanced capitalist city' and only appears 'on the agenda after the industrial revolution'.

2   The quote by Le Corbusier in this sentence is attributed by Woudstra (2014) to a letter that Le Corbusier wrote. The letter is lodged with the Fondation Le Corbusier, Paris, and references to it can be found in the article by Woudstra (2014).

3   Robert Moses was a significant public figure in shaping urban renewal in the US. He wielded considerably political influence, particularly in New York City and its environs. One of the best accounts of Robert Moses is by Robert Caro (2015) in *The Power Broker*.

4   It has been estimated that over 90 million people worldwide were forced to move in the 1990s due to development projects involving construction (see Robinson, 2003).

⁵ 'Nail house' is an expression to denote a person and/or a household that uses a variety of actions to try and hold out against a demolition order and development proposal (Hess, 2010). Hess (2010: 908) argues that the notion of 'nail house' has been coined by developers to describe households that resist development as akin to 'stubborn "nails"…on a plank of wood that cannot be easily hammered down'.

⁶ The project was self-funded and I originally developed the work in 1998 when I moved to Esher. Over an 18-year period, I kept a research diary based on my observations from walks around the area, documenting changes to its social and physical fabric. I spoke to numerous local people on my walks, engaging in conversations about changes to the place, and took photographs to document the process of the demolition and rebuilding of the neighbourhood, including Wootton Place. In mid-2014, with a research partner, Dr Luna Glucksberg, a small number of interviews took place with key actors about Wootton Place, including meetings with local planners, a representative from Elmbridge Housing Trust, local councillors and residents.

Chapter 6

¹ Despite the COVID-19 pandemic, and the potential for a slowdown in building and related activities, industry reports about the state of the demolition industry are optimistic. Cunningham (2020: 1) outlines industry views from the US, noting that 'for many, there has been an increase in work in the past year', with 40 per cent of respondents saying that they will increase investment over the next year into 2021. Layoffs were not envisaged: '85 percent of participants say they'll either keep the same number of employees or hire more' (Cunningham, 2020: 1).

² I have been collecting information about the changing character of the neighbourhoods of Esher since the late 1990s, when I first noticed teardown development. I have documented the teardown process on regular walks around the neighbourhood, recording changes by writing my thoughts and reactions, and taking photographs to show the 'before' and 'after' of specific teardown projects.

Chapter 7

¹ An interesting illustration of the build-for-rent market is the involvement of financial sector service companies, such as Legal and General Investment Management (LGIM). They have established a portfolio of 14 build-for-rent schemes in 11 cities, totalling over 4,900 apartments, and fund a mixture of schemes, including homes for 'later life'. Most of the apartments are expensive to rent, with a two-bed apartment in the Blackhorse Mills development in Walthamstow, London, renting *from* £1,990 per month, or just under £500 per week (see: www.blackhorsemills.com/apartments/2-bedroom).

² The debate about land banking is characterised by dispute and controversy, and it is difficult to sort out fact from fiction. Research by Ruddick (2015) claims that in 2015, builders had enough land to construct over 600,000 homes but were sitting on it as part of a process to benefit from increases in land values. This contrasts with a report by the HBF (2014a: 2), noting 'that land hoarding does not occur in any systematic or concerted way by house builders'. The Letwin (2018: 28) report on UK house building concurred, suggesting that developers were not withholding land from the market. Letwin's report, which commands authority in UK planning and property circles, does not correspond with many academic papers. In the Australian context, Murray's (2020: 1) analysis of over 200,000 housing lots led to the conclusion that 'housing developers routinely delay

housing production to capitalise on market cycles'. There are many other papers published that share this view, a fact not reflected in, or evaluated by, the Letwin report.

3   Second-homeownership is addressed in a number of countries, where there are policies to try and mitigate its harmful effects. In Denmark, purchasers of second homes have to provide evidence of its continuous habitation and use, while in New Zealand, the government banned foreign people from buying homes in 2018 to alleviate house price inflation (see Agerholm, 2018). In the UK, there are no such restrictions, or any strong or effective approach by local tiers of government to ward off the negative consequences of second-homeownership.

4   Wyatt (2008), in a comprehensive review of empty dwellings in England, notes that housing can be left empty while undergoing refurbishment because an owner cannot afford its upkeep or the cost of repairs and maintenance, or for less obvious reasons because a person may be working overseas, in prison or otherwise living elsewhere. There are dwellings that are temporarily unoccupied because they are holiday lets and second homes. In other instances, dwellings are bought purely for investment and not to be lived in. There is, therefore, complexity to the vacancy rates relating to dwellings and no singular solution or response that will enable a comprehensive uptake or occupancy of housing.

5   In England, local authorities have powers to encourage the occupancy of empty homes. Shepperson (2016) notes that local authorities can double the rate of council tax on homes left empty for more than two years, compulsory purchase empty properties or use an Empty Dwelling Management Order. The latter can be issued to a dwelling's owner if a property has been empty for more than two years, and where it is a focus for anti-social activity and vandalism. Very few orders have been issued, and Shepperson (2016) suggests that most legal powers relating to empty properties are either unused or ineffective.

Chapter 8

1   The testimonials from Ann and Reiko were generated from two different research projects. Ann was a research participant in a project about accessible housing and the built environment (Imrie, 2006). I met Reiko in Tokyo in July 2014, and she accompanied me as an interpreter to interviews that I was conducting in Japan. As a vision-impaired person, she was knowledgeable about navigation and wayfinding issues around Tokyo, and I accompanied her on walks, where she provided me with insights into how a vision-impaired person is able to interact with the environment, and the problems and issues that this entails (see Imrie and Kullman, 2014).

2   Construction is a high-risk industry that may undermine and debilitate bodies. In the UK, construction contributes to around 40 per cent of occupational cancer deaths and registrations (Construction Industry Training Board, 2019). Past exposures to toxic substances in the construction sector cause over 5,000 occupational cancer cases per year in the UK, primarily related to exposure to asbestos, silica, paint and diesel engine fumes. Construction is ranked as the third most dangerous industry in the UK, with 30 deaths in the sector in 2019 (see Steed, 2019).

3   In October 2013, I started a three-year European Research Council project entitled 'Universalism, universal design and equitable access to the designed environment' (project number 323777). The project studied how far universal design (UD) was a panacea to the problems that result from the design of environments inattentive to the needs of disabled people. The project investigated the extent to which the principles and practices of UD had permeated public discourses and socio-institutional networks, and how these were shaping the form and performance of designed environments.

⁴ Mike Westley is head of Westley Design, an inclusive landscape consultancy specialising in community-based public space and healthcare and learning environments, with the commitment to creating accessible, multi-sensory places of benefit to all users. His ideas and work can be viewed at: http://westleydesign.co.uk

⁵ FLW used the term 'Usonia' to refer to an idealised territorial formation in the US, characterised by the decentralisation of power from federal to regional state structures as part of a process to facilitate political self-determination. It formed part of his broader political and architectural philosophy of seeking to create a society living off the land, conserving the environment and using natural, uncontaminated resources. Part of FLW's vision for Usonia was the provision of modest, low-cost dwellings situated in acres of land, enabling people to be connected to nature. A total of 140 Usonian-style houses were built, though they were not necessarily modest in size or price (see Lind, 1994).

⁶ I met Paul Hede in October 2015 in Melbourne, Australia. He spoke about his work with autistic people, particularly school students, and how he has developed a particular sensitivity and skills in relation to designing for people with a range of different sensory and cognitive impairments. Paul developed his practice, Hede Architects, in 1982, and in 2019, he became Senior Principal at the Bickerton Masters (BM) Group. His ideas and work can be viewed at: www.hedearchitects.com.au/projects/

Chapter 9

¹ Construction sites are a major source of air pollution. The supplementary planning guidance for the London plan (Greater London Authority, 2014) on construction and demolition cites information generated by the London Atmospheric Emissions Inventory, which notes that construction was responsible for 12 per cent of nitrogen dioxide emissions and 15 per cent of dangerous fine particulates in 2013 (see also Gardiner, 2017). Most of these emissions come from equipment used on construction sites, including diesel digging machines and energy generators.

² The construction industry is culpable because it is the world's biggest contributor to carbon emissions and global warming, and generates high energy use at every stage of the building process. This includes: the excavation and transport of raw building materials; their processing and manufacture into thousands of building products; their transport to building sites for use in construction; site preparation, including demolition and waste disposal; the construction of a building and/or infrastructure; interior fittings, including decoration and the installation of heating, lighting and other ancillary services; and the use and operation of a building.

³ For Büscher and Fletcher (2016: 1), the valuing of nature as natural capital is 'putting nature to work for capitalist growth', is 'inherently anti-ecological' and does not make a break with instrumentalist values. Rather than addressing the problems of the destruction of the earth's ecology, there are dangers that the application of natural capital principles may exacerbate them.

⁴ The International Energy Agency (2018: 1) notes that 'the cement sector is the third-largest industrial energy consumer' in the world, responsible for 7 per cent of industrial energy use, and the second-largest industrial CO_2 emitter, responsible for about 7 per cent of global CO_2 emissions. Global cement production continues to grow, and despite increasing efficiencies to reduce levels of embodied carbon contained within its manufacture and material composition, direct carbon emissions from the cement industry are expected to increase by 4 per cent globally by 2050. Cement is the main constituent of the carbon

footprint in concrete, and it is estimated that 5 per cent of human-induced carbon emissions originate from the use of cement (see International Energy Agency, 2018).

5   For at least the last 3,000 years, building structures known as wind catchers have been used to create natural ventilation and enable passive cooling in buildings. They are widespread in North Africa and the Middle East, and a common feature in Iranian settlements. Windcatchers are chimney-like structures that capture cool air and direct it down vents into buildings. They are effective at reducing air temperatures inside buildings and demonstrate that there is no need for energy-intensive air-conditioning systems (for further details, see Saadatian et al, 2012).

6   An example of a social grouping that rejects high-energy-embodied products is the 'de-paving' movement. De-paving is a reaction to the unliveable conditions rendered by concrete, and its despoilation of nature. The movement has emerged in the US to counter concrete places by encouraging the removal of pavements (see: https://depave.org/about/mission/).

Chapter 10

1   'Arcology' is a term coined by Paolo Soleri (1969) in his book, *Arcology: The City in the Image of Man*. The book outlines Soleri's utopian vision for a better, humane and nature-sensitised society. Arcology is the fusion of architecture and ecology, and one of the objectives is to create self-sustaining communities that are not parasitic on the earth and its resources. A good source of information about arcology and its applications can be found at: www.arcosanti.org/history/#

References

Abu-Lughod, J. (1971) *Cairo: 1001 Years of the City Victorious*, Princeton, NJ: Princeton University Press.

Adham, K. (2004) 'Cairo's urban deju vu: globalisation and urban fantasies', in Y. Elsheshtawy (ed) *Planning Middle Eastern Cities: An Urban Kaleidoscope*, London: Routledge, pp 134–68.

Ae, J., Suzuki, M. and Yamaguchi, R. (2020) 'Japan', in A. Synett (ed) *The Public Competition Enforcement Review, Edition 12*, The Law Reviews, London: LBR.

Agerholm, H. (2018) 'New Zealand bans sales of homes to foreign buyers', *The Independent*, 15 August.

Ahmed, I. (2014) 'Factors in building resilience in urban slums of Dhaka, Bangladesh', *Procedia Economics and Finance*, 18: 745–53.

Ahn, Y.H., Pearce, A.R., Wang, Y. and Wang, G. (2013) 'Drivers and barriers of sustainable design and construction: the perception of green building experience', *International Journal of Sustainable Building, Technology and Urban Development*, 4(1): 35–45.

Akers, J., Beal, V. and Rousseau, M. (2020) 'Redefining the city and demolishing the rest: the techno-green fix in post-crash Cleveland, Ohio', *Environment and Planning E*, 3(1): 207–27.

Albanesi, S., De Giorgi, G. and Nosal, J. (2017) *Credit Growth and the Financial Crisis: A New Narrative*, Working Paper 23740, NBER working paper series, Cambridge, MA: NBR.

Alberga, H. (2017) 'Out with the old – Forest Hill gets a facelift', *Toronto Storeys*, 24 July.

Aldrete, G. (2006) *Floods of the Tiber in Ancient Rome*, Baltimore, MD: Johns Hopkins University Press.

Alexander, S. (2015) *Prosperous Descent: Crisis as Opportunity in an Age of Limits*, Melbourne: Simplicity Institute.

Al-Kodmany, K. (2020) *Tall Buildings and the City: Improving the Understanding of Placemaking, Imageability, and Tourism*, New York, NY: Springer.

Allegra, M. (2017) ' "Outside Jerusalem – yet so near": Ma'ale Adumim, Jerusalem, and the suburbanization of Israel's settlement policy', in M. Allegra, A. Handel and E. Maggor (eds) *Normalizing Occupation: The Politics of Everyday Life in the West Bank*, Bloomington, IN: Indiana University Press, pp 48–63.

Allegra, M., Handel, A. and Maggor, E. (eds) (2017) *Normalizing Occupation: The Politics of Everyday Life in the West Bank*, Bloomington, IN: Indiana University Press.

Almacantar (2020) 'About', https://almacantar.com/about/

Alpert, D. (2013) *The Age of Oversupply: Overcoming the Greatest Challenge to the Global Economy*, London: Penguin Publishing Group.

American Enterprise Institute (2019) 'China global investment tracker', www.aei.org/china-global-investment-tracker/

Amin, A. (2006) 'The Good City', *Urban Studies*, 43(5/6): 1009–23.

Ammon, F. (2016) *Bulldozer: Demolition and Clearance of the Postwar Landscape*, New Haven, CT, and London: Yale University Press.

Antaki, G. (2005) *Piping and Pipeline Engineering: Design, Construction, Maintenance, Integrity and Repair*, New York, NY: Taylor and Francis.

Asenova, D. and Beck, M. (2010) 'Crucial silences: when accountability met PFI and finance capital', *Critical Perspectives on Accounting*, 21(1): 1–13.

Asher, L., Aresu, M., Falaschetti, E. and Mindell, J. (2012) 'Most older pedestrians are unable to cross the road in time: a cross-sectional study', *Age and Ageing*, 41(5): 690–4.

Atkins, G., Wajzer, C., Hogarth, R., Davies, N. and Norris, E. (2017) *What's Wrong with Infrastructure Decision Making? Conclusions from Six UK Case Studies*, London: Institute for Government.

Atkinson, R. (2019) 'Necrotecture: lifeless dwellings and London's super-rich', *International Journal of Urban and Regional Research*, 43(1): 2–13.

Atkinson, R. (2020a) *Alpha City: How London Was Captured by the Super-Rich*, London: Verso.

Atkinson, R. (2020b) 'How the superrich conquered London', *The Conversation*, 28 May.

Austen, B. (2018) *High-Risers: Cabrini-Green and the Fate of American Public Housing*, New York, NY: Harper.

Ayouba, K., Breuille, M.-L., Grivault, C. and Le Gallo, J. (2020) 'Does Airbnb disrupt the private rental market? An empirical analysis for French cities', *International Regional Science Review*, 43(1–2): 76–104.

Bach, J. (2016) 'China's infrastructural fix', *Limn*, Issue 7, Public Infrastructures/Infrastructural Publics, https://limn.it/articles/chinas-infrastructural-fix/

Badger, E. (2018) 'Anonymous owner, L.L.C.: why it has become so easy to hide in the housing market', *New York Times*, 30 April.

Badger, E. and Bui, Q. (2019) 'Cities start to question an American ideal: a house with a yard on every lot', *New York Times*, 18 January.

Baldwin, S., Holroyd, E. and Burrows, R. (2019) *Luxified Troglodytism? Mapping the Subterranean Geographies of Plutocratic London*, Newcastle University eprints, Newcastle Upon Tyne: University of Newcastle.

Balfour Beatty (2019) *Our Sustainability Blueprint*, London: Balfour Beatty.

Balfour Beatty (2020) 'Sustainability', www.balfourbeatty.com/sustainability

Barcott, B. (2008) *The Last Flight of the Scarlet Macaw: One Woman's Fight to Save the World's Most Beautiful Bird*, New York, NY: Random House.

Bar-Hillel, M. (2007) '£8m homes left empty for years', *Mail Online*, 30 January.

Barker, K. (2008) 'Planning policy, planning practice and housing', *Oxford Review of Economic Policy*, 24(1): 34–49.

Barkham, P. (2020) 'HS2 will destroy or damage hundreds of UK wildlife sites, says report', *The Guardian*, 15 January.

Barry, K. (2017) 'A symbol of Spain's housing crisis finds a community', *Bloomberg CityLab*, 9 August.

Barton, C. and Wilson, W. (2020) 'Tackling the under-supply of housing in England', research briefing, UK Parliament, House of Commons Library, 9 March.

Batabyal, A. (2019) 'China's worldwide investment project is a push for more economic and political power', *The Conversation*, 17 October.

Bates, C., Imrie, R. and Kullman, K. (eds) (2017) *Care and Design: Bodies, Buildings, Cities*, Chichester: Wiley-Blackwell.

Batty, D. (2018) 'Fury as housing associations redevelop and sell affordable homes', *The Guardian*, 13 June.

Bautista, L. (2011) 'Building sense out of households: migrants from Chuuk (re)create local settlements in Guam', *City and Society*, 23(1): 66–90.

BBC (British Broadcasting Corporation) (2020) 'Flooding: anger as people flee homes after third flood', *BBC News*, 18 June.

Bebbington, D., Verdum, R., Gamboa, C. and Bebbington, A. (2018) 'The infrastructure–extractives–resource governance complex in the pan-Amazon: roll backs and contestations', *European Review of Latin American and Caribbean Studies*, 106(July–December): 183–208.

Beech, A. (2019) 'Tokyo proves that housing shortages are a political choice', *City Metric*, 31 May.

Been, V., Gould Ellen, I. and O'Regan, K. (2019) 'Supply skepticism: housing supply and affordability', *Housing Policy Debate*, 29(1): 25–40.

Beiser, V. (2018) 'Dramatic photos show how sand mining threatens a way of life in Southeast Asia', *National Geographic*, 15 March.

Bell, A., Brooks, C. and Killick, H. (2019) 'Medieval property investors, ca. 1300–1500', *Enterprise and Society*, 20(3): 575–612.

Bellah, R. (1968) 'Meaning and modernization', *Religious Studies*, 4(1): 37–45.

Benjamin, W. (1969) 'Paris: capital of the nineteenth century', *Perspecta*, 12: 163–72.

Berg, N. (2017) 'Raze, rebuild, repeat: why Japan knocks down its houses after 30 years', *The Guardian*, 16 November.

Berman, M. (1982) *All That Is Solid Melts into Air, the Experience of Modernity*, New York, NY: Penguin.

Bernardi, M. (2018a) 'Millennials, sharing economy and tourism: the case of Seoul', *Journal of Tourism Futures*, 4(1): 43–56.

Bernardi, M. (2018b) 'The impact of Airbnb on our cities: gentrification and "Disneyfication" 2.0', *LabGov*, 2 October.

Berners-Lee, M. (2010) 'What's the carbon footprint of … building a house', *The Guardian*, 14 October.

Berney, R. (2017) *Learning from Bogotá: Pedagogical Urbanism and the Reshaping of Public Space*, Austin, TX: University of Texas Press.

Betsky, A. (2015) 'The Design School lecture', Herberger Institute for Design and the Arts, Arizona State University, 4 November, https://design.asu.edu/events/design-school-lecture-series-presents-aaron-betsky

Betsky, A. (2017) 'Make it alive: beyond new buildings', lecture, CMU School of Architecture, 25 September, https://vimeo.com/286400696

Betsky, A. (2019) 'What bothers many people is the sense of an alien culture', *Dezeen*, 9 August.

Betsky, A. (2020) 'The 2020s "will see the return of the real"', *Dezeen*, 2 January.

Bibby, P., Henneberry, J. and Halleux, J. (2018) 'Under the radar? "Soft" residential densification in England, 2001–2011', *Environment and Planning B: Urban Analytics and City Science*, 4(1): 102–18.

Birchall, C. (2014) 'Radical transparency?', *Cultural Studies*, 14(1): 77–88.

Black, D. (2015) 'Urban resettlement exposes Angola's neglect of social programs', *Pulitzer Center Newsletter*, 14 October.

Black, W. (2004) 'The "Dango" tango: why corruption blocks real reform in Japan', *Business Ethics Quarterly*, 14(4): 603–23.

Blake, P. (1960) *Frank Lloyd Wright: Architecture and Space*, London and New York, NY: Penguin Books.

Blewitt, J. and Cunningham, R. (eds) (2014) *The Post-growth Project, How the End of Economic Growth Could Bring a Fairer and Happier Society*, London: Green House.

Bloomfield, R. (2018) 'Builders behaving badly: Chelsea neighbours fight back in basement wars with fines for disruptive renovations', *Evening Standard*, 16 May.

Bohlen, C. (1999) 'Earthquake in Turkey: rage; survivors lead a chorus of demands to punish the builders', *The New York Times*, 20 August.

Bolleter, J. (2019) *Desert Paradises: Surveying the Landscapes of Dubai's Urban Model*, London: Routledge.

Bookchin, M. (1979) 'Ecology and revolutionary thought', *Antipode*, 10(3): 21–32.

Booth, K.M., Pinkston, M.M. and Poston, W.S.C. (2005) 'Obesity and the built environment', *Journal of the American Dietetic Association*, 105(5 Supplement): 110–17.

Booth, R. (2014) 'London council plans to fine "buy-to-leave" investors', *The Guardian*, 31 March.

Booth, R. and Bengtsson, H. (2016) 'The London skyscraper that is a stark symbol of the housing crisis', *The Guardian*, 24 May.

Booth, R. and Wahlquist, C. (2017) 'Grenfell Tower residents say managers "brushed away" fire safety concerns', *The Guardian*, 14 June.

Bosetti, N. and Colthorpe, T. (2018) *Meanwhile, in London: Making Use of London's Empty Spaces*, London: Centre for London.

Bourdieu, P. (1984) *Distinction: A Social Critique of the Judgement of Taste*, London: Routledge.

Bourdieu, P. (1998) *Acts of Resistance: Against the New Myths of Our Time* (trans R. Nice), Cambridge: Polity Press.

Bowen, A. and Fankhauser, S. (2011) 'The green growth narrative: paradigm shift or just spin?', *Global Environmental Change*, 21(4): 1157–9.

Boyd, V. and Pfeiffer, B. (2007) *Frank Lloyd Wright & The House Beautiful: Designing an American Way of Living*, Washington, DC: International Arts & Artists.

Bozikovic, A. (2015) ' "Design empathy" builds inclusive spaces for people with autism', *The Globe and Mail*, 16 April.

Bradbury, P. and Cumber, R. (2014) 'Safety fears after green man crossing time cut to six seconds', *My London*, 16 January.

Bradley, Q. (2021) 'The financialisation of housing land supply in England', *Urban Studies*, 58(2): 389–404.

BREEAM (Building Research Establishment Environmental Assessment Method) (2018) *BREEAM UK New Construction: Non Domestic Buildings (UK), Technical Manual, SD5078*, Watford: BREEAM UK.

Briney, A. (2019) 'Geography and history of Tuvalu: Tuvalu and the impacts of global warming', *ThoughtCo*, 20 February.

British Property Federation (2020) *Build-to-Rent Sector Set Sights on UK Regions for New Housing Supply*, 20 August, London: BPF.

Brooks, S., Jabour, J., van den Hoff, J. and Bergstrom, D. (2019) 'Our footprint on Antarctica competes with nature for rare ice-free land', *Nature Sustainability*, 2: 185–90.

Brown, A. (2019) 'Strong growth for Indian construction industry', *KHL Group, International Construction*, 18 March.

Brune, P., Perucchio, R., Ingraffea, A. and Jackson, M. (2010) 'The toughness of imperial Roman concrete', in B. Oh, O. Choi and L. Chung (eds) *Fracture Mechanics of Concrete and Concrete Structures: Recent Advances in Fracture Mechanics of Concrete*, Seoul: Korea Concrete Institute, pp 38–45.

Bubeck, P., Dillenardt, L., Alfieri, L., Feyen, L., Thieken, A. and Kellermann, P. (2019) 'Global warming to increase flood risk on European railways', *Climatic Change*, 155(1): 19–36.

Buhayer, N. and Cannon, C. (2019) 'How California became America's housing market nightmare', *GVWIRE*, 11 November.

Building Services Research and Information Association (2020) 'Circular economy', www.bsria.com/uk/information-training/information-centre/circular-economy/

Bulliet, R. (2009) *Cotton, Climate, and Camels in Early Islamic Iran: A Moment in World History*, New York, NY: Columbia University Press.

Buranyi, S. (2019) 'The air conditioning trap: how cold air is heating the world', *The Guardian*, 29 August.

Büscher, B. and Fletcher, R. (2016) 'Nature is priceless, which is why turning it into "natural capital" is wrong', *The Conversation*, 21 September.

Butler, R. (2012) 'Amazon has nearly 100,000 km of roads', *Mongabay*, 8 December.

Call, R., Powell, D. and Heck, S. (2014) *Blackstone: Atlanta's Newest Landlord*, Atlanta, GA: Occupy Our Homes Atlanta.

Camões, A. and Ferreira, R. (2010) 'Technological evolution of concrete: from ancient times to ultra high-performance concrete', in P. da Sousa Cruz (ed) *Structures and Architecture*, London: Routledge, pp 1571–8.

Campanella, T. (2008) *The Concrete Dragon: China's Urban Revolution and What it Means for the World*, New York, NJ: Princeton Architectural Press.

Campbell, S. (2019) 'The care home market: economically viable for investors?', *Property Investor Today*, 4 November.

Carlisle, S. (2006) 'The practice of movement, final report', Watson Fellowship, August, www.nomadicarchitecture.com/final-report

Carmon, N. (1999) 'Three generations of urban renewal policies: analysis and policy implications', *GeoForum*, 30(2): 145–58.

Caro, R. (2015) *The Power Broker: Robert Moses and the Fall of New York*, London: The Bodley Head.

CBRE (2020) 'One Blackfriars, Southbank SE1', www.cbreresidential.com/uk/en-GB/new-developments/one-blackfriars-southbank-se1

Ceballos, G., Ehrlich, P., Barnosky, A., García, A., Pringle, R. and Palmer, T. (2015) 'Accelerated modern human-induced species losses: entering the sixth mass extinction', *Science Advances*, 1(5): e1400253.

Chance, T., Chapman, A. and de Souza, M. (2016) 'Tackling our housing crisis: why building more houses is not the answer', *The Land*, 19: 55–8.

Charles, S. (2014) 'The spatio-temporal pattern of housing redevelopment in suburban Chicago, 2000–2010', *Urban Studies*, 51(12): 2646–64.

Chartered Institute of Building (2013) *No Decrease in Corruption, as Survey Claims Bribery Act Ineffective*, London: CIOB.

Cheer, T., Kearns, R. and Murphy, L. (2002) 'Housing policy, poverty, and culture: "discounting" decisions among Pacific peoples in Auckland, New Zealand', *Environment and Planning C*, 20(4): 497–516.

Chen, S. (2020) 'The people vs. big development', *New York Times*, 7 February.

Cheshire, P. (2014) 'Turning houses into gold: the failure of British planning', *LSE Blog*, 7 May.

Cheshire, P. (2018) 'Broken market or broken policy? The unintended consequences of restrictive planning', *National Institute Economic Review*, 245(1): 9–19.

Cheshire, P. and Buyuklieva, B. (2019) *Homes on the Right Tracks: Greening the Green Belt to Solve the Housing Crisis*, London: Centre for Cities Report.

Choi, J. (2007) 'Governance structure and administrative corruption in Japan: an organizational network approach', *Public Administration Review*, 67(5): 930–42.

Choi, N. (2016) 'Metro Manila through the gentrification lens: disparities in urban planning and displacement risks', *Urban Studies*, 53(3): 577–92.

Chorshanbiyev, P. (2017) 'China expected to award a grant worth US$230m to Tajikistan for construction of parliamentary complex', *Asia Plus*, 19 July.

Cidell, J. (2009) 'A political ecology of the built environment: LEED certification for green buildings', *Local Environment: The International Journal of Justice and Sustainability*, 14(7): 621–33.

Clawson, M. (1962) 'Urban sprawl and speculation in suburban land', *Land Economics*, 38(May): 99–111.

Cleveland City Council and Gaylord Consulting (2012) 'Through demolition ... Cleveland rebuilds value', www.clevelandcitycouncil.org/media/documents/publication/Ward12/urbanrebuild-final4-linksrev.pdf

CMAP (Chicago Metropolitan Agency for Planning) (2008) *Teardown Strategy Report*, Chicago: CMAP.

Collins, J. and Johnson, N. (2019) 'California needs more housing, but 97% of cities and counties are failing to issue enough RHNA permits', *Los Angeles Daily News*, 10 December.

Conant, J. (2018) 'Is land speculation helping destroy Brazil's "birthplace of waters"?', *Grassroots International*, 19 May.

Construction Industry Training Board (2019) *Construction Health & Safety Awareness 2020*, Peterborough: CITB.

Corley, C. (2006) 'Teardown trend altering historic neighborhoods', *NPR*, 25 September.

Cousins, S. (2018) 'How can construction kick its plastics habit?', *Construction Manager*, 28 March.

Cousins, S. (2019) 'Shifting sand: why we're running out of aggregate', *Construction Research and Innovation*, 10(3): 69–71.

Covey, A. (2006) 'The Inca Empire', in H. Silverman and W. Isbell (eds) *The Handbook of South American Archaeology*, New York, NY: Springer, pp 809–30.

Coward, M. (2009) *Urbicide: The Politics of Urban Destruction*, London: Routledge.

Cox, S. (2010) *Losing Our Cool: Uncomfortable Truths About Our Air-Conditioned World*, New York, NY: The New Press.

Craver, S. (2010) 'Urban real estate in late republican Rome', *Memoirs of the American Academy in Rome*, 55: 135–58.

Crocker, S. (2019) 'Dam nation: Fortis in Belize, part 1', *The Independent Newfoundland & Labrador*, 27 May.

Crosland, A. (1972) *Hansard, Parliamentary Debates (Commons)*, 26 June, 839: 1091.

Crownshaw, T., Morgan, C., Adams, A., Sers, M., dos Santos, N., Damiano, A., Gilbert, L., Haage, G. and Greenford, D. (2019) 'Over the horizon: exploring the conditions of a post-growth world', *The Anthropocene Review*, 6 (1–2): 117–41.

Cunningham, K. (2020) 'The state of the demolition industry', *Construction and Demolition Recycling*, 2 September.

Cunningham, S. (2018) 'San Antonio mega-dam on Brazil's Madeira River disrupts local lives', *Mongabay*, 3 December.

Curry, A. (2008) 'Göbekli Tepe: The World's first temple?', *Smithsonian Magazine*, November.

Dahl, M. (2011) *Failure to Thrive in Constructivism: A Cross-Cultural Malady*, Transgressions: Cultural Studies and Education, vol 62, Leiden, Netherlands: Brill.

Dahmen, J., von Bergmann, J. and Das, M. (2018) 'Teardown Index: impact of property values on carbon dioxide emissions of single family housing in Vancouver', *Energy and Buildings*, 170: 95–106.

Daily Record (2013) 'Glasgow tower block residents reveal their thoughts on soon-to-be demolished flats', 21 December.

Dale, G. (2015) 'Origins and delusions of green growth', *International Socialist Review*, 97, https://isreview.org/issue/97/origins-and-delusions-green-growth

Dan Gavriletea, M. (2017) 'Environmental impacts of sand exploitation. Analysis of sand market', *Sustainability*, 9(7): 1118–44.

Da Silva, M. (2019) 'Build to rent homes cost 15% more than other private rentals', *Landlord Today*, 26 June.

Davies, R., Connolly, K. and Sample, I. (2017) 'Cladding for Grenfell Tower was cheaper, more flammable option', *The Guardian*, 16 June.

Davis, W. (2019) 'Thousands left homeless in Bangladeshi capital after fire burns hundreds of shanties', *NPR News*, 18 August.

Dawkins, C. and Nelson, A. (1992) 'Urban containment policies and housing prices: an international comparison with implications for future research', *Land Use Policy*, 19(1): 1–12.

DCLG (Department for Communities, and Local Government) (2012) *National Planning Policy Framework*, London: Her Majesty's Stationery Office.

DCLG (2016) *Housing and Planning Act 2016, Explanatory Notes*, London: The Stationery Office.

Dean, B., Dulac, J., Morgan, T., Remme, U. and Motherway, B. (2018) *The Future of Cooling: Opportunities for Energy-Efficient Air Conditioning*, Paris: International Energy Agency.

De Jong, M., Henry, W. and Stansbury, N. (2009) 'Eliminating corruption in our engineering/construction industry', *Leadership and Management in Engineering*, 9(3): 105–11.

Delmendo, L. (2020) 'Canada: slowdown before a new boom?', *Global Property Guide, Canada*, 29 March.

Demissie, F. (1997) 'Book review of *African Nomadic Architecture: Space, Place and Gender* by Labelle Prussin', *The International Journal of African Historical Studies*, 30(2): 395–8.

Department for Environment, Food and Rural Affairs (2020) *UK Statistics on Waste*, 19 March, London: Government Statistical Service.

Desai, U. (2020) 'Huge investment in "new infra" key to China's recovery', *Asia Times*, 27 April.

DETR (Department for the Environment, Transport and the Regions) (1997) *PPG1, General Policy and Principles*, London: DETR.

Dobrowolski, A. and Dobrowolski, J. (2006) *Heliopolis: Rebirth of the City of the Sun*, Cairo: American University of Cairo Press.

Douglas, R. (2007) 'Growthism and the green backlash', *The Political Quarterly*, 78(4): 547–55.

Drury, C. (2020) 'HS2 will destroy ancient woodlands and "huge swathes of irreplaceable" wildlife, report warns', *Independent*, 15 January.

Dudley, G. and Banister, D. (2014) *The Economic Case for HS2*, Working Paper No. 1067, Oxford: Transport Studies Unit, School of Geography and the Environment, Oxford University.

Dufton, A. (2019) 'The architectural and social dynamics of gentrification in Roman North Africa', *American Journal of Archaeology*, 123(2): 263–90.

Dunphy, S. (2018) 'Dark side of dams: social and environmental costs of hydropower may outweigh the energy benefits', *European Scientist*, 6 November.

Dye, J. (2019) *Dam Building by the Illiberal Modernisers: Ideology and Changing Rationales in Rwanda and Tanzania*, Future DAMS Working Paper 005, Manchester: University of Manchester.

Dyos, H. (1967) 'The slums of Victorian London', *Victorian Studies*, 11(1): 5–40.

Dzhambov, A. and Lercher, P. (2019) 'Road traffic noise exposure and birth outcomes: an updated systematic review and meta-analysis', *International Journal of Environmental Research and Public Health*, 16(21): 4134.

Edwards, P. (2003) 'Infrastructure and modernity: force, time and social organisation in the history of sociotechnical systems', in T. Misa, P. Brey and A. Feenberg (eds) *Modernity and Technology*, Cambridge, MA: MIT Press, pp 185–226.

Ehrlich, A. and Ehrlich, P. (1980) 'Ecoscience: the Greeks and Romans did it, too!', *Mother Earth News*, May/June.

Eisenman, J. and Kurlantzick, J. (2006) 'China's Africa strategy', *Current History*, 105(691): 219–24.

Elinoff, E. (2017) 'Concrete and corruption: materialising power and politics in the Thai capital', *City*, 21(5): 587–96.

Elinoff, E., Sur, M. and Yeoh, B. (2017) 'Constructing Asia: an introduction', *City*, 21(5): 580–6.

Ellsworth-Krebs, K. (2018) 'Fixing the housing crisis: it's time to challenge our thirst for more living space', *The Conversation*, 18 July.

Ely, R. (1920) 'Land speculation', *American Journal of Agricultural Economics*, 2(3): 121–35.

Engels, F. (1975 [1954]) *The Housing Question*, Moscow: Progress.

English, J. (1982) *The Future of Council Housing*, London: Croom Helm.

Escobar, A. (2001) 'Culture sits in places: reflections on globalism and subaltern strategies of localization', *Political Geography*, 20(2): 139–74.

European Commission (2019) *Waste: Construction and Demolition Waste (CDW)*, Brussels: European Commission.

European Environment Agency (2019) *The European Environment – State and Outlook 2020: Knowledge for Transition to a Sustainable Europe*, Luxembourg: Publications Office of the European Union.

Evans, G. (2003) 'The built environment and mental health', *Journal of Urban Health: Bulletin of the New York Academy of Medicine*, 80(4): 536–55.

Evans, I., Smiley, L. and Smith, M. (2002) *The Hand-Sculpted House: A Philosophical and Practical Guide to Building a Cob Cottage*, White River Junction, VT: Chelsea Green Publishing Company.

Evenson, N. (1979) *Paris: A Century of Change, 1878–1978*, New Haven, CT: Yale University Press.

Faiola, A. (2003) 'Waste puts Japan on road to nowhere', *The Washington Post*, 9 November.

Fan, Y. (2008) 'Soft power: power of attraction or confusion?', *Place Branding and Public Diplomacy*, 4(2): 147–58.

Fearnside, P. (2014) 'Viewpoint – Brazil's Madeira River dams: a setback for environmental policy in Amazonian development', *Water Alternatives*, 7(1): 256–69.

Feldhoff, T. (2002) 'Japan's construction lobby activities – systemic stability and sustainable regional development', *ASIEN*, 84: 34–42.

Fernández Muñoz, S. and Collado Cuerto, L. (2017) 'What has happened in Spain? The real estate bubble, corruption and housing development: a view from the local level', *Geoforum*, 85: 206–13.

Fielding, J. (2018) 'Flood risk and inequalities between ethnic groups in the floodplains of England and Wales', *Disasters: The Journal of Disaster Studies, Policy and Management*, 42(1): 101–23.

Fingleton, B., Fuerst, F. and Szumilo, N. (2019) 'Housing affordability: is new local supply the key?', *Environment and Planning A: Economy and Space*, 51(1): 25–50.

Flyvbjerg, B. and Molloy, M. (2011) 'Delusion, deception and corruption in major infrastructure projects: causes, consequences and cures', in S. Rose-Ackerman and T. Søreide (eds) *International Handbook on the Economics of Corruption, Volume Two*, Cheltenham: Edward Elgar, pp 81–107.

Ford, J. and Gomez-Lanier, L. (2017) 'Are tiny homes here to stay? A review of literature on the tiny house movement', *Family and Consumer Sciences Research Journal*, 45: 394–405.

Foucault, M. (1976) *The History of Sexuality Volume 1: The Will to Knowledge*, Paris: Hachette.

Fournier, V. (2008) 'Escaping from the economy: the politics of degrowth', *International Journal of Sociology and Social Policy*, 28(11–12): 528–45.

Frampton, K. (1998) *Alvar Aalto: Between Humanism and Materialism*, New York, NY: Museum of Modern Art.

Frearson, A. (2013) 'Space-wasting "vanity" skyscrapers revealed', *Dezeen*, 5 September.

Fredrickson, T. (2012) 'Investigation begun into Hopewell collapse', *Bangkok Post*, 2 March.

Fry, T. (2005) 'Rematerialisation as a prospective project', *Design Philosophy Papers*, 3(2): 119–29.

Fry, T. (2009) *Design Futuring: Sustainability, Ethics and New Practice*, Oxford: Berg Publishers.

Fry, T. (2011) *Design as Politics*, Oxford: Berg Publishers.

Fullilove, M.T. (2004) *Root Shock: How Tearing Up City Neighborhoods Hurts America*, New York, NY: Random House.

Funes, Y. (2019) 'The Amazon forest fires are a form of "genocide"', Guardians of the Forest, Gizmodo, https://gizmodo.com/tag/guardians-of-the-forest

Gallent, N., Durrant, D. and May, N. (2017) 'Housing supply, investment demand and money creation: a comment on the drivers of London's housing crisis', *Urban Studies*, 54(10): 2204–16.

GAN Integrity (2020) 'Thailand corruption report', www.ganintegrity.com/portal/country-profiles/thailand/

Gardiner, J. (2017) 'How to stop the construction industry choking our cities', *The Guardian*, 20 April.

Garside, M. (2020) 'Major countries in worldwide cement production 2015–2019', www.statista.com/statistics/267364/world-cement-production-by-country/

Gelardi, D. (2019) 'Denver issued demolition permits for more than 400 homes last year', *The Denver Channel*, 30 January.

Gibson-Graham, J.K. and Miller, E. (2015) 'Economy as ecological livelihood', in K. Gibson, D.B. Rose and R. Fincher (eds) *Manifesto for Living in the Anthropocene*, Brooklyn, NY: Punctum Books, pp 7–16.

Glaeser, E. and Gyourko, J. (2002) *The Impact of Zoning on Housing Affordability*, NBER Working Paper 8835, Cambridge, MA: National Bureau of Economic Research.

Glantz, A. (2019) 'Unmasking the secret landlords buying up America', *Reveal; The Center for Investigative Reporting*, 17 December.

Glasgow Housing Association (2020) *Demolitions*, Glasgow: Glasgow Housing Association.

Glotzer, P. (2019) 'Book review of Yates, A. (2015) *Selling Paris: Property and Commercial Culture in the Fin-de-Siècle Capital*, Cambridge, Massachusetts: Harvard University Press', *Enterprise and Society*, 20(3): 719–21.

Glover, C. (2017) 'Spain has fourth largest number of empty homes in the world', *The Olive Press*, 26 February.

Glowacz, B. (2020) 'Boom town to ghost town', *Deloitte Blog: Real Estate*, 5 June.

GoContractor (2017) 'How does construction impact the environment?', *GoContractor Blog*, 21 June.

GoContractor (2019) 'State of U.S and Canadian construction industry in 2018', *GoContractor Blog*, 20 December.

Godoy-Shimizu, D., Steadman, P., Hamilton, I., Donn, M., Evans, S., Moreno, G. and Shayesteh, H. (2018) 'Energy use and height in office buildings', *Building Research & Information*, 46(8): 845–63.

Goldman, M. (2011) 'Speculative urbanism and the making of the next world city', *International Journal of Urban and Regional Research*, 35(3): 555–81.

Goldthwaite, R.A. (1982) *The Building of Renaissance Florence: An Economic and Social History*, Baltimore, MD: Johns Hopkins University Press.

Goodman, M. (2019) 'The bulldozers are coming to your neighborhood', *D Magazine*, July.

Gordillo, G. (2014) *Rubble: The Afterlife of Destruction*, Durham: Duke University Press.

Gotham, K. (2000) 'Growth machine up-links: urban renewal and the rise and fall of a pro-growth coalition in a U.S. city', *Critical Sociology*, 26(3): 268–300.

Gotham, K. (2001) 'A city without slums: urban renewal, public housing, and downtown revitalization in Kansas City, Missouri', *The American Journal of Economics and Sociology*, 60(1): 285–316.

Graedel, T. (2011) 'The prospects for urban mining', *The Bridge*, 41(1): 43–50.

Graham, S. (2015) 'Life support: the political ecology of urban air', *City*, 19(2–3): 192–215.

Graham, S. (2016) 'City ground', *Places Journal*, November.

Grand View Research (2018) *Green Building Materials Market Size, Share & Trend Analysis Report By Product, By Application (Framing, Insulation, Roofing, Exterior Siding, Interior Finishing), and Segment Forecasts, 2012–2022*, San Francisco: GVR.

Greater London Authority (2008) *Planning for a Better London*, London: GLA.

Greater London Authority (2014) *The Control of Dust and Emissions During Construction and Demolition*, London: GLA.

Green, K., Filipowicz, J., Lafleur, S. and Herzog, I. (2016) 'The impact of land-use regulation on housing supply in Canada', *Fraser Institute*, 7 July.

Green, P. (2005) 'Disaster by design: corruption, construction and catastrophe', *British Journal of Criminology*, 45(4): 528–46.

Greenpeace (2020) 'The biggest problem with carbon offsetting is that it doesn't really work', 26 May.

Grimwood, G. (2020) *Planning for the Future: Planning Policy Changes in England in 2020 and Future Reforms*, briefing paper, Number 8981, 8 October, London: House of Commons Library.

Gual, J. (2019) 'Ruins. A visual motif of the Spanish real estate crisis', *Comparative Cinema*, 7(12): 53–175.

Habraken, N.J. (1972) *Supports: Alternatives to Mass Housing*, London: Architectural Press.

Habraken, N.J. (2005) *Palladio's Children: Essays on the Everyday Environment and the Architect*, Abingdon: Taylor and Francis.

Hackworth, J. (2016) 'Demolition as urban policy in the American Rust Belt', *Environment and Planning A*, 48(11): 2201–22.

Haff, P. (2013) 'Technology as a geological phenomenon: implications for human well-being', in C. Waters, J. Zalasiewicz, M. Williams, M. Ellis and A. Snelling (eds) *A Stratigraphical Basis for the Anthropocene*, London: Geological Society, pp 301–9.

Hallaq, E. (2003) 'An epidemic of violence', *Palestine–Israel Journal*, 10(4).

Hannah, F. (2016) 'How speculation shaped the housing market', *The Independent*, 7 September.

Harding, R. (2016) 'Why Tokyo is the land of rising home construction but not prices', *Financial Times*, 3 August.

Harlan, C. (2013) 'Apartments a scale for South Koreans' progress', *The Seattle Times*, 21 September.

Harvey, D. (1975) 'The political economy of urbanization in advanced capitalist societies: the case of the United States', in G. Gappert and H. Rose (eds) *The Social Economy of the City*, Sage Urban Affairs Annual Review 9, Beverly-Hills, CA: Sage, pp 119–64.

Harvey, D. (2006) *The Limits to Capital*, London and New York, NY: Verso.

Harvie, G. (2019) 'The history of fabric structures', Conservation Wiki, www.designingbuildings.co.uk/wiki/The_history_of_fabric_structures

Havlíček, F. and Morcinek, M. (2016) 'Waste and pollution in the Ancient Roman Empire', *Journal of Landscape Ecology*, 9(3): 33–49.

Hays, J. (2012) 'Infrastructure and public works in Japan', http://factsanddetails.com/japan/cat23/sub152/item842.html

HBF (Home Builders Federation) (2005) *Making Sustainability in Housebuilding Work*, 20 July, London: HBF.

HBF (2014a) *Use Autumn Statement to Speed Up the Planning Process and Support Small Builders to Boost Housing Numbers*, London: HBF.

HBF (2014b) *Permissions to Land: Busting the Myths about House Builders and 'Land Banking'*, London: HBF.

He, S. and Wu, F. (2007) 'Socio-spatial impacts of property-led redevelopment on China's urban neighbourhoods', *Cities*, 24(3): 194–208.

Heerwagen, J. (2009) 'Bioplilia, health and well-being', in L.K. Campbell and A. Wiesen (eds) *Restorative Commons: Creating Health and Well-being Through Urban Landscapes*, Gen Tech Rep NRS-P-39, Madison: US Department of Agriculture, Forest Service, Northern Research Station, pp 38–57.

Heffernan, E., Pan, W., Liang, X. and de Wilde, P. (2015) 'Zero carbon homes: perceptions from the UK construction industry', *Energy Policy*, 79: 23–36.

Hemingway, W. (2018) 'Smaller homes make developers rich – but they are shrinking our lives', *The Guardian*, 28 August.

Herbling, D. and Li, D. (2019) 'China's Belt and Road leaves Kenya with a railroad to nowhere', *The Economic Times*, 19 July.

Herriges, D. (2018) 'Why are developers only building luxury housing?', *Strong Towns*, 25 July.

Herscher, A. (2008) 'Warchitectural theory', *Journal of Architectural Education*, 61(3): 35–43.

Herstad, K. (2017) '"Reclaiming" Detroit: demolition and deconstruction in the Motor City', *The Public Historian*, 39(4): 85–113.

Hess, S. (2010) 'Nail-houses, land rights, and frames of injustice on China's protest landscape', *Asian Survey*, 50(5): 908–26.

Higgins, P. (2010) *Eradicating Ecocide: Laws and Governance to Prevent the Destruction of Our Planet*, London: Shepheard-Walwyn.

Highsmith, A. (2009) 'Demolition means progress: urban renewal, local politics, and state-sanctioned ghetto formation in Flint, Michigan', *Journal of Urban History*, 35(3): 348–68.

Hilber, C. (2018) 'Second home investments', *CentrePiece*, Autumn: 25–8.

Hilber, C. and Vermeulen, W. (2016) 'The extraordinarily rigid planning system is the main reason homes in England are unaffordable', *LSE BPP*, 12 March.

Hill, D. (1996) *A History of Engineering in Classical and Medieval Times*, London: Routledge.

Hirt, S. (2018) 'Alternative peripheries: socialist mass housing compared with modern suburbia', in R. Harris and U. Lehrer (eds) *The Suburban Land Question: A Global Survey*, Toronto: University of Toronto Press, pp 43–61.

Ho, V. (2020) 'Silicon Valley has pledged billions to fight the housing crisis. It won't be enough', *The Guardian*, 6 January.

Hodges, P. (2015) 'Speculators exit London's high-price property developments', *Independent Commodity Intelligence Services*, 24 July.

Hohfelder, R., Oleson, J. and Brandon, C. (2007) 'Constructing the harbour of Caesarea Palaestina, Israel: new evidence from the ROMACONS field campaign of October 2005', *The International Journal of Nautical Archaeology*, 36(2): 409–15.

Hoisington, A., Stearns-Yoder, K., Schuldt, S., Beemer, C., Maestre, J., Kinney, K., Postolache, T., Lowry, C. and Brenner, L. (2019) 'Ten questions concerning the built environment and mental health', *Building and Environment*, 155: 58–69.

House of Commons Public Accounts Committee (2019) *Planning and the Broken Housing Market*, 26 June, London: House of Commons.

Howell, S. (2019) 'Land banking: construction companies still hoarding land', *The Big Issue*, 30 July.

Huang, J., Shen, G. and Zheng, W. (2015) 'Is insufficient land supply the root cause of housing shortage? Empirical evidence from Hong Kong', *Habitat International*, 49: 538–46.

Huang, Y. (2016) 'Understanding China's Belt & Road initiative: motivation, framework and assessment', *China Economic Review*, 40: 314–21.

Huang, Z. and Chen, X. (2016) 'Is China building Africa?', *European Financial Review*, June–July: 41–7.

Humphreys, S. (2008) *Architecture and Autism*, 3 October, Hasselt: UDDA.

Hurley, J., Morris, S. and Portelance, G. (2019) 'Examining the debt implications of the Belt and Road initiative from a policy perspective', *Journal of Infrastructure, Policy and Development*, 3(1): 139–75.

Huxley, A. (1930) *Brave New World*, London: Chatto and Windus.

Ibisch, P., Hoffmann, M., Kreft, S., Pe'er, G., Kati, V., Biber-Freudenberger, L., DellaSala, D., Vale, M., Hobson, P. and Selva, N. (2016) 'A global map of roadless areas and their conservation status', *Science*, 354(6318): 1423–27.

Ibis World (2019) 'Demolition in the UK industry trends (2014–2019)', 14 September.

Ibis World (2020) 'Demolition & wrecking in the US, market size 2003–2026', www.ibisworld.com/industry-statistics/market-size/demolition-wrecking-united-states/

IDMC (Internal Displacement Monitoring Centre) (2017) 'Internal displacement: what's development got to do with it?', July.

ILFI (International Living Future Institute) (2020) Te Kura Whare, https://living-future.org/lbc/case-studies/te-kura-whare/

Imrie, R. (2003) 'Architects' conception of the human body', *Environment and Planning D: Society and Space*, 21(1): 47–65.

Imrie, R. (2006) *Accessible Housing*, London: Routledge.

Imrie, R. and Kullman, K. (2014) 'Universal design policy and practice in Japan', *Access by Design*, 141: 28–33.

Imrie, R. and Thomas, H. (1999) 'Assessing urban policy and the urban development corporations', in R. Imrie and H. Thomas (eds) *British Urban Policy: An Evaluation of the Urban Development Corporations*, London: Sage Publications, pp 3–43.

International Energy Agency (2018) *Technology Roadmap: Low-Carbon Transition in the Cement Industry*, Paris: IEA.

International Olympic Committee (2020) 'Olympic Games to become "climate positive" from 2030', 4 March, www.olympic.org/news/olympic-games-to-become-climate-positive-from-2030

International Rivers Network (2007) *The World Bank's Big Dam Legacy*, Berkeley: IRN.

IPCC (Intergovernmental Panel on Climate Change) (2018) *Special Report: Global Warming of 1.5 °C*, Geneva: Intergovernmental Panel on Climate Change.

IPIM (IP Investment Management) (2020) 'Home page', www.ip-im.com/hk/

Iqbal, N. (2018) 'In desirable Southwold, locals rise up against blight of empty holiday homes', *The Guardian*, 24 June.

Irwin, S. (2013) 'Qualitative secondary data analysis: ethics, epistemology and context', *Progress in Development Studies*, 13(4): 295–306.

Ishak, N. (2019) '34 unforgettable photos of China's massive, uninhabited ghost cities', *All That's Interesting*, 28 April.

Jackson, B. (2017) 'A complex issue: the apart-ization of South Korea', *Korea Expose*, 20 November.

Jackson, J. (2019) 'First-time buyers crowded out of booming German housing market', *DW*, 19 April.

Jacobs, J. (1961) *The Death and Life of Great American Cities*, New York, NY: Vintage Books.

Jameson, F. (1998) *The Cultural Turn: Selected Writings on the Postmodern, 1983–1998*, London: Verso.

Ja-young, Y. (2020) 'Government renews war on real estate speculation', *The Korea Times*, 24 August.

Jedwab, R. and Moradi, A. (2016) 'The permanent effects of transportation revolutions in poor countries: evidence from Africa', *Review of Economics and Statistics*, 98(2): 268–84.

Jeffreys, P. (2016) 'Land banking: what's the story? (Part 1)', *Shelter Blog*, 14 December.

Jeong-su, K. (2013) 'The environmental fallout of the Four Major Rivers Project', *Hankyoreh*, 3 August.

Jessel, E. (2020) 'Student housing: time for a reckoning?' *Architects Journal*, 3 February.

Johansson, B. (2011) 'The post-war destruction of Swedish cities', *Building Research and Information*, 39(4): 412–29.

Johnson, B. (2020) *PM Economy Speech: 'Build, Build, Build'*, 30 June, London: Prime Minister's Office.

Jones, R., Leuenberger, C. and Regan Wills, E. (2016) 'The West Bank wall', *Journal of Borderlands Studies*, 31(3): 271–9.

Jones Lang LaSalle (2020) *Vauxhall Nine Elms Battersea: UK Living Research*, 7 February, London: JLL Residential UK.

Jongerden, J. (2010) 'Dams and politics in Turkey: utilizing water, developing conflict', *Middle East Policy*, 17(1): 137–43.

Jordan, D. (1992) 'The city: Baron Haussmann and modern Paris', *The American Scholar*, 61(1): 99–106.

Karuka, M. (2019) *Empire's Tracks: Indigenous Nations, Chinese Workers, and the Transcontinental Railroad*, Oakland, CA: University of California Press.

Kellert, S., Heerwagen, J. and Mador, M. (eds) (2008) *Biophilic Design: The Theory, Science and Practice of Bringing Buildings to Life*, Chichester: Wiley.

Kellett, J.R. (1969) *The Impact of Railways on Victorian Cities*, London: Routledge & Kegan Paul.

Kemman, A. (2015) 'Open the floodgates: will dams in South-eastern Turkey be used as weapons of war?', *Slate*, 9 October.

Kendall, R. and Tulip, P. (2018) *The Effect of Zoning on Housing Prices*, Research Briefs in Economic Policy, 124, Washington, DC: CATO Institute.

Kenner, D. (2014) *Who Should Value Nature?*, London: Institute of Chartered Accountants in England and Wales.

Khrushchev, N. (2009) 'Industrialised building speech, 1954', *Archis*, no. 3, 1 March.

Kill, J. (2013) *Carbon Discredited: Why the EU Should Steer Clear of Forest Carbon Offsets*, Moreton-in-Marsh: Fern and Les Amis de la Terre.

Kinton, C., Smith, D. and Harrison, J. (2016) 'De-studentification: emptying housing and neighbourhoods of student populations', *Environment and Planning A: Economy and Space*, 48(8): 1617–35.

Knapton, S. and Horton, H. (2019) 'Carbon offsetting may increase pollution as experts warn the rich: "You can't buy a clean conscience"', *The Daily Telegraph*, 20 August.

Knight Frank (2019) 'Residential investment report, 2019', www.knightfrank.co.uk/research/residential-investment-report-6404.aspx

Koc, C. (2018) 'Builder of $200 million Turkish chateaux project goes bankrupt', *Bloomberg Real Estate*, 26 November.

Komlos, J. (2017) 'Has creative destruction become more destructive?', *The B.E Journal of Economic Analysis & Policy*, 16(4), https://doi.org/10.1515/bejeap-2016-0179

Korcheck, K. (2015) 'Speculative ruins: photographic interrogations of the Spanish economic crisis', *Arizona Journal of Hispanic Cultural Studies*, 19: 91–110.

Koutamanis, A., van Reijn, B. and van Bueren, E. (2018) 'Urban mining and buildings: a review of possibilities and limitations, resources', *Conservation and Recycling*, 138(November): 22–39.

Koziarz, J. (2018) 'Dozens of new town homes headed to vacant Cabrini Green parcels', *CURBED Chicago*, 20 November.

KPMG (Klynveld Peat Marwick Goerdeler) (2013) *HS2 Regional Economic Impacts*, London: High Speed Two (HS2) Limited.

Kyung-min, L. (2020) 'Government tightens property rules to stem speculation', *The Korea Times*, 17 June.

Lahtinen, M., Huuhtanen, P. and Reijula, K. (1998) 'Sick building syndrome and psychosocial factors – a literature review', *Indoor Air*, 4: 71–80.

Lai, R.N. and Wang, K. (1999) 'Land-supply restrictions, developer strategies and housing policies: the case in Hong Kong', *International Real Estate Review*, 2(1): 143–59.

Lam, W., Wong, K., Fulks, M. and Holsti, L. (2008) 'Obsessional slowness: a case study', *Canadian Journal of Occupational Therapy*, 75(4): 249–54.

Laming, S. (2018) 'Five-fold growth leaves build to rent set to become a mainstream asset class', *Savills News*, 24 October.

LaMore, R., Berghorn, G. and Syal, M. (2018) 'The next big thing in architecture? Buildings that never die', *Fast Company*, 21 November.

Lanciani, R. (1899) *The Destruction of Ancient Rome: A Sketch of the History of the Monuments*, New York, NY: The MacMillan Co.

Landscape Institute (2013) *Public Health and Landscape: Creating Healthy Places*, London: Landscape Institute.

Lane, M. (2019) 'Why 2020 could be a strong year for the UK's PBSA sector', *Property Investor Today*, 13 December, https://www.propertyinvestortoday.co.uk/breaking-news/2019/12/why-2020-could-be-a-strong-year-for-the-uks-pbsa-sector

Lapidus, I. (1973) 'The evolution of Muslim urban society', *Comparative Studies in Society and History*, 15(1): 21–50.

Larkin, B. (2013) 'The politics and poetics of infrastructure', *Annual Review of Anthropology*, 42: 327–43.

Laubin, R. and Laubin, G. (2012) *The Indian Tipi: Its History, Construction, and Use*, Norman, OK: University of Oklahoma Press.

Laurance, W. and Salt, D. (2018) 'Opinion: environmental impact assessments aren't protecting the environment', Ensia, University of Minnesota Institute on the Environment, 6 December.

Laver, R. (2014) 'Systemic corruption: considering its cultural drivers in second-generation reforms', Working Paper 45, Edward J. Safra Center for Ethics, Harvard University.

LBM (Living Building Movement) (2014) *Living Building Challenge 3.0: A Visionary Path to a Regenerative Future*, Seattle, WA: International Living Future Institute.

Le Corbusier (2004) *The Modulor and Modulor 2*, Basel and Boston, MA: Birkhäuser.

Lee, J. and Tang, W. (2017) 'The hegemony of the real estate industry: redevelopment of 'government/institution or community' (G/IC) land in Hong Kong', *Urban Studies*, 54(15): 3403–22.

Lee, S. (2015) 'Assessing South Korea's green growth strategy', in R.L. Bryant (ed) *The International Handbook of Political Ecology*, Camberley: Edward Elgar Publishing, pp 345–58.

Lees, L. and White, H. (2019) 'The social cleansing of London council estates: everyday experiences of "accumulative dispossession"', *Housing Studies*, https://doi.org/10.1080/02673037.2019.1680814

Lefebvre, H. (1991) *The Production of Space*, Oxford: Blackwell.

Legacy, C., Pinnegar, S. and Wiesel, I. (2013) 'Under the strategic radar and outside planning's "spaces of interest": knockdown rebuild and the changing suburban form of Australia's cities', *Australian Planner*, 50(2): 117–22.

Leick, G. (2002) *Mesopotamia: The Invention of the City*, London: Penguin Books.

Leigh, D. and Evans, R. (2009) 'British firm Mabey and Johnson convicted of bribing foreign politicians', *The Guardian*, 25 September.

Letto, J. (1995) 'TV lets corporations pull green wool over viewers' eyes', *Fairness and Accuracy in Reporting*, 1 July.

Letwin, O. (2018) *Independent Review of Build Out Rates: Draft Analy*sis, London: Ministry of Housing, Communities and Local Government.

Levien, M. (2012) 'The land question: special economic zones and the political economy of dispossession in India', *The Journal of Peasant Studies*, 39(3–4): 933–69.

Levien, M. (2018) *Dispossession without Development: Land Grabs in Neoliberal India*, Oxford: Oxford University Press.

Levin, M. (2020) 'The pandemic hasn't killed California's big housing plans – but they have mutated', *Capradio*, 24 May.

Levin, M. and Christopher, B. (2017) 'Californians: here's why your housing costs are so high', *Cal Matters*, 21 August.

Levina, M. (2019) 'Can Central Asia countries pay their external debts?', *The Times of Central Asia*, 17 March.

Lewis, S. and Maslin, M. (2015) 'Defining the Anthropocene', *Nature*, 519(7542): 171–80.

Leyshon, A. and French, S. (2009) ' "We all live in a Robbie Fowler house": the geographies of the buy to let market in the UK', *British Journal of Politics and International Relations*, 11(3): 438–60.

LGA (Local Government Association) (2019) *LGA Briefing: Building Out Extant Planning Permissions, House of Commons*, 30 October, London: Local Government Association.

Li, D., Lu, D., Moran, E. and da Silva, R. (2020) 'Examining water area changes accompanying dam construction in the Madeira River in the Brazilian Amazon', *Water*, 12(7): 1–22.

Li, Y., Yang, L., He, B. and Zhou, D. (2014) 'Green building in China: needs great promotion', *Sustainable Cities and Society*, 11: 1–6.

Lind, C. (1994) *Frank Lloyd Wright's Usonian Houses*, Rohnert Park, CA: Pomegranate Art Books.

Lindsey, R. (2020) 'Climate change: global sea level', *NOAA Climate.gov*, 14 August.

Lipuma, L. (2019) 'Roman mining activities polluted European air more heavily than previously thought', *AGU Blogosphere*, 7 May.

Liss, H. (2000) *Demolition: The Art of Demolishing, Dismantling, Imploding, Toppling and Razing*, New York, NY: Black Dog & Leventhal Publishing.

Lloyd Wright, F. (1908) 'In the cause of architecture', *Architectural Record*, 23(3): 155–63.

Lloyd Wright, F. (1931) *To the Young Man in Architecture, Two Lectures on Architecture*, Architectural Record, August, Chicago, IL: Art Institute of Chicago.

Lloyd Wright, F. (1932) *An Autobiography*, London: Longmans, Green.

Lloyd Wright, F. (1939) *An Organic Architecture: The Architecture of Democracy*, London: Lund Humphries & Co.

Lloyd Wright, F. (1954) *The Natural House*, New York, NY: Horizon Press.

Lloyd Wright, F. (1992 [1894]) 'The architect and the machine', in B. Pfeiffer (ed) *Frank Lloyd Wright: Collected Writings, Volume 1, 1894–1930*, New York, NY: Rizzoli, pp 20–6.

Lloyd Wright, F. (1994 [1947]) 'Planning man's physical environment' (lecture given at Princeton University Bicentennial Conference, 5 March), in B. Pfeiffer (ed) *Frank Lloyd Wright: Collected Writings, Volume 4, 1939–1949*, New York, NY: Rizzoli, pp 311–14.

Locatelli, G., Mariani, G., Sainati, T. and Greco, M. (2017) 'Corruption in public projects and megaprojects: there is an elephant in the room!', *International Journal of Project Management*, 35(3): 252–68.

Lopez, G. (2015) 'Hurricane Katrina, in 7 essential facts', *Vox*, 28 August.

Lord, A. and Tewdwr-Jones, M. (2018) 'Getting the planners off our backs: questioning the post-political nature of English planning policy', *Planning Practice and Research*, 33(3): 229–43.

Lorinc, J. (2006) 'Meltdown in Mansionville', *The Globe and Mail*, 7 January.

Lowe, T. and Gardiner, J. (2020) 'RIBA tells Jenrick to "urgently reconsider" planning reforms', *Building Design*, 4 August.

Luhn, A. (2017) 'Moscow's big move: is this the biggest urban demolition project ever?', *The Guardian*, 31 March.

Lupton, K., Colwell, J. and Bayley, M. (2002) 'Aspects of children's road crossing behaviour', *Municipal Engineer*, 151(2): 151–7.

Lynch, K. (1960) *The Image of the City*, Cambridge, MA: Harvard–MIT Joint Center for Urban Studies.

Lynch, K. (1981) *Good City Form*, Cambridge, MA: MIT Press.

Lynch, K. (1990) 'The waste of place', *Places*, 6(2): 10–23.

MacKerron, G. and Mourato, S. (2009) 'Life satisfaction and air quality in London', *Ecological Economics*, 68(5): 1441–53.

MacPherson, C. (1997) 'A Samoan solution to the limitations of urban housing in New Zealand', in J. Renoel and M. Rodma (eds) *Home in the Islands: Housing and Social Change in the Pacific*, Hawaii: University of Hawaii Press, pp 151–74.

Macrotrends LCC (2020) 'Nairobi, Kenya Metro Area Population 1950–2020', www.macrotrends.net/cities/21711/nairobi/population

Magnus, B. (1978) *Nietzsche's Existential Imperative*, Bloomington, IN, and London: Indiana University Press.

Mahadevan, P. (2019*) Sand Mafias in India: Disorganized Crime in a Growing Economy*, Geneva: Global Initiative Against Transnational Organized Crime.

Malhi, Y. (2017) 'The concept of the Anthropocene', *Annual Review of Environment and Resources*, 42: 77–104.

Mallach, A. (2011) 'Demolition and preservation in shrinking US industrial cities', *Building Research and Information*, 39(4): 380–94.

Mallowan, M. (1970) 'The development of cities from Al 'Ubaid to the end of Uruk 5', *Ancient History*, 1(1): 327–462.

Mangold, S. and Zschau, T. (2019) 'In search of the "good life": the appeal of the tiny house lifestyle in the USA', *Social Sciences*, 8(26): 1–21.

Mansell, J. (2016) *The Age of Noise in Britain: Hearing Modernity*, Champagne, IL: University of Illinois Press.

Marais, H. and Labuschagne, J.-P. (2019) 'If you want to prosper, consider building roads: China's role in African infrastructure and capital projects', *Deloitte Insights*, 22 March.

Marí, A. (2016) 'La ruina', in J. Balló and A. Bergala (eds) *Motivos visuales del cine*, Barcelona: Galaxia Gutenberg, pp 214–19.

Mark, R. and Hutchinson, P. (1986) 'On the structure of the Roman pantheon', *The Art Bulletin*, 68(1): 24–34.

Marosi, R. (2017) 'A failed vision', *Los Angeles Times*, 26 November.

Marshall, C. (2015) 'The world's first skyscraper: a history of cities in 50 buildings', *The Guardian*, 2 April.

Martin, A., Moral-Benito, E. and Tom Schmitz, T. (2019) *The Financial Transmission of Housing Bubbles: Evidence from Spain*, Working Paper Series, Frankfurt: European Central Bank.

Martínez, M. (2018) '5 million houses empty due to their location, insecurity', *Mexico News Daily*, 29 October.

Maven (2018) 'Maven & IPIM build Stirling's 1st purpose built student accommodation', 21 February.

May, N. (2016) 'Building more houses cannot solve the housing crisis', *UCL Sustainable Cities Blog*, March.

Mayer, C. and Somerville, C. (2000) 'Land use regulation and new construction', *Regional Science and Urban Economics*, 30(6): 639–62.

Mayhew, L. (2020) *Too Little, Too Late: Housing for an Ageing Population*, London: Centre for the Study of Financial Innovation.

Mazumdar, S. (2008) *Crony Capitalism and India: Before and after Liberalization*, ISID Working Paper No: 2008/04, Munich: Munich Personal RePEc Archive.

McAuliffe, M. (2020) *Paris, City of Dreams: Napoleon III, Baron Haussmann, and the Creation of Paris*, Lanham, MD: The Rowman and Littlefield Publishing Group.

McCormack, G. (1995) 'Growth, construction, and the environment: Japan's construction state', *Japanese Studies Bulletin*, 15(1): 26–35.

McCormack, G. (2001) *The Emptiness of Japanese Affluence*, New York, NY: East Gate Book.

McCormick, J. (1997) *Carl Schmitt's Critique of Liberalism: Against Politics as Technology*, Cambridge: Cambridge University Press.

McElroy, J. (2016) 'One chart shows how unprecedented Vancouver's real estate situation is', *Global News*, 4 August.

McIntyre, D. (2019) 'There are over 17 million vacant homes in America', *24/7 Wall St*, 30 September.

McLennan, J. (2012) *Transformational Thought: Radical Ideas to Remake the Built Environment*, Kansas City, KS: Ecotone Publishing.

McLennan, J. (2019) 'Living buildings for a living planet', *Reflections*, New Haven, CT: Yale University, https://reflections.yale.edu/article/crucified-creation-green-faith-rising/living-buildings-living-planet

Mehan, A. (2017) ' "Tabula rasa" planning: creative destruction and building a new urban identity in Tehran', *Journal of Architecture and Urbanism*, 41(3): 210–20.

Mehra, D. and Batra, L. (2006) 'Neoliberal Delhi: through the lens of the Yamuna Pushta demolitions', in C. Broius and R. Ahuja (eds) *Megacities: Approaches to Metropolitan Cities in India*, Heidelberg: Draupadi Verlag, pp 173–91.

Mensch, J. (2008) 'Violence and embodiment', *Symposium*, 12(1): 4–15.

Merchant, C. (1992) *Radical Ecology: The Search for a Liveable World*, New York, NY: Routledge.

Merleau-Ponty, M. (1962) *Phenomenology of Perception*, London: Routledge.

Metcalf, S. (2018) 'Council claims oversupply of student accommodation is "mythical"', *The Business Desk*, 24 May.

Milani, B. (2000) *Designing the Green Economy: The Post-industrial Alternative to Corporate Globalization*, New York, NY: Rowan and Littlefield Publishers.

Millard, P. (ed) (2000) *Notes of Me: The Autobiography of Roger North*, Toronto: University of Toronto Press.

Ministry of Water Resources (2011) *2010 Statistic Bulletin on China Water Activities*, Beijing, China: Water Power Press.

Minkjan, M. (2019) 'Degrowth is about redistribution by design, not by collapse', *Failed Architecture*, 17 September.

Mohl, R. (1993) 'Race and space in the modern city', in A.R. Hirsch and R.A. Mohl (eds) *Urban Policy in Twentieth-Century America*, New Brunswick, NJ: Rutgers University Press, pp 100–58.

Mohl, R. (2004) 'Stop the road: freeway revolts in American cities', *Journal of Urban History*, 30(5): 674–706.

Mollenkopf, J. (1975) 'Theories of the state and power structure research', *Insurgent Sociologist*, 5(3): 245–2.

Molotch, H. (1976) 'The city as a growth machine: toward a political economy of place', *American Journal of Sociology*, 8(2): 309–32.

Monbiot, G. (2014) 'Put a price on nature? We must stop this neoliberal road to ruin', *The Guardian*, 24 July.

Monk, S., Pearce, B. and Whitehead, C. (1996) 'Land-use planning, land supply, and house prices', *Environment and Planning A*, 28(3): 495–511.

Monkkonen, P. (2019) 'Understanding and challenging opposition to housing construction in California's urban areas', UCLA, https://luskin.ucla.edu/person/paavo-monkkonen

Monkkonen, P. and Livesley-O'Neill, W. (2017) *Overcoming Opposition to New Housing*, Los Angeles, CA: UCLA California, Ralph and Goldy Lewis Center for Regional Policy Studies.

Moore, R. (2012) *Why We Build*, London: Picador – Pan Macmillan.

Moore-Bick, M. (2019) *Grenfell Tower Inquiry*, London: House of Commons.

Morin, C.R. and Fischer, C.R. (2006) 'Kansas City Hyatt Hotel skyway collapse', *Journal of Failure Analysis and Prevention*, 6: 5–11.

Morris, L. and Beck, L. (2020) 'Berlin is taking radical measures to control rents. Can it hold back the tide?', *The Washington Post*, 30 January.

Morris, R. (2010) 'Anthropogenic impacts on tropical forest biodiversity: a network structure and ecosystem functioning perspective', *Philosophical Transactions of the Royal Society B*, 365(1558): 3709–18.

Mörtenböck, P. and Mooshammer, H. (2018) 'Urban frontiers in the global struggle for capital gains', *Finance and Society*, 4(1): 108–25.

Mortice, Z. (2016) 'When public housing goes private', *Curbed*, 28 September.

Morton, H. (1980) 'Who gets what, when and how? Housing in the Soviet Union', *Soviet Studies*, 32(2): 235–59.

Moss and Co (2019) 'London's luxury ghost towers: why are they empty?', Blog, Moss & Co, http://blog.mosswimbledonhill.co.uk/londons-luxury-ghost-towers-why-are-they-empty/

Mulheirn, I. (2019) 'Why building 300,000 houses per year won't solve the housing crisis – and what will', *LSE Blogs*, 28 August.

Mumford, L. (1956) 'The natural history of urbanization', in W. Thomas (ed) *Man's Role in Changing the Face of the Earth*, Chicago, IL: University of Chicago Press, pp 387–98.

Mumford, L. (1961) *The City in History*, New York, NY, and London: Penguin Books.

Murphy, K. (2015) 'When a house is demolished, more than the home is lost', *The Conversation*, 21 July.

Murphy, N. (2018) 'Why are so many of the UK's homes under-occupied?', *RSA Blog*, 1 February.

Murray, C. (2020) 'Time is money: how land banking constrains housing supply', *Journal of Housing Economics*, 49: 1–10.

Murshed, S.M. (2020) 'Capitalism and COVID-19: crisis at the crossroads', *Peace Economics, Peace Science and Public Policy*, 26(3): 1–8.

Myers, J. (2019) 'Yes, Britain does have a bloody housing shortage – and we obviously do need to build more homes', *City Metric*, 3 September.

Nadj, D. (2019) 'Deregulation, the absence of the law and the Grenfell Tower fire', *Human Rights Law Review*, 5(2), www.qmul.ac.uk/law/humanrights/media/humanrights/docs/Nadj-final.pdf

Nasar, J., Evans-Cowley, J. and Mantero, V. (2007) 'McMansions: the extent and regulation of super-sized houses', *Journal of Urban Design*, 12(3): 339–58.

Nash, G. (1999) *The Federal Landscape: An Economic History of the Twentieth-Century West*, Tucson, AZ: University of Arizona Press.

National Autistic Society (2020) 'What is autism?', www.autism.org.uk/advice-and-guidance/what-is-autism

National Commission for Urban Problems (1969) *Building the American City*, Washington, DC: Government Printing Office.

Natural Capital Coalition (2020) *Natural Capital*, London: Natural Capital Coalition.

Neate, R. (2014) 'Scandal of Europe's 11m empty homes', *The Guardian*, 23 February.

Neate, R. (2017) 'High living, low sales: Shard apartments still empty, five years on', *The Guardian*, 5 July.

Neate, R. (2018a) 'Park Modern: flats for super-rich leave key workers in the cold', *The Guardian*, 13 August.

Neate, R. (2018b) 'Brutalist market: flats at London's Centre Point taken off market', *The Guardian*, 31 October.

Nestor, O. and Moser, C. (2018) 'The importance of play', *Journal of Occupational Therapy, Schools, and Early Intervention*, 11(3): 247–62.

Newbold, R. (1974) 'Some social and economic consequences of the A.D. 64 fire at Rome', *Latomus*, 33: 858–69.

New Economics Foundation (2018) *What Lies Beneath: How to Fix the Broken Land System at the Heart of Our Housing Crisis*, London: New Economics Foundation Report.

New Gorbals Housing Association (2016) *Norfolk Court Demolition*, 8 May.

New London Architecture (2019) *London Tall Building Survey*, London: NLA.

Newman, G. and Saginor, J. (2014) 'Four imperatives for preventing demolition by neglect', *Journal of Urban Design*, 19(5): 622–37.

Newman, P. and Kenworthy, J. (1999) *Sustainability and Cities: Overcoming Automobile Dependence*, Washington, DC: Island Press.

Nguyen, V. (2017) 'Slow construction: alternative temporalities and tactics in the new landscape of China's urban development', *City*, 21(5): 650–62.

Nienaber, M. (2019) 'Germany builds 285,900 new dwellings, highest in 16 years', *Reuters*, 29 May.

Norberg-Schultz, C. (1988) *Architecture: Meaning and Place*, New York, NY: Rizzoli.

Norberg-Schultz, C. (2019) 'Genius-loci: towards a phenomenology of architecture', in J. Cody and F. Siravo (eds) *Readings in Conservation, Historic Cities: Issues in Urban Conservation*, Los Angeles, CA: The Getty Conservation Institute, pp 31–45.

Nye, J. (2008) 'Public diplomacy and soft power', *Annals, AAPSS*, 616(1): 94–109.

O'Brien, F. (2018) '1 in 4 Vancouver houses sold will be demolished', *Vancouver is Awesome*, 22 June.

OECD (Organisation for Economic Co-operation and Development) (2011) *Towards Green Growth*, Paris: OECD.

OECD (2019) *Global Material Resources Outlook to 2060: Economic Drivers and Environmental Consequences*, Paris: OECD.

Öktem, K. (2019) 'Erasing palimpsest city: boom, bust, and urbicide in Turkey', in H. Yacobi and M. Nasasra (eds) *Routledge Handbook on Middle East Cities*, London: Routledge, pp 295–318.

Olukoju, A. (2004) 'Nigerian cities in historical perspective', in T. Falola and Steven J. Salm (eds) *Nigerian Cities*, Asmara and Trenton: Africa World Press, Inc, pp 11–46.

Ong, A. (2011) 'Hyper building: spectacle, speculation, and the hyperspace of sovereignty', in A. Roy and A. Ong (eds) *Worlding Cities: Asian Experiments and the Art of Being Global*, London: John Wiley & Sons, pp 205–26.

ONS (Office for National Statistics) (2020a) *Construction Output in Great Britain: August 2020*, London: ONS.

ONS (2020b) *Private Rental Market Summary Statistics in England: April 2019 to March 2020*, London: ONS.

Opie, J. (1987) 'Renaissance origins of the environmental crisis', *Environmental Review*, 11(1): 2–17.

Orr, D. (1999) 'Architecture as pedagogy', in C. Kibert (ed) *Reshaping the Built Environment: Ecology, Ethics, and Economics*, Washington, DC: Island Press, pp 212–18.

Paccoud, A. (2017) 'Buy-to-let gentrification: extending social change through tenure shifts', *Environment and Planning A*, 49(4): 839–56.

Pallasmaa, J. (1984) *Alvar Aalto Furniture*, Helsinki: Museum of Finnish Architecture.

Pallasmaa, J. (2017) 'Embodied and existential wisdom in architecture: the thinking hand', *Body and Society*, 23(1): 96–111.

Papanek, V. (1984) *Design for the Real World: Human Ecology and Social Change*, London: Thames & Hudson.

Parker, C. (1911) 'Governmental regulation of speculation', *The Annals of the American Academy of Political and Social Science*, 38(2): 126–54.

Parker, J. (2020) 'Architecture is yet to come to terms with trans bodies', *Failed Architecture*, 26 May.

Parsons, M. (2012) 'Nicholas Barbon (1637–98): FRCP, property developer', *Journal of Medical Biography*, 20: 62–4.

Pearce, F. (1997) 'Forum: land of the rising concrete – the concrete pourers of Japan are going berserk', *New Scientist*, 11 January.

Pene, G., Peita, M., Howden-Chapman, P. and Oranga, H.K. (2009) 'Living the Tokelauan way in New Zealand', *Social Policy Journal of New Zealand*, 35(June): 79–92.

Pennington, M. (2000) *Planning and the Political Market: Public Choice and the Politics of Government Failure*, London: Athlone Press.

Pennington, M. (2002) *Liberating the Land*, Hobart Papers 143, London: Institute of Economic Affairs.

Pettifor, A. (2018) 'Why building more homes will not solve Britain's housing crisis', *The Guardian*, 27 January.

Phillips, J. (2017) 'The "whys and wherefores" of citizen participation in the landscapes of HS2', *Planning Theory and Practice*, 18(2): 328–33.

Pinnegar, S., Freestone, R. and Randolph, B. (2010) 'Suburban reinvestment through "knockdown rebuild" in Sydney', in M. Clapson and R. Hutchison (eds) *Suburbanization in Global Society (Research in Urban Sociology, Vol 10)*, Melbourne: Emerald Group Publishing Ltd, pp 205–29.

Place Alliance (2020) *A Housing Design Audit for England*, London: Place Alliance.

Platt, C. (1976) *The English Medieval Town*, London: Secker and Warburg.

Poon, L. (2019) 'China's huge number of vacant apartments is causing a problem', *Bloomberg CityLab*, 27 February.

Portland Cement Association (2020) 'Cement and concrete sustainability', www.cement.org/sustainability

Pow, C. (2017) 'Courting the "rich and restless": globalisation of real estate and the new spatial fixities of the super-rich in Singapore', *International Journal of Housing Policy*, 17(1): 56–74.

Power, A. (2010) 'Housing and sustainability: demolition or refurbishment?', *Urban Design and Planning*, 163(DP4): 205–16.

Preston, D. (2015) *The New Single Family Home Renters of California: A Statewide Survey of Tenants Renting from Wall Street Landlords*, San Francisco, CA: Tenants Together.

PricewaterhouseCoopers (2020) *Real Estate 2020: Building the Future*, London: PWC.

Prisco, J. (2019) 'Ryugyong Hotel: the story of North Korea's "Hotel of Doom"', *CNN Style*, 10 August.

Property Shark (2016) 'Who lives largest? The growth of urban American homes in the last 100 years', *Property Shark*, 8 September.

Pullen, T. (2020) 'What is an eco home?', *Homebuilding and Renovating*, 3 June.

Pyne, S. (2001) *Fire: A Brief History*, Seattle: University of Washington Press and Weyerhaeuser Environmental Books.

Quigley, J. and Raphael, S. (2005) 'Regulation and the high cost of housing in California', *American Economic Review*, 95(2): 323–8.

Rabeneck, A., Sheppard, D. and Town, P. (1973) 'Housing flexibility?', *Architectural Design*, 43(11): 698–727.

Rae, D. (2003) *City: Urbanism and Its End*, New Haven, CT, and London: Yale University Press.

Rahman, K. (2014) 'Flipping heck! £1 million luxury flat inside Battersea Power Station goes BACK on the market for £1.5 million just six months later – and it hasn't even been built yet', *Mail Online*, 29 November.

Railton, W. (2016) 'The economics of iceberg homes: are mega-basements just a sunk cost?', *CityA.M.*, 26 October.

Rainforest Relief (2013) 'Long Beach is destroying nine square miles of rainforests', 14 July.

RAU Architects (2020) 'Triodos Bank/RAU Architects', *Arch Daily*, www.archdaily.com/926357/triodos-bank-rau-architects?ad_source=search&ad_medium=search_result_projects

Reid, S. (2006) 'Khrushchev modern: agency and modernization in the Soviet home', *Cahiers du Monde russe*, 47(1/2): 227–68.

Reuters (2019) 'Court orders Thai rail authority to pay $370 mln to HK's Hopewell', 22 April.

Rhodes, C. (2019) 'The construction industry: statistics and policy', Briefing Paper, Number 01432, House of Commons Library, 16 December.

Richter, A., Göbel, H. and Grubbauer, M. (2017) 'Designed to improve? The makings, politics and aesthetics of "social" architecture and design', *City*, 21(6): 769–78.

RICS (Royal Institution of Chartered Surveyors) (2020) *Life after Lockdown Part 8: Build, Build, Build: for Better or for Worse?*, 28 July, London: RICS.

Rielage, R. (2017) 'The origins of the Santa Rosa wildfire', *Fire Rescue-1*, 12 October.

Rightmove (2020) 'House prices in Esher', www.rightmove.co.uk/house-prices/esher.html

Rios, S. (2009) 'Integration and the environment on the Rio Madeira', *The North American Congress on Latin America Magazine*, 9 March.

Ritchie, H. and Roser, M. (2019) 'Urbanization', Our World in Data, November, https://ourworldindata.org/urbanization

Rivoalen, E. (1882) 'Promenades à travers Paris: Maisons et Locataires', *Revue générale de l'architecture* 9: 258–60.

Roberts, T. (2018) 'The living building challenge: epitomizing optimism in our future', *Rise*, 7 August.

Robinson, G., Betts, M., Burton, C., Leonard, J. Sharda, A. and Whittington, T. (2015) *Global Construction 2030: A Global Forecast for the Construction Industry to 2030*, London: Global Construction Perspectives and Oxford Economics.

Robinson, W. (2003) *Risks and Rights: The Causes, Consequences, and Challenges of Development-Induced Displacement*, Washington, DC: The Brookings Institution.

Roebuck, J., Kroemer, K. and Thomson, W. (1975) *Engineering Anthropometry Methods*, New York, NY: John Wiley & Sons.

Rogers, L. (2018) 'Climate change: the massive CO2 emitter you may not know about', *BBC News*, 17 December.

Rogers, S. (2009) 'Urban geography: urban growth machine', in R. Kitchin and N. Thrift (eds) *International Encyclopaedia of Human Geography*, Oxford: Elsevier, pp 40–5.

Rosenberg, M. (2016) 'A teardown a day: bulldozing the way for bigger homes in Seattle, suburbs', *The Seattle Times*, 26 August.

Rosenman, E. and Walker, S. (2016) 'Tearing down the city to save it? "Back-door regionalism" and the demolition coalition in Cleveland, Ohio', *Environment and Planning A*, 48(2): 273–91.

Rosenzweig, R. and Blackmar, E. (1992) *The Park and the People: A History of Central Park*, Ithaca, NY: Cornell University Press.

Roth, A. (2018) 'Putin opens 12-mile bridge between Crimea and Russian mainland', *The Guardian*, 15 May.

Ruddick, G. (2015) 'Revealed: housebuilders sitting on 600,000 plots of land', *The Guardian*, 30 December.

Russell, M. (2004) *Creating the New Egyptian Woman: Consumerism, Education, and National Identity 1863–1922*, New York, NY: Palgrave Macmillan US.

Ryan, J. (1902) 'The ethics of speculation', *International Journal of Ethics*, 12(3): 335–47.

Saadatian, O., Chin Haw, L., Sopian, K. and Sulaiman, M. (2012) 'Review of windcatcher technologies', *Renewable and Sustainable Energy Reviews*, 16: 1477–95.

Sanchez, A. (2016) *Criminal Capital: Violence, Corruption and Class in Industrial India*, New York, NY: Routledge.

Sandilands, A. (2018) 'Construction waste: "Out of site", out of mind?', *Resource*, 8 June.

Saroglou, T., Meir, I., Theodosiou, T. and Givoni, B. (2017) 'Towards energy efficient skyscrapers', *Energy and Buildings*, 149: 437–49.

Sayer, A. (2011) *Why Things Matter to People: Social Science, Values and Ethical Life*, Cambridge: Cambridge University Press.

Scally, C. and Tighe, R. (2015) 'Democracy in action? Nimby as impediment to equitable affordable housing siting', *Housing Studies*, 30(5): 749–69.

Schrader, B. (2013) 'Māori housing – te noho whare', *Te Ara The Encyclopaedia of New Zealand*, https://teara.govt.nz/en/maori-housing-te-noho-whare/print

Schultheis, E. (2019) 'The radical way Berlin plans to solve its housing crisis', *Huffington Post*, 12 April.

Schumpeter, J. (1943) *Capitalism, Socialism and Democracy*, London: G. Allen & Unwin.

Scott-Fine, A. and Lindberg, J. (2002) *Protecting America's Historic Neighborhoods: Taming the Teardown Trend*, Washington, DC: National Trust for Historic Preservation.

Segú, M. (2018) 'Do short-term rent platforms affect rents? Evidence from Airbnb in Barcelona', MPRA Paper, 84369, University Library of Munich, Germany.

Sen, A. (1977) 'Starvation and exchange entitlements: a general approach and its application to the great Bengal famine', *Cambridge Journal of Economics*, 1(1): 33–59.

Shabrina, Z., Arcaute, E. and Batty, M. (2019) 'Airbnb's disruption of the housing structure in London', Cornell University, March, https://arxiv.org/abs/1903.11205

Shan, M., Le, Y., Chan, A. and Hu, Y. (2020) *Corruption in the Public Construction Sector: A Holistic View*, Singapore: Springer.

Sharman, J. (2018) 'Construction waste and materials efficiency', *NBS*, 6 April.

Shatkin, G. (2008) 'The city and the bottom line: urban megaprojects and the privatization of planning in Southeast Asia', *Environment and Planning A*, 40(2): 383–401.

Shelton, T. (2010) 'The highway and the American city', in C.A. Brebbia, S. Hernandez and E. Tiezzi (eds) *The Sustainable City VI: Urban Regeneration and Sustainability*, Southampton: WIT Press, pp 323–34.

Shen, L., Zhang, Z. and Long, Z. (2017) 'Significant barriers to green procurement in real estate development', *Resources, Conservation and Recycling*, 16: 160–8.

Shepard, W. (2015a) 'During its long boom, Chinese cities demolished an area the size of Mauritius every year', *City Metric*, 22 September.

Shepard, W. (2015b) ' "Half the houses will be demolished within 20 years": on the disposable cities of China, *CityMetric*, 21 October.

Shepperson, T. (2016) 'Three ways we could deal with the scandal of empty homes', *The Landlord Law Blog*, 10 May.

Shi, L., Wurm, M., Huang, X. and Tauberboch, H. (2020) 'Urbanization that hides in the dark – spotting China's "ghost neighborhoods" from space', *Landscape and Urban Planning*, 200: art 103822.

Shin, H.B. (2013) 'China's speculative urbanism and the built environment', *China Policy Institute Blog*, University of Nottingham, 24 April.

Shin, H.B. and Kim, S.-H. (2016) 'The developmental state, speculative urbanisation and the politics of displacement in gentrifying Seoul', *Urban Studies*, 53(3): 540–59.

Shiva, V., Jani, S. and Fontana, S. (2011) *The Great Indian Land Grab*, New Delhi: Navdanya.

Short, J. (2018) *The Unequal City: Urban Resurgence, Displacement and the Making of Inequality in Global Cities*, Abingdon: Routledge.

Silzer, K. (2019) 'Understanding Frank Lloyd Wright through 5 key works', *Visual Culture*, 10 September.

Simpson, L. (2020) 'Our why: marketing the value of construction', *Insynth*, 21 February.

Sinclair, B. (2017) 'Japanese spirituality, flexibility and design: influences and impacts on agile architecture + open building', in M. Couceiro da Costa, F. Roseta, J. Pestana Lages and S. Couceiro da Costa (eds) *Architectural Research Addressing Societal Challenges Volume 2: Proceedings of the EAAE ARCC 10th International Conference (EAAE ARCC 2016), 15–18 June 2016*, Lisbon, Portugal: CRC Press, pp 833–40.

Sinclair, I. (2011) *Ghost Milk: Calling Time on the Grand Project*, London: Penguin Group.

Sisson, P. (2017) 'How air conditioning shaped modern architecture – and changed our climate', *CURBED Architecture*, 9 May.

Skeggs, B. (2014) 'Values beyond value? Is anything beyond the logic of capital?', *British Journal of Sociology*, 65(1): 1–20.

Slowey, K. (2018) 'Global construction waste will almost double by 2025', *Construction Dive*, 13 March.

Smith, A. (1776) *An Inquiry into the Nature and Causes of the Wealth of Nations*, London: Strahan and Cadell.

Snook, J. (2018) 'Why green construction is here to stay', https://gocontractor.com/blog/green-construction/

Soleri, P. (1969) *Arcology: The City in the Image of Man*, Cambridge, MA: MIT Press.

Soleri, P., Kim, Y., Anderson, C., Nordfors, A., Riley, S. and Tamura, T. (2012) *Lean Linear City: Arterial Arcology*, Mayer, AZ: Cosanti Press.

Staccioli, R. (2003) *The Roads of the Romans*, Los Angeles, CA: J. Paul Getty Museum.

Stahl, L. (2014) 'China's real estate bubble', *CBS News*, 3 August.

Stallmeyer, J. (2011) *Building Bangalore: Architecture and Urban Transformation in India's Silicon Valley*, London: Routledge.

Stambaugh, J. (1988) *The Ancient Roman City*, Baltimore, MD: Johns Hopkins University Press.

Statista (2019) 'Construction industry spending worldwide from 2014 to 2025 (in trillion U.S. dollars)', Statista Research Department, New York, 9 August.

Statista (2020) 'Value added by the construction industry as a percentage of U.S. GDP 2007–2019', Statista Research Department, New York.

Statista (2021) 'Airbnb listings in select major cities worldwide as of September 2018', Statista, Hamburg.

St Denis, J. (2018) 'Vancouver's rapid cycle of house teardowns comes with environmental cost', *The Star Vancouver*, 23 May.

Steed, L. (2019) 'Construction is third most dangerous UK industry', *Construction Europe*, 26 November.

Steele, W. (2017) 'Constructing the construction state: cement and post-war Japan', *The Asia-Pacific Journal*, 15(11): 1–11.

Steffen, W., Broadgate, W., Deutsch, L., Gaffney, O. and Ludwig, C. (2015) 'The trajectory of the Anthropocene: the great acceleration', *The Anthropocene Review*, 2(1): 81–98.

Stein, S. (2019) *Capital City: Gentrification and the Real Estate State*, London: Verso.

Steiner, E. (2017) 'Building blocs: why Moscow is pursuing its apartment renovation program', *Vocal Europe*, 2 January.

Stone, P. (2020) 'The westward growth of London in the 17th century', *The History of London*, www.thehistoryoflondon.co.uk/the-aristocratic-growth-of-london-in-the-late-17th-century/

Storlazzi, C.D., Gingerich, S.B., van Dongeren, A., Cheriton, O.M., Swarzenski, P.W., Quataert, E., Voss, C.I., Field, D.W., Annamalai, H., Piniak, G.A. and McCall, R. (2018) 'Most atolls will be uninhabitable by the mid-21st century because of sea-level rise exacerbating wave-driven flooding', *Science Advances*, 4(4): EAAP9741.

Strang, V. (2005) 'Knowing me, knowing you: Aboriginal and European concepts of nature as self and other', in J. Miller (ed) *Worldviews: Global Religions, Culture, and Ecology*, Leiden, Netherlands: Brill, pp 25–56.

Sukhdev, P. (2014) 'Who should value nature? Interview with Pavan Sukhdev', *Why Green Economy*, https://whygreeneconomy.org/information/who-should-value-nature-interview-with-pavan-sukhdev/

Sullivan, S. (2016) 'Nature is being renamed "natural capital" – but is it really the planet that will profit?', *The Conversation*, 13 September.

Swinney, P. (2018) 'Yes, supply is the cause of the housing crisis – and we do need to build more homes in successful cities', *City Metric*, 3 April.

Tacconi, L., Boscolo, M. and Brack, D. (2003) *National and International Policies to Control Illegal Forest Activities*, Jakarta, Indonesia: Center for International Forestry Research.

Tafel, E. (1979) *Years with Frank Lloyd Wright: Apprentice to Genius*, New York, NY: McGraw-Hill Book Company.

Talen, E. (2014) 'Housing demolition during urban renewal', *City and Community*, 13: 233–53.

Tansel, C. (2018) 'Authoritarian neoliberalism and democratic backsliding in Turkey: beyond the narratives of progress', *South European Society and Politics*, 23(2): 197–217.

Taylor, M. (2015) *California's High Housing Costs Causes and Consequences*, Sacramento, CA: California Legislative Analyst's Office Report.

Taylor, P. (2020) 'Want more affordable housing in Canada? Build more houses', *C2C Journal*, 27 March.

Thomsen, A., Schultmann, F. and Kohler, N. (2011) 'Deconstruction, demolition and destruction', *Building Research & Information*, 39(4): 327–32.

Till, K. (2012) 'Wounded cities: memory-work and a place-based ethics of care', *Political Geography*, 31: 3–14.

Tilley, C. (1996) *An Ethnography of the Neolithic: Early Prehistoric Societies in Southern Scandinavia*, Cambridge: Cambridge University Press.

Toynbee, P. (2017) 'We could end the buy-to-leave scandal – if the political will was there', *The Guardian*, 3 August.

Transparency International (2017) *Faulty Towers: Understanding the Impact of Overseas Corruption on the London Property Market*, London: TI.

Tricario, A. and Sol, X. (2016) 'Re-building the world: the structural adjustment through mega-infrastructures in the era of financialization', *Development*, 59(1): 53–8.

Trubiano, F., Onbargi, C., Rinaldi, A. and Whitlock, Z. (2019) *Fossil Fuels, the Building Industry, and Human Health*, Pennsylvania, PA: University of Pennsylvania, Kleinman Center for Energy Policy.

Turner, J. (1976) *Housing by People: Towards Autonomy in Building Environments, Ideas in Progress*, London: Marion Boyars.

Tweedie, N. (2018) 'Is the world running out of sand? The truth behind stolen beaches and dredged islands', *The Guardian*, 1 July.

UNEIEA (United Nations Environment and International Energy Agency) (2017) *Towards a Zero-Emission, Efficient, and Resilient Buildings and Construction Sector. Global Status Report 2017*, Paris: UNEIEA.

United Nations (2019) *World Urbanization Prospects: The 2018 Revision*, New York, NY: United Nations, Department of Economic and Social Affairs Population Division.

United Nations Environment Programme (2019) *Global Status Report for Buildings and Construction: Towards a Zero-Emission, Efficient and Resilient Buildings and Construction Sector*, Nairobi, Kenya: United Nations Environment Programme.

United Nations Habitat (2016) *Urbanization and Development: Emerging Futures: World Cities Report 2016*, Nairobi, Kenya: United Nations Human Settlements Programme (UN-Habitat).

US Census Bureau (1996) *Statistical Brief: Who Owns the Nation's Rental Properties?*, Washington, DC: US Census Bureau.

US Census Bureau (2015) *2015 Rental Housing Finance Survey: National Summary Tables*, Washington, DC: US Census Bureau.

US Census Bureau (2018) *American Community Survey for 2018*, Washington, DC: US Census Bureau.

US Department of Justice (2016) 'Lumber Liquidators Inc. sentenced for illegal importation of hardwood and related environmental crimes', Office of Public Affairs, US Department of Justice, 1 February.

Vale, L. (2012) 'Housing Chicago: Cabrini-Green to Parkside of Old Town', *Places Journal*, February.

Valenzuela, F. and Bohm, S. (2017) 'Against wasted politics: a critique of the circular economy', *Ephemera: Theory and Politics in Organization*, 17(1): 23–60.

Van de Rijdt, S. (2020) 'Can the circular economy make construction more sustainable? Planning News Today', *pbc today*, 6 April.

Van Dijck, P. (2008) 'Troublesome construction: the rationale and risks of IIRSA', *European Review of Latin American and Caribbean Studies*, 85: 101–120.

Van Loon, J. and Aalbers, M. (2017) 'How real estate became "just another asset class": the financialization of the investment strategies of Dutch institutional investors', *European Planning Studies*, 25(2): 221–240.

Vidal, J. (2018) 'The 100 million city: is 21st century urbanisation out of control?', *The Guardian*, 19 March.

Wagenaar, M. (2010) 'Haussmann, Baron Georges-Eugène', in R. Hutchison (ed) *Encyclopaedia of Urban Studies*, Thousand Oaks, CA: SAGE Publications, Inc, pp 345–6.

Waley, P. (2005) 'Ruining and restoring rivers: the state and civil society in Japan', *Pacific Affairs*, 78(2): 195–215.

Walker, J. (2015) 'The wound in West Baltimore: how city planners killed a community', *Reason*, 5 August.

Walker, P. (1972) 'Parliamentary debates (Commons)', *Hansard*, 839: column 1094, 26 June.

Walker, P. (2020) 'Councils say 1m homes given go-ahead but not yet built', *The Guardian*, 20 February.

Walsh, J. (2019) *The Great Fire of Rome: Life and Death in the Ancient City*, Baltimore, MD: Johns Hopkins University Press.

Walsh, M. (2019) 'In Old Shanghai, a last spring festival before the bulldozers', *Sixth Tone*, 5 February.

Warner, J. (2012) 'The struggle over Turkey's Ilısu Dam: domestic and international security linkages', *International Environmental Agreements: Politics, Law and Economics*, 12: 231–50.

Warnock, A. (2017) 'How Tuhoe is leading the way in sustainable design', *This New Zealand Life*, https://thisnzlife.co.nz/tuhoe-leading-way-sustainable-design/

Washington, E. (2012) 'Historic preservation and its costs', *City Journal*, 2 May.

Watson, B. (2016) 'The troubling evolution of corporate greenwashing', *The Guardian*, 20 August.

Watts, J. (2014) 'Belo Monte, Brazil: the tribes living in the shadow of a megadam', *The Guardian*, 16 December.

Watts, J. (2019) 'Concrete: the most destructive material on earth', *The Guardian*, 25 February.

Weaver, R. (2018) 'A guide to our property investment asset classes', *Property Partner*, 30 August.

Webb, J. and Murphy, L. (2020) *Renting Beyond Their Means? The Role of Living Rent in Addressing Housing Affordability*, London: Institute for Public Policy Research.

Weiler, P. (2013) 'Labour and the land: the making of the Community Land Act, 1976', *Contemporary British History*, 27(4): 389–420.

Weisse, M. and Goldman, E. (2020) 'We lost a football pitch of primary rainforest every 6 seconds in 2019', World Resources Institute, 2 June.

Weizman, E. (2004) 'The geometry of occupation', Centre of Contemporary Culture of Barcelona 2004, conference, 1 March, www.cccb.org/rcs_gene/geometry_occupation.pdf

West, M. (2013) 'Almost all 866 flats in Battersea Power Station development sold to foreign investors for £675m – and they haven't even been built yet', *This is Money*, 21 May.

Westwater, H. (2019) 'There are enough empty homes in England to meet 72% of the new homes target', *The Big Issue*, 23 September.

While, A., Jonas, A. and Gibbs, D. (2004) 'The environment and the entrepreneurial city: searching for the urban "sustainability fix" in Manchester and Leeds', *International Journal of Urban and Regional Research*, 28(3): 549–69.

White, A. (2016) 'One Blackfriars: an exclusive look inside the Vase, London's newest skyscraper', *The Daily Telegraph*, 19 November.

White, D. (2018) 'Urban wildfires are the new normal and everyone should be prepared', *Berkeleyside*, 21 May.

White, T. (2018) 'Build-to-rent: how developers are profiting from Generation Rent', *The Guardian*, 11 April.

Whitehand, J. and Larkham, P. (1991) 'Housebuilding in the back garden: reshaping suburban townscapes in the Midlands and South East England', *Area*, 23(1): 57–65.

Whyte, A. (1932) 'Reflections on the age of noise', *Fortnightly Review*, 132: 72–82.

Wijburg, G. (2020) 'The de-financialization of housing: towards a research agenda', *Housing Studies*, 22 May.

Williams, P. and Smith, N. (1986) 'From "renaissance" to restructuring: the dynamics of contemporary urban development', in N. Smith and P. Williams (eds) *Gentrification of the City*, London: Allen & Unwin, pp 204–24.

Williams, R. (1989) 'Socialism and ecology', in R. Gable (ed) *Resources of Hope*, London: Verso, pp 210–26.

Wiman, P. and Zuckerman, N. (2019) 'Savills: Sweden on track for a bumper 2019 due to record investment in residential real estate,' *Savills News*, https://news.euro.savills.co.uk/sweden/mim-sweden-investment-q3-2019-final.pdf

Winter, C. and Blackman, A. (2020) 'No city hates its landlords like Berlin does', *Bloomberg Businessweek*, 4 February.

Witcher, T. (2018) 'Reinforced concrete rises: the Ingalls Building', *Civil Engineering Magazine Archive*, 88(11): 4–43.

Wohl, A. (1977) *The Eternal Slum*, London: Edward Arnold.

Wong, D. (2020) 'How can foreign technology investors benefit from China's new infrastructure plan?', *China Briefing*, 7 August.

Wood, H. (2020) 'Sino-African architecture; a look at the rise of Chinese-built projects across the African continent', *Archinect Features*, 18 February.

Woodland Trust (2020) 'Ancient woodland', www.woodlandtrust.org.uk/trees-woods-and-wildlife/habitats/ancient-woodland/

Woodworth, M. (2017) 'Landscape and the cultural politics of China's anticipatory urbanism', *Landscape Research*, 43(7): 891–905.

Woodworth, M. and Wallace, J. (2017) 'Seeing ghosts: parsing China's "ghost city" controversy', *Urban Geography*, 38(8): 1270–81.

World Commission on Dams (2000) *Dams and Development: A New Framework for Decision-Making*, London: Earthscan.

World Economic Forum (2016) *Shaping the Future of Construction: A Breakthrough in Mindset and Technology*, Cologny: WEF.

World Forum on Natural Capital (2020) 'What is natural capital?', https://naturalcapitalforum.com/about/

World Green Building Council (2016) *Towards Zero-Emission Efficient and Resilient Buildings, Global Status Report 2016*, Paris: Global Alliance for Buildings and Construction.

World Health Organisation (2020) *Air Pollution*, Geneva: World Health Organisation, www.who.int/health-topics/air-pollution#tab=tab_1

Woudstra, R. (2014) 'Le Corbusier's vision for fascist Addis Ababa', *Failed Architecture*, 9 October.

Wu, W. and Gaubatz, P. (2013) *The Chinese City*, London: Routledge.

Wyatt, P. (2008) 'Empty dwellings: the use of council-tax records in identifying and monitoring vacant private housing in England', *Environment and Planning*, 40(5): 1171–84.

Xu, K., Shen, G.Q., Liu, G. and Martek, I. (2019) 'Demolition of existing buildings in urban renewal projects: a decision support system in the China context', *Sustainability*, 11(2): 1–22.

Yanfeng, Q. (2010) 'China must replace half its homes in 20 years', *China Daily*, 8 July.

Yates, A. (2011) 'Developing knowledge, the knowledge of development: real estate speculators and brokers in late nineteenth-century Paris', *Business and Economic History Online*, 9(Fall).

Yates, A. (2015) *Selling Paris: Property and Commercial Culture in the Fin-de-Siècle Capital*, Cambridge, MA: Harvard University Press.

Yavetz, Z. (1958) 'The living conditions of the urban plebs in republican Rome', *Latomus*, 17(3): 500–17.

Yin, L. and Silverman, R.M. (2015) 'Housing abandonment and demolition: exploring the use of micro-level and multi-year models', *ISPRS International Journal of Geo-Information*, 4(3): 1184–200.

Young, I. (1990) *Justice and the Politics of Difference*, Princeton, NJ: Princeton University Press.

Yu, H. (2016) 'Motivation behind China's "One Belt, One Road" initiatives and establishment of the Asian Infrastructure Investment Bank', *Journal of Contemporary China*, 26(105): 353–68.

Zalasiewicz, J., Williams, M., Waters, C., Barnosky, A. and Haff, P. (2014) 'The techno-fossil record of humans', *The Anthropocene Review*, 1(1): 34–43.

Zeller, T. (2007) *Driving Germany: The Landscape of the German Autobahn, 1930–1970*, New York, NY: Berghahn Books.

Zhu, M. (2011) 'City without city: urbanisation development model is urgently in need of change', *China Housing Magazine*, 21: 42–5.

Zibechi, R. (2012) *Territories in Resistance: A Cartography of Latin American Social Movements*, Oakland, CA: AK Press.

Index

commons 84–5
community 49, 83, 101, 103, 105, 106, 110,
    116, 117, 119, 121–2, 123, 139, 141–2,
    193, 208, 216–17, 223, 230, 233
community opposition 141–2
community resistance 83
comprehensive renewal 96–7
computer graphics 164
concrete
    acceleration in production of 13
    Bangkok 55
    building block of construction 2
    carbon footprint of 233–4
    cement 24
    dwellings 98, 174
    embodied energy of 234
    environmental credential of 187, 204
    hostile spaces 170
    immovable objects 131
    infrastructure 165, 203
    Japanese usage of 49–50, 56
    plasticity of 18
    pollution 34, 228
    Roman society 17, 18–19, 228
    slip forming 23
    staple material of building 22–3
    supply of 2
    techno-fossils 17, 35
    Tokyo 1
    volume construction 46–7
    waste 28, 30, 228
    West Bank barrier 39
Connecticut 119
conspicuous consumption 27, 128
construction booms 60
construction conflicts 99–100
construction lobby 49, 120
construction sector 17, 29–30, 35, 43–4,
    50–1, 186–7, 196, 199, 200, 208, 213,
    224–5, 232
construction state 36, 37, 43–54, 56,
    60–1, 229
containment policies 142–3
contamination 185, 210–11
continuous construction 5–6, 169, 186
conventional building 168, 173
Copenhagen 165
corporate landlords 147, 148, 152–3
corruption 30–1, 37, 54–61
cost–benefit analysis 58, 109
COVID-19 60, 69, 211, 217–18, 229, 231
craftwork 174
creative destruction 112, 118
crime 8, 25, 37, 54, 57, 114
Crimean Bridge 41
critical pedagogy 225–6
cultural imperialism 160

culture of construction 27, 35, 133–4,
    212, 226

D
Dallas 124
daytime economy 9
debilitating 10, 157, 165
deforestation 7, 19, 24, 50, 186, 192, 197,
    206–7, 210
degradation 3, 111, 135, 186, 192, 194, 200,
    202, 207, 209, 215, 226
Delhi 114
democracy 201
democratic 4, 88, 95, 117, 167, 177,
    212, 223
democratisation 3
demolition 2, 3, 4, 6, 9–10, 27–8, 36, 44, 47,
    52, 68, 91–2, 93–4, 99, 109, 110–36, 158,
    211, 228, 231, 233
demolition paradigm 9–10, 109, 111, 112,
    113–23, 130–1, 133, 136
demountable 165, 168, 196, 220
Denmark 232
Denver 124
de-paving 234
destruction
    of Chinese housing 120
    comprehensive urban renewal 95
    creative forms of 112, 118
    dominance in the building process 112,
        118, 130
    ecosystems 27, 184, 187, 188, 189, 194,
        200, 202, 226, 233
    end of life 113
    fishing habitats 29
    gentrification 121
    Glasgow 110–11
    habitation 107
    Haussmann 93
    indigenous communities 36
    local ecologies 9
    normality of 118
    Rome 115
    state legitimation of 122
    Stockholm 47
    teardown 123
    tropical forests 184
    urban heterogeneity 111
    warcraft 114
    warfare 128
    waste 29
    wildlife 188
Detroit 49, 120
Deutsche Wohnen 148
developers 5, 47–8, 49, 52, 54, 64, 68, 69,
    70–2, 77–8, 99, 109, 123, 141–2, 146–7,
    188, 198, 229, 231–2
development politics of building 108

Gulf Coast 90
illegal use of hardwoods 184
intra-urban roads 96–7
low-cost dwellings 45–6
luxury homes 124
mass clearances 135
native American lands 67
New Deal 44–5
opposition to high density housing
    141–2, 143
Public Works Administration 44
rental properties 147–8
road building 96–7, 107
scale of urbanisation 23
shell companies 147–8
shrinking cities 120
size of new homes 220
speculation 67, 69, 82, 219
state-led growth coalitions 48–9
sub-prime mortgages 229
suburbanisation 45–6, 69
teardown 123–5, 126–7
tiny homes 220
unprecedented house building 144
vacant sites 119
value of construction activity 44, 228
users 30, 72, 94, 111, 132–3, 158, 161, 162,
    164, 167, 169, 170, 171, 173, 174, 182,
    195, 222, 224, 233
Usonian house 174, 233
utilitarian 19, 25, 34

V
vacant buildings 118
vacant sites 113, 119, 120
valuation 98, 100–1, 103, 109, 192, 200
valuation practices 101
valuing of nature 233
Vancouver 124–5, 130
vanity projects 33, 42–3, 82, 94, 127,
    214, 219
ventilation 203, 204, 234
vernacular 15, 27, 72, 80, 109, 120, 131,
    167–8, 177, 208
vertical building 69
verticality boom 69
Vietnam 29
violence 121, 4, 31, 88, 94, 108, 128, 157,
    164, 215
vison impaired 164, 182, 232
vulnerability 31
vulnerable population 107

W
Wales 140, 190
walking 80, 81, 157, 165, 206
Wall Street 5, 148
Wandsworth 79

waste 3, 9, 14, 17, 25, 28–35, 44, 72, 81, 87,
    112, 123, 127, 130, 134–5, 158, 177, 184,
    185, 187, 194, 195–6, 199, 203, 214, 217,
    220, 223, 228, 233
waste disposal 135, 233
wastefulness 3, 28, 32, 216, 217
wasting 28–30, 219
water
    bottled forms of 192
    China 13
    conservation of 185
    dam projects 39
    degradation of 192, 215
    demand for 213
    flooding 89, 90–1
    fresh sources of 210
    guarantee of life 13
    infrastructure 25
    levees 90
    localised forms of 222
    pipelines 1, 165
    pollution of 4, 35, 158, 186, 187, 210, 229
    poor quality of 29, 200, 223, 229
    purification of 203
    riverbanks 29
    source of disease 217
    speculation 218
    sprinkler systems 31
    supplies of 29, 98, 186
    transporting of 13, 22
    underground tanks 2–3
    untreated forms of 217
    usage of 24, 197
wayfinding 232
welfare 33, 38, 41, 60, 74, 117, 155,
    156, 208
well-being 4, 11, 14, 20, 28, 30, 37, 44, 60,
    156, 157–8, 165, 166, 169–70, 177–8,
    182, 187, 192–3, 195, 201, 211, 218,
    222, 226
West Baltimore 96, 98
West Bank 39, 41, 229
West Bank barrier 39
Western culture of architecture 132
wetlands 189
wheelchairs 156, 164, 170
wilderness 12, 25
wildlife 188–9
Williams, R. 84, 226
windcatchers 234
windfall gains 51, 64
Wisconsin 174–5
working class 93
World Bank 5, 36, 47, 50
World Commission on Dams 87
World Economic Forum 44
World Health Organisation 186